Russian
Intelligence Services

Vladimir Plougin

Russian
Intelligence Services

—

Volume I: The Early Years

9th — 11th centuries
(882 — 1069)

Translated by Gennady Bashkov

Edited by Claudiu A. Secara

Algora Publishing
New York

Algora Publishing, New York
© 2001 by Algora Publishing
All rights reserved. Published 2000.
Printed in the United States of America
ISBN: 1-892941-52-X
Editors@algora.com

Library of Congress Cataloging-in-Publication Data 00-010746

Plougin, Vladimir.
 Russian intelligence services / by Vladimir Plougin ; translated by
Gennady Bashkov ; edited by Claudiu A. Secara.
    p. cm. — (A history of Russian intelligence ; v. 1)
  ISBN 1-892941-52-X (v. 1 : alk. paper)
 1. Intelligence service—Russia—History. 2. Intelligence
Service—Soviet Union—History. 3. Intelligence service—Russia
(Federation)—History. I. Secara, Claudiu A. (Claudiu Adrian) II.
Title. III. Series.
 UB256.R8 P56 2000
 327.1247—dc21

00-010746

Front Cover: *Zaporozhian Cossacks* by Ilya Repin (1880-1891)
Back Cover: *Yermak's Conquest of Siberia* (fragment) by Vasily Surikov (1895)

New York
www.algora.com

THE RIURIK DYNASTY
RULERS OF KIEV AND NOVGOROD

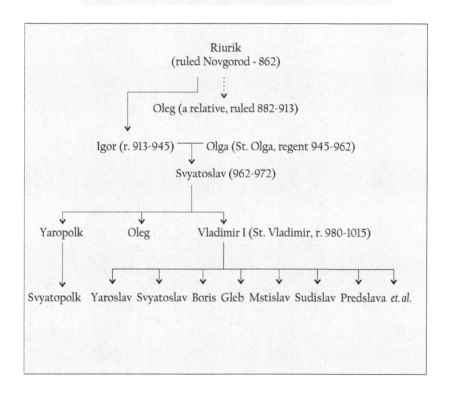

Riurik
(ruled Novgorod - 862)

Oleg (a relative, ruled 882-913)

Igor (r. 913-945) ⎯⊤⎯ Olga (St. Olga, regent 945-962)

Svyatoslav (962-972)

Yaropolk   Oleg   Vladimir I (St. Vladimir, r. 980-1015)

Svyatopolk Yaroslav Svyatoslav Boris Gleb Mstislav Sudislav Predslava *et. al.*

Kievan Russia in the Eleventh Century

ROUTE OF VARANGIANS
800 - 900

FINNS

ESTHS

Iuriev

LITHUANIANS

BALTIC SLAVS

PRUSSIANS

POLES

CARPATHIAN

HUNGARIANS

MTS.

Baltic Sea

Ladoga

Belozero

NOVGOROD

Pskov

Rostov

Suzdal

Murom

Polotsk

Smolensk

Chernigov

Vladimir in-V.

KIEV

Pereiaslavl

PECHENEGS

Olbia

Chersonesus

Tmutorakan

Black Sea

Constantinople

BYZANTINE

EMPIRE

Mediterranean Sea

VOLGA
Gt. Bulgar

BULGARS

KHAZARS

Sarkil

Itil

Caspian Sea

CAUCASUS MTS.

Kura

Araks

ARABIAN CALIPHATE

N. Dvina

Kama

Volga

Ural

Don

Donets

Kuban

Danube

Niemen

Vistula

Pripet

Dniester

Prut

Dnieper

0   500 miles

What trait in a person's character do you, dear reader, find most appealing? I, for one, think, it is curiosity. That is the real engine of social development, the mother of sciences, arts, and crafts, midwife of intellectual and moral reflection. Unfortunately, curiosity is rather rarely found among men. "We are lazy and lack curiosity", said the poet — and the more widespread that condition is, the more precious is the exception.

These sketches, offered to your attention are, to a certain extent, nothing more than an extended eulogy (there was such a genre in the ancient art of speech), that is, praise of those people for whom curiosity was the basic property of their nature and a tool that enabled them to serve their country, and make a living for themselves, and (in some cases) stand out as textbook cases of professionalism. As the reader may have guessed, we shall speak about intelligence agents in the broadest sense of the term.

The ancient history of the institutions where these people worked and are still working, that is, the secret and special services of Russia (political, economic and military reconnaissance services and the intelligence arm of the secret police and the diplomatic corps) has not been written and has not attracted much attention so far — even by the literature of the cold war. Only fiction writers have ventured from time to time to intrude into this sphere that is for the most part covered with a dark veil. And sometimes they have done it successfully. One may recollect, for instance, Sergey Borodin's novel *Dmitry Donskoy*, in which it is asserted that the role of the head of the great prince's intelligence service was played by the boyar Mikhail Andreevich Brenk, a wise and watchful person who liked to keep his place in the shadows (one of the professional requirements of these good-hearted and appealing people). The role of the executive agent is played by a huge warrior Grisha Kapoustin, a large man with a child's smile on a small face. Both characters existed, in reality, but the author's recording of their activity came by ways inaccessible to historians. Reading such books on Russia's past one gets the impression that security services in their various manifestations were already flourishing long ago, not only in the service of Russia proper but also of the nations of the near abroad. One may recollect Lavrin Kapusta, who guarded Bogdan Khmelnitsky against Polish encroachments, as described in *Pereyaslav rada*, a book by Nathan Rybak, then prince Baaka Kherkheulidze, head of King Georgy's court guard and his secret police as described by Anna Antonovskaya in her epic *The Great Mouravi*. One may also recall King Dodon's guard in *The Golden Cockerel* (*Le Coq D'Or* or *Zolotoy Petushok*, rf. Pushkin's fairytale and Rimsky-Korsakov's opera) who diligently served their sovereign, perched on the high domes of competent institutions, intently surveying both the faraway (overseas) and the close-at-hand (domestic) affairs.

But fiction writers are rather *impatient* people. The overwhelming majority does not depict history as it was but shows how it could have been, if this or that event had not happened (they are the precursors of modern theoreticians who speculate about the many twists in historical development) — while chroniclers and lovers of the documented truth maintain a touching silence.

One should mention, though, a half-fiction book by A. Gorbovsky and Y. Semenov, *Without a Single Shot*, published in the early 1980s, on the history of the Russian military reconnaissance services. Several pages are dedicated to Old Russia. And in the late 1990s under the aegis of the (Russian) Director of Foreign Intelligence Services Academician E. M. Primakov (later Prime Minister), publication began on a six-volume work called *Sketches from the History of Russian Foreign Intelligence*. But it was not by accident that the publisher of the book did not mention, in the foreword, the most ancient period of Russian secret services activities — as if it did not exist. And the first volume of "Sketches", dealing with the period up to 1917, seems rather weak. Only a cursory glance is given to certain episodes from the times of Sviatoslav and Vladimir, and then the study jumps at once to Dmitry Donskoy, Vasily II "The Dark" and Ivan III. Then, the book extends, more or less coherently, from the 16ᵗʰ century, the epoch of Ivan the Terrible, onward. One may be left with the impression that we Russians know a lot less about this period of our history than some foreign researchers (consider the books published in Great Britain in 1987 and 1990 by Richard Deacon — *A History of the Russian Secret Service*, and by Peter Hopkirk — *The Great Game: the Secret Services in High Asia*).

I will not pronounce any judgment on the authors' reasons for such choices. In any case, the surviving sources from epochs past are no longer secret (and most of them never were). Still, the facts they contain remain secret to a large extent. I did not set out to produce a systematic or coherent description of the structure and activities of the Russian special services from the 10ᵗʰ to the 18ᵗʰ centuries. These sketches have a much more modest aim — to give the reader a glance at the life and "activities" of some members of the intelligence and investigative services and at certain features of the secret (both old and modern) wars within Russia

A few words about terminology: E. Cherniak, in his book *Five Centuries of Secret War* suggests making a distinction (though with some qualifications) between intelligence operations (i.e. acquisition of secret political, military and other information, together with counterintelligence, the struggle with enemy agents) on the one hand, and active engagement in secret wars on the other. The latter refers to the different ways of conducting acts of subversion, up to and including provoking mutinies and fomenting the overthrow of states. Such a distinction seems to him more important than theoretical differences between "noble" reconnaissance and "base" espionage, which distinction is still much in use by many Western authors. I cannot but agree with Cherniak. After all, who is in a position to find out who is a scout, a snoop, a spook or a spy anyway? All of them are fellows in the same trade and they do the same thing, only under labels that carry a different moral load.

As to the difference between intelligence and secret wars. . . First of all, "pure" intelligence very often turns "dirty" under the influence of mere circumstances, even when both actions were conducted by the same people. Second, intelligence as such is only one of the means (and stages) of a secret war, and without reference to its ultimate function intelligence-gathering itself loses its meaning, to a great extent.

All this considered, I shall follow Cherniak's approach in using the more-inclusive definition.

Some clarification about the moral aspects of intelligence work: The fate of detectives and scouts is quite often a sad one; also, not all of them strove for the glory of the Fatherland. Some worked for its shame — though such abundant examples of treachery as are manifest amongst their modern heirs were unthinkable in the old days.

Ivan Eganov, an ordinary soldier on the "invisible front," served the Great Prince of Moscow Vasily Ivanovich III and, after the latter's death in 1533, was taken into custody "while on active duty". We will never know if Ivan Eganov suffered for a just cause, yet he could have been speaking for the majority of those who engage in intelligence activities when he wrote the following, from prison, to the future Ivan the Terrible, heir and namesake of Vasily Ivanovich. "For my Lord (Vasily III) told me to pursue my quest everywhere and in doing so I have exhausted my means to a great extent. I am serving you and I wish well in my land; you may punish all of us but do not allow us to end our lives without repentance and absolution."

One must appreciate the sincerity of these words, their bitter irony and the ill-fated agent's high understanding of his moral duty. These words were written not in the 1930s but in the 16th century.

Chapter I.
AT THE SOURCES

1. A Commotion on the Rhine or, How the Russians Alarmed Europe for the First Time

I can imagine that some readers might expect clear answers to many such questions as: Who was the first Russian spy? When was the first reconnaissance service active? What did the first "security organs" in Russia look like? etc. I should admit I do not have the answers to satisfy such curiosity.

Who was the first spy or certified snoop, the precursor of all the systems of secret services, the first secret agent? Some point to Ephialt. But was he really the first intelligence agent in the world? One doubts it very much. Even if he was such a reconnaissance agent at all, that does not mean that there had been no such activity well before his time.

Still, the Russian intelligence services were first mentioned in a very precise year and even on a very precise day. As the court priest of the Frankish emperor Louis I, Pius Prudentius, has it (in what is known as *The Bertine Annals*), on May, 18, 839 AD, His Majesty received, in the small town of Ingelheim, on the banks of the Rhine, messengers from the nation of Rhos — that is, the state of Rus', which nowadays most historians duly identify geographically with the Kiev power (this is also one of the first times Rus' is mentioned in surviving documents). The unexpected guests arrived along with the embassy of the Byzantine emperor Theophilus, but they were distinct from the Greeks and made Louis suspicious. Representatives of an altogether unfamiliar eastern power, their looks and language resembled, at least to him, the too well-known Normans, Danes and Norwegians who often encroached the northern coast of the empire, as well as the Swedes that he had had the pleasure to receive some ten years earlier. "Having investigated the cause of their arrival," notes Prudentius, "the emperor learned that they really belonged to the nation of Sweons. Taking them, at first, for intelligence officers of Byzantium, not seekers of friendship, he decided to detain them and find out for sure whether they arrived with good intentions or not." The imperial security services must have taken part in the matter and produced some preliminary recommendations. That is, they concluded that these men might well be ambassadors and not spies, although they looked like spies rather very much. And therefore the investigation should be prolonged. When the Greeks were about to leave, Louis asked them to tell His Most August Brother (and he also sent a letter to that effect to Constantinople) that "out of his love for him he gladly received" guests from the Rhos country "and if they prove to be people of goodwill and if there is a chance for them to go safely back to their motherland (and Theophilus had asked about that), they would be sent there with an honor guard. Otherwise he would send them back to His Majesty so that the latter could decide for himself what was to be done with them." What was proven in the end and where the envoys of the Rhos state were sent, to Constantinople or Kiev, remains a mystery. In the end, we do not know at all whether the first formal representatives of Kiev to the Empire of the Franks were intelligence officers or not — but we know that Louis I, Emperor of the Franks, was indeed unsettled by their presence.

Could it be, as a matter of fact, that Varangians and not Slavs were sent to Constantinople and from there to Ingelheim? It seems likely, because the powerful Russian state (in the annals its ruler was called "Chaganus" or "kagan") did not have, among the local noblemen, many individuals qualified to undertake such a difficult ambassadorial mission. One must know the languages, customs and the ways of life of the various nations involved, diplomatic etiquette, routes and logistical options and many other things. The seasoned Vikings who used to roam all over Europe were far better suited to such a purpose, though it might not have been easy to find such persons in Kiev at the time — the Varangians appeared in force there only some half century later. But the Russian "Chaganus," who was the descendant of the legendary Kiy, managed somehow to secure such men. They must have been sent first to Byzantium and, since they did not cause any trouble there, Emperor Theophilus might have put in a good word for them with Louis the Pious.

The Carolingian emperor's suspicions would not have been entirely unsubstantiated. If the Russians were seeking to investigate any of the empire's secrets, one can surmise that those secrets could only have been about the Eastern Roman Empire, which they invaded two decades later. Russia was separated from the Carolingian (Carlovingian) State by a strip of western Slavic lands and their visit must be seen clearly from that geographic perspective. A "get-acquainted" mission would not have been unthinkable; but it could, too, have been aiming to extract some secret information from the common knowledge shared among the ruling court establishment. At all times, before and after, foreign ambassadors and embassies in every country have always been under close surveillance and have been subject to suspicion (quite often unsubstantiated). It is only fair to assume that if the Franks really wanted to implicate the Kiev representatives, the Varangians, on charges of spying, only the gods could have helped them escape. (Louis I the Pious' suspicions also seemed quite fair to the respected Russian Church historian, E. E. Golubinsky, who wrote that it was "customary" for Russians to investigate a Catholic state by covert means.)

In any event, the story, as it came to be related to us, is quite representative of how the Russians made their first documented appearance in Europe: they scared the Europeans.

2. Strange Customs of the Arsanians

Oriental sources, mostly Arabic, of the 10th and later centuries mention three groups or types of Russians, each having its own state territory, a capital and a king. For instance, Ibn Khaukal wrote in his *Book of Ways and Countries*, "Russians: There are three groups of them. One of them is nearest to Bulgar and their king sits in the city under the name of Kuyaba . . . The farthest of them is called Slavia, and (the third) group is called Arsania; and their king sits in Ars. People from there come to Kuyaba for trading purposes. As for Ars, it is not known that any foreigner has reached it, for they kill any stranger coming to their land. They go downstream to trade but do not tell anyone about their affairs or about their goods, they do not allow anybody to follow them or enter their country. From Ars they export black sable and tin. . . Those Russians trade with Khazars, Rome (Byzantium) and Great Bulgar."

Some suppose that this information dates back to the second half of the 9th century. The location of the first two groups does not involve much controversy. They have been identified with Kiev and Novgorod. However, it is different in regard to Arsania, for historians have placed it in various parts of Eastern Europe. Currently most oriental researchers tend to locate Ars in the North, probably in the vicinity of Rostov/Belo-ozero where archaeological investigations indicate that there was a trade and a handicraft center at the Sars place (I. G. Konovalov). This point of view seems most plausible. Why did Arsania elicit the interest of medieval Arabic writers? As distinct from Kiev and Novgorod, Arsania presented an enigma, which for various reasons one such as Ibn Khaukal would have wanted to unveil. It should be remembered that Ibn Khaukal himself, who traveled nearly all over the Moslem world, from Spain to India, in the middle of the 10th century, made his travels according to some reports as a political agent — first of the Egyptian Fatimids, then of Baghdad's Abbasids and then of Spanish Omeyads. (I. G. Konovalov).

What can one deduce from the story of the strange customs of Arsania's population? This is a vivid example of a closed society with pronounced xenophobia. The latter property does not seem attractive to anyone from the outside, especially when those curious foreigners are treated to a *take-no-prisoners* approach. Such societies have existed in every era (many legends have been spread about them) and no society on Earth has been totally open. The composition of the conflicting components may have varied, but "iron curtains" have appeared in history far more often than one may think. They emerge not because of ill will but out of necessity. One may also mention "softer curtains" that have guarded a state or an ethnic entity against the danger (real or imaginary) of the environment and provided added defense to aid survival in adverse situations.

Coming back to Ibn Khaukal, Al Istarkhy and other authors, we should add that northeastern Russia in the 9th - 10th centuries was under intensive colonization by Slavs (migrating populations settling in new territories). The process was not without conflicts — and rather mortal ones for the Finnish and Ugric population that had settled there earlier and given rise to the unwelcome feelings mentioned above. Kievan princes kept a watchful eye on the northeastern lands, where Svyatoslav organized a "visit" to the Vyatiches. Even more, a constant threat was perceived as coming from the strong and cunning states along the Volga and the Don rivers: Bulgaria and Khazaria. It follows that the Arsania people developed an "allergy" to strangers, irrespective of their state or tribal establishments.

As we know, in ancient and medieval times, not only spies but merchants were often used for such purposes and very often the distinction between the two was rather vague. Merchants were major information sources for the historians of the time, as they were the first to establish contacts with those who came from the mysterious countries, eagerly penetrating beyond the "iron curtain". That is why Ibn Khaukal and his fellow writers were able to deal with the issues in so great detail. His description is so vivid that one can imagine the servants of the god Mercury (the tradesmen) trying to strike up conversations with the taciturn people from the North. At some oriental marketplace or caravanserai they would try to find out where these goods originated, how difficult it was to procure them, whether the effort was worthwhile and whether the profit was sufficient, etc. But the taciturn men with beards did not yield either to flattery or to inquisitive approaches; and for seekers of the black sables and tin from the Volga River or its tributaries, only swords rattled.

There can be two levels of xenophobia: one at the grassroots and the other as a state policy. Both may have co-existed and they may have reinforced each other. If that was the case, this provides us with some insight. We can establish, even if with some reservations, a certain social and psychological profile of the people. Closed societies breed xenophobia, xenophobia breeds potential and actual counterintelligence.

3. A Ballad to the Intelligence Services of the Prophetic Oleg

The Russian-German conflict of 839 AD reflected an evident truth: that one of the ways that reconnaissance activity has always been masked is through the use of the diplomat, the functions of an ambassador. Intelligence officers were often infiltrated among the members of the diplomatic staff or an ambassadorial rank was just a cover for a "coq d'or"; that is, when one is speaking about formal diplomacy.

As to clandestine activity, foreign envoys often engage in conspiratorial affairs among themselves — at least in those cases when their plots targeted not their host country, but a common enemy. The very nature of such activity has always required qualities other than those inherent to the "etiquette" of state ambassadors. One needed not so much nobility of looks or of family tree, eloquence or even a penetrating mind, but dexterity, shrewdness, the ability to appear and disappear without notice, acquaintance with the demands of fraud, bribery and other "irregularities". These are qualities inherent to the ambassadors seeking to fulfill "His lordship's service", without which they could not get by in this world.

"Secret ambassadorial talks" were in wide use in ancient Russia as well as in all other countries of Europe. That might explain the secret action that Rus' was able to undertake in 860 when it learned about the Byzantine troops marching out of Constantinople, the capital, into Asia Minor at the same time that the Byzantine fleet was setting out for Cyprus. Some sort of "tip-off" by a well-acquainted envoy must have made possible the attack on Constantinople by a Russian fleet consisting of about 200 boats sailing for Byzantium under the command of Emperor Mikhail. That event led the chronicler to speak for the first time about the Russian lands, as mentioned in the Greek annals, and about how the Russian tsar got his name. For we learned that during the rule of the Byzantine Emperor Michael, the Rus' came to *Tsargrad*, in the words of the Greek chronicles.

There is little doubt that such an undertaking could have been possible only due to some successful intelligence operation pursued under strict military secrecy; although we do not know who arranged it and who helped in the execution of this difficult project. Likewise, we do not know much about other reconnaissance operations undertaken during the previous military campaigns of Surozh by Novgorod's Prince Bravlin at the end of the 8th or beginning of the 9th century, nor about the campaign of Amastrida (between 825 and 842). In short, after the 830s, the next information as to intelligence activity coming out of Russia (this time domestic in nature) appears only at the end of the 9th century. This is the earliest documented information on the nature of domestic intelligence gathering operations in Russia.

At the end of the same 9th century, we learn for first time of a military and political action that took place with some agents spying and disseminating false information about the enemy and in collusion with former close neighbors. That action led to an overthrow of state, probably for the first time recorded in the annals of the eastern lands. It was arranged and led by the prophetic Oleg, and the neighbor this time was the "state of Rhos".

According to early chronicles, two years after the death of the founder of the (Varangian) House of Riurik, in the year of 6389 since the Earth's creation (or 6390) — that is, in 881 (or 882) AD — Oleg and another young fellow, Prince Igor, left the pleasant banks of the Volkhov River at the head of a large legion of Varangians, Novgorod Slovens, Kriviches and Chud', Merya and Ves. He went out to conquer the Slav Kiev (or maybe he was just moved by desire to roam around). Having invaded Smolensk and Liubech, he went by boat down the river Dnieper and found himself "at the bluffs of Kiev". He liked the place. He sent someone to find out who was its happy owner. The first intelligence officer disembarked; he was, most probably, a Slav or a Varangian (his name at the time the chronicle was written was still a secret). It is easy to assume that he did not wear any military insignia, as his mission must have been that of a civilian scout or a spy, as we would call him now. The envoy made inquiries and brought back the answer — the rulers are two brothers: Askold and Dir.

Oleg ordered most of his troops to stay in hiding and then, with the rest of his men "feigning to be passersby", disembarked at the dock. Agents were sent to the princely brothers to inform them that the Russians were merchants heading "to the Greeks, on behalf of Prince Oleg and young Igor". That was definitely the first recorded act of disinformation on behalf of Russian authorities.

Having deceived Askold and Dir as to the broader scope of their mission, the two Russians also managed to further deceive them and bring them both to the wharf, where they captured them. The troops sprang out from the boats and detained the local rulers. Oleg (or maybe Igor) rebuked Askold and Dir for having usurped power without any right to it since, according to the Russian princes, neither Askold nor Dir belonged to a princely house. And that was how Askold and Dir came to be murdered.

That is also how the first Kievan coup d'etat took place — but the Nikon chronicle of the 16th century puts it somewhat differently, emphasizing mystery and additional intelligence ploys. Oleg himself is said to have stayed in the boat and "ordered his men to go ashore, telling them something in secret". That is to say, he gave them secret service-type instructions. Probably the chronicler did not have any additional information (although he may have had some historical evidence that has been lost by now); he just understood the character he was describing the same way as does the author of these pages.

It is quite possible that Oleg put out a rumor alleging that he was ill; it would have been his way of explaining why an ordinary merchant had the nerve to invite the prince to visit his premises rather than rushing to the palace himself to present his bows. He thus got away with violating hierarchical etiquette, at least as it was understood in the 16th century under Vasily III and Ivan IV.

In other words, the chronicler invented a "psychological portrait" around Oleg's ruse. One reads with great interest Oleg's own instructions to his reconnaissance operatives. "I am a guest from a faraway land and I travel to the Greeks on the orders of Oleg and Igor. Right now I am ill. Tell the envoys of Askold and Dir that I have lots of pearls and embroidery and I have a message for you that must be transmitted orally, so do please come here".

"Oral message", "pearls" — fascinating, to say the least. The medieval writer had a penchant for fiction and he made the short story of his predecessor even more picturesque by embellishing it. Little doubt, the chroniclers belonged to those well-informed circles (Metropolitan Daniel and his closest colleagues) who were knowledgeable about the 'ways and means' of intelligence in use among their contemporaries.

Professional spies would agree that a lure in the form of "treasure" (quite natural on the part of a merchant) and confidential information would not be lost on clever individuals even nowadays. It is clear that neither Askold nor Dir could stay in their palace, given such a chance to get a first-hand look at such an important messenger. "So they appeared at the dock, unawares", and according to the logic of the story they may have "boarded the boat" to "see the infirm guest" (and his pearls) and to hear the promised secret messages. (In early chronicles, the place of meeting is not defined clearly; but one may well assume the riverbank.) The reader already knows the rest of the story.

The events described here were definitely construed under the auspices of an intelligence operation and with the intent of overthrowing a "legitimate government".

But let us ask: did Oleg have any counterintelligence services also?

One should go back to the year 907, when Oleg went to Tsargrad "in great force" "both on horseback and in boats". He had with him Varangians, Slovens, Kriviches, Severians, Drevlians, Radimiches, Vyatiches, Croats, Doulebys, Tivertsy, Meri, and Chud'. The Greeks had a common name for them: the "Great Scythians". Though Oleg's intentions were, as he put it, of a peaceful nature — he wanted only to lay the richest "Empire of Eastern Romans" under his tribute, and to fix his shield on the city gate (for beauty's sake and for remembrance) — he may have slaughtered everything in the vicinity (it was customary to wage war in such a way at the time). For their part, the Greeks met him with hostility.

Still, they could not resist two thousand sailboats placed on wheels and marching onto the capital; they agreed to pay the tribute. But they cherished the hope of eliminating the cheeky Barbarian by presenting him with poisoned victuals and wine. The Byzantine civilization was in full flower at the time. The laws and rules of secret war were highly developed. The Russian chronicler made a point of it: "The Greeks are crafty till this day." The Barbarian, however, did not accept the gifts. And the Byzantines, scared by his prophetic powers, began whispering among themselves that he was not Oleg, but Demetrius of Salonicas, sent by God to punish them. So, at least, the chronicler explained; he did not say anything about one Lavrin Kapusta, who may have helped the prince to sniff out the crafty designs of the Greeks.

But we know one more thing for sure. Judging by the chronicles, Oleg's expeditionary fleet appeared at Constantinople unexpectedly and played havoc and ignited panic in the city. Yet Oleg's small boats could navigate the Black Sea only along the coastline, and would have had to make frequent stops. How could the Eastern Roman guards have missed them? We may come here to a conclusion that Oleg had a powerful system of counterintelligence. First, he would have had to establish a sailing plan with designated moorings, second, to arrange a safe system of lookouts. He may have intercepted the heralds who spotted the boats. The chronicle also mentions Oleg's men on horseback near Tsargrad. He could not have brought the horses in such small boats! One may imagine a special detachment on horseback that went along the seacoast and prevented any information leak. We do not exclude probable assistance from the Bulgarians.

At last, the Eastern Romans learned about the danger that was awaiting them and locked the mouth of the Golden Horn Bay with chains. That was the most vulnerable access to the city. But it was too late. The fleet entered unimpeded into the Sea of Marmara.

4. Intelligence Among Slavs and Russians According to Early Medieval Authors

Standards in the intelligence services in Russia in general could hardly have been satisfactory for long. Besides the social and political level of development, they were definitely influenced by specific ethnic and psychological traits. The renowned Byzantine historian Procopius of Caesaria, in describing the ancient Slavs, Ants and Sclavics (who "are all tall, and very strong; their countenance is not very fair, they are not auburn though not black and close to reddish) noted that they " are not at all perfidious and evil-minded"). Some time later, the Eastern Roman emperor Mauricius, in his "*Strategicon*", asserts something quite the opposite, intimating that "the Ants and Sclavics tribes are rather treacherous and unreliable in agreements". He also makes the observation that they would more likely yield to fear than to gifts. He also mentions some of the tricks and practices of Slavic military reconnaissance: they used ambushes, surprise-attacks and various cunningly devised subterfuges day and night. But their tactical reconnaissance was not always on a par with their cunning strategies. Thus one of the oriental historians, Ibn Isfendiyar, early in the 10th century, relates one unfortunate outcome for the Russians (Varangians and Slavs) during a maritime campaign along the southern coast of the Caspian Sea in 909 or 912. During the night, some of them that had disembarked; they were taken by surprise by the people of Gilian and were slaughtered; the rest, who were in the boats, hastened to raise sail and depart. But the people of Gilian managed to warn King Shirvanshakh of the escapees' route. Having received this precious intelligence he ordered his men to lay an ambush at sea and in the end none of the Russians escaped alive.

Another Arabic scholar, Al Masoudi, presented a similar situation. According to him, sometime after 912 a whole contingent of Russians sailing in some 500 boats, in collusion with the Khazar ruler, were on the move from the Black Sea to the Caspian in order to pillage the vicinity. They were to share the plunder equally. But once the plundered gold reached the Khazar treasury, the allies' ruler lost all interest in the Russians and allowed the Moslems (and some Christians) under him to attack the boats that had come to the Volga River. He notified his "partners" about the planned campaign at the last minute and then washed his hands in despair. Evidently the warning arrived too late and the Russians could not mount any serious defense.

Here is another episode. In 943-944 (or 944-945), one of the Russian detachments invaded the Azerbaijan city of Berdaa near the Koura River and wanted to make it a Russian stronghold. The Persian historian Ibn Miskaveikh wrote (in Arabic) that the ruler of Marzban province was unsuccessful in his attempts to retake the Russian stronghold, though Moslems who had remained in the city actively helped him. But all of a sudden, the invaders developed stomach trouble and deemed it better to get into their boats with the loot and leave the city at night, without much ado. According to the Armenian contemporary historian Movses Kagakatvatsi, the Russians' illness did not come about by itself. The unwelcome invaders had just been poisoned. So much for the Russians' counterintelligence!

5. A Woman Saves the City

The first counterintelligence operation may date back to the beginning of Olga's rule. Otherwise, how can one evaluate her actions in 945, right after the murder of her husband Igor, in the land of Derevskaya? She managed to entice the guilty (and she considered all the Drevlian nobility guilty of complicity) to come to her own province, detained them and pronounced a verdict. According to the chronicle, the Drevlian walked into the trap of their own free will, for (having censured the greedy Igor Riurikovich, Olga's husband) they had only the happy thought of sending a delegation to the widow with a proposal to marry their "good" prince (as it were). Knowing from the chronicles about Olga's "famous craftiness" (she later managed to delude even the Byzantine emperor), one may assume that she found a way to provoke the Drevlians to such a risky affair (for instance, she may have disseminated false rumors).

She did not act single-handedly, of course. The men who were digging the great hole in the ground, in Olga's courtyard, must have known what they were doing. As did those of her people who were invited to the palace the next morning to attend the royal feast. For they never disputed the Drevlians' insolent proposal to take them to Olga's palace, by carrying the boat in which they had arrived on their shoulders. So her people must have known that such were Olga's orders. They claimed that since their prince was no longer alive and their princess was about to marry another prince, there was not much to dispute. And they carried their enemies in their boat. But having entered the court-yard, they suddenly heaved the boat into the pit. The scenario must have been written beforehand and all the roles assigned clearly. Olga managed to inquire of her envoys whether they were pleased with the reception; then the twenty simpletons were buried alive.

In the miniature picture of the Radzivil chronicle, three sturdy men are shown who, like Atlantes, are carrying on their shoulders a boat full of peacefully conversing Drevlians. The artist must have imag-ined that Kiev was full of heroes and he did not care to take into ac-count the weight they were carrying. Indeed, if we take the weight of each man in a boat to be about 70 kilos (150 pounds) then the total would be about two tons, not counting the vessel itself. The chronicle treats lightly a world record in weight lifting that is unattainable nowadays. But that is not our concern . . . Olga is shown in the picture twice: once on the balcony of her palace, witnessing the event, and then looking down at the offenders hopelessly trapped in the pit. In both cases she is stern and calm as a person performing an important and naturally right act.

The first Russian history writer Vasily Nikitich Tatishchev, who was a young aide of Peter the Great, described the events according to some other chronicles that have not survived to our day (and some-times he added his own commentaries to the text). He wrote in "Russian History" that after the execution of the Drevlians, Olga, the charismatic ruler of Kiev, immediately imposed "strong cordons" on the frontier with the Drevlians so that "nobody could send a word about the story there". At the same time she sent "some reliable men" as am-bassadors. According to the lost revelations, a new lineup of "security services" came into existence at this time: frontier guards and inter-cepting detachments, and, of course, the envoys themselves — the "reliable men" — the ambassadors, who were also partners in the power-game.

They asked the Drevlians to send to Kiev a delegation of the no-blest of their people; otherwise the Kievan citizens would not let the princess leave the city. The Drevlians sent there "the best men that were in their land". When the guests arrived, they were invited to go to the bathhouse; the door was shut behind them and then the place was set on fire. The executioners must have been the same men as the first time. The artists of the time depicted them similarly. We see the same three men; two of them are setting the naive Drevlian "nobility" afire, and the third one, portrayed as possessing an ample crown of hair and clad in a coat (the sign of a dignitary), strikes the pose of a guardian angel descended to earth (familiar in medieval icons) and discusses with Olga the progress of the "operation", pointing with his hand to the flaming "bathhouse".

The last act of the "revenge" operation took place on the enemy's territory. Olga once again sent a message to the Drevlians to the effect that she wanted to visit the grave of her husband to mourn and to pray (after which she could think about marriage). Let the Drevlians come to the place and bring with them "wine and victuals". The latter did not blink an eye, and went to Igor's grave near Iskorosten' with a host of about five thousand men. Olga arrived with a "small detachment", cried over her spouse's grave, then ordered a mound to be made over it and a sermon given. The Drevlians sat down to drink the wine they had brought along and which was "plentiful". Olga's men served them. Some of them asked Olga where were their former ambassadors. The princess answered calmly that they were coming, presently, with Igor's troops. Having noticed that her would-be relatives were already giddy, she ordered her men to accelerate the process of inebriation by repeatedly calling to toast their health. She then slipped away under some pretext and gave a sign to her guard. The five thousand Drevlians remained forever at the place where they had feasted.

Let us once again have a look at the illustrated book. This time the artist must have made some kind of blunder. Instead of Olga, he showed the Drevlian Prince toasting with a huge cup of wine. The artist must have thought that the "bridegroom" was also present at the occasion (he did not read the text carefully enough). At the same time, two other men are slashing the drunken Drevlians with swords, others are already on horseback ready to go back to Kiev. Here again we see three people in action. Maybe the artist had some inside information about the events, as he did not always follow the text. In that case, we should only regret that the names of such valiant men were lost.

The business was finally sealed by a military campaign led by the teenaged Svyatoslav, his uncle Asmud, and army leader Sveneld. They managed the campaign in the usual way, defeating the Drevlians in an open battle and then laying siege to their capital. In order to ultimately crush them, as before, they relied on Olga's wit (unleashing pigeons and sparrows that set the city on fire).

Curiously enough, such influential men as Sveneld and Asmud are mentioned in the chronicle only in connection with the armed hostilities. Their participation in Olga's previous actions must have been insignificant. Describing the events, the chronicler mentioned only "the Kievans, men and host", that is the citizens, palace servants and troops whose names were of no relevance, for they were just ordinary operatives (the reliable people mentioned by Tatishchev may have been boyars). Emotional, strong-willed, dominating, witty and legendarily beautiful, the princess handled the reins throughout a complex and crafty counterintelligence operation. In the final analysis, should we not call her the founder of domestic counterintelligence services?

Of course there were no permanent "competent entities" at the time, and for a long time to come. When there was a need, suitable people were selected. When the necessity was over, they engaged in more mundane affairs. Citizens went about their business as usual, their professional crafts or trades, tended to the royal court or went into the military. The host "sharpened their swords" and "deliberated" with the princess (but about other things).

6. How a Lad, Together with Voivode Pretich, Saved Kiev
or, Disinformation as a Factor in Victory

By the end of her life, the aging princess once again demonstrated her will and her wit. In the summer of 968 AD, the Pechenegs, having allowed the Kievan host of Prince Svyatoslav pass through their lands on their way to the Danube, suddenly appeared at the gates of Kiev and laid siege to it with a great number of troops. On the other side of the Dnieper was the Chernigov commander Pretich, but he did not dare to rescue the besieged city for, apparently, his forces were insufficient. Then the local citizens sought a brave individual who could pass through the Pechenegs lines and tell Pretich that if he did not come to the rescue the next day, the Kievans would have to surrender because of lack of victuals and water. A volunteer was found. So he went at night to carry out the dangerous mission. He set out with a horse's halter in his hand and inquired among the enemy solders about his lost horse. He managed to reach the riverbank, "pulled off his pants and waded into the water, and made it to the opposite side". The Pechenegs, realizing the charade, went after him and started to shoot arrows, but in vain. Russian boats came to his aid and the scout's deed succeeded.

This unknown character is also shown in the picture in the Radziwill chronicle. He is wading the Dnieper, naked, holding in his hand something resembling a scepter. Maybe the artist wanted to emphasize that he was not an accidental volunteer but a formal envoy from Olga, who had to show Pretich some tangent symbol of his mission. On the left one can see Kiev, and a soldier who is sending the messenger off. A bit closer stands a Pecheneg, using his bow and looking a bit like a modern "Mafioso". On the right a man helps the messenger get into the boat.

When Pretich learned about the disastrous situation of the besieged city, he decided "early the next morning to come to the city by boat, to break through the guards and, having rescued the princess and her three grandsons Yaropolk, Oleg and Vladimir, to get them to the opposite bank of the river."

Tatishchev in "History of Russia" tells us about all this in more detail but somewhat differently. "Voivode Pretich", we read in his book, "convened a council where nearly everybody agreed that with so few troops they could not defend the city against so numerous an enemy, and just to enter it without supplies would not bring any benefit but would be a disaster. Pretich argued that while they were in their boats the Pechenegs could not do them much harm; therefore he proposed they go in boats and if they did not manage to defend the city, they could at least rescue the princess and her grandsons. 'If we do not do this', he is quoted as saying, 'Svyatoslav will then castigate us. I am afraid of him, for he is an extremely fierce man.'"

The Lavrientiev chronicle tells it differently. "The Russians started out at dawn and hailed the people in the city. The Pechenegs thought the Prince had come back and fled from the city. Olga with her grandsons and some other men managed to get to the boats."

Tatishchev writes that the Russians embarked at night and as soon as the dawn arose, they moved to the city shouting very loudly.

The citizens organized a sortie and started fighting the enemy.

Which version is closer to the truth? Either way, this was clearly a well-planned simultaneous operation, in which Olga and her grandsons had to appear on the riverbank as soon as the Pretich host arrived, so that they could cross the river at once.

The artist of the Radzivil chronicle (to be more accurate, the ancient chronicle from which he copied) had the same understanding. He depicted Olga with her men walking out of the city to meet Pretich's boat. In front of Olga two little princes are walking (evidently Yaropolk and Oleg). One of them is holding the hand of a man who is conversing with Pretich. Behind him another boyar, addressing either him or Pretich, points at Olga. Otherwise, if she did not know the intentions of her Voivode, who broke into the city, she would hardly have dared to leave the fortress. That confirms the description of the Kievan scout's mission and sheds additional light on his actions.

They managed at first to deceive the Pechenegs, but when their leader learned that the Russian force was not numerous he came back to inquire who they were. Pretich gave a diplomatic answer: "We are people from the other bank". When asked if he was the prince, he said, "I am his man and am head of a reconnaissance detachment. Behind me comes the Prince with a great many troops." The scribe added that he threatened them. The new false information had its effect. After exchanging sabers as a token of friendship, the Pechenegs lifted the siege (in the Radzivil chronicle there is a picture showing Pretich donating a huge saber). Later on, Svyatoslav did, indeed, come to their rescue and chased off the nomads into the steppes.

Chapter II.

UNEQUAL COMPETITION:
SVYATOSLAV'S INTELLIGENCE AGAINST BYZANTIUM AND ITS ALLIES

1. The First Balkan Campaign. Voivode Volk

Svyatoslav appeared at the Danube following an agreement with Nicephorus II Phocas, in order to destroy the Bulgarians, who were the enemies of the Eastern Roman Empire. According to the agreement of 944 AD, Russian princes were to accord military assistance to Constantinople's rulers in the event that any "hot spot" should emerge within their vast possessions. And Russian troops, in alliance with the Greeks, reached Syria, Crete and Sicily. Besides wishing to use good pagan swords for the glory of the leader of all Christians, the Byzantine emperor was eager to distract the attention of the too-militant prince from his traditional prey along the Black Sea coast and Crimea. Svyatoslav, for his part, heeded calls of his highly placed "friend", but not because he was deluded by his gifts (15 hundredweight of gold — i.e. about 455 kg — brought to Kiev by the emperor's ambassador Calokir to be divided among the prince and his troops), as we are assured by the Byzantine chroniclers Leo Diacon of Caloy and John Scylitzes.

Svyatoslav himself is believed to have been indifferent to treasure (with the exception, perhaps, of ornamented weapons!). He had his own and rather significant interests in the Balkans. Historians consider them in different ways. Some think that he wanted to conquer at least all of Bulgaria and become a close neighbor to the Eastern Romans, so that he could more easily and expeditiously levy tribute from the

Greeks and exert more influence on the Empire's political and trade relations with Russia. Others maintain that he simply wanted to control the lower reaches of the Danube, which was the major trade and transportation artery of southeast Europe. This may be credible, as Svyatoslav's immediate goal; or maybe he wanted to surround the core of his possessions with friendly (first of all Bulgarian) lands, that is to act in the Balkans as a Slavic patron.

Most probably, the Kievan prince thought to align his political and military strategy with the prevailing situation, though Leo Diacon assures us that, during the negotiations with Calokir, Svyatoslav "dreamed" of becoming the ruler of the Moesian (Bulgarian) lands. . . Unfortunately, we do not know the contents of the agreement concluded between Kiev and Constantinople. Russian chronicles do not mention it and do not even discuss the Byzantine diplomatic mission's arrival at the Dnieper. Maybe such an agreement, if there was one, was never committed to writing. According to A. N. Sakharov, "Alliances at the time were implemented either by oral negotiations or by mail, using specials envoys." One should also bear in mind that the parties had to observe certain precautions of military nature. Kiev and Constantinople were full of foreigners: merchants, travelers, mercenaries of all sorts. That might have led to "an information leak" if there were open talk of such and such potential alliances. By contrast, a military affair prepared in secret promised to yield success. Such ambassadorial missions were in wide usage long ago, and Calokir's agreement in Kiev is one such. Calokir's mission remained unknown to Russian chroniclers; only very few people must have known of his talks with the Russian prince. The essence of the Russian-Byzantine agreement was that Svyatoslav came to the Balkans as the "Empire's friend". That is all the more interesting, given that historical literature holds that the Pecheneg attack on Kiev during Svyatoslav's absence took place with the help of Byzantine intelligence, which informed some of the chiefs of the nomadic hordes that their stars had spun into favorable alignment.

If this premise is not false, one may think that the imperial secret service acted on an impulse, tempted by the opportunity to trip up an ally at the earliest possible occasion.

Of course the Pechenegs might have managed without the help of the "crafty" Greeks and Bulgarians (according to another version); they were, at the time, greatly interested in subverting the Russians at their most vulnerable point. For the Pechenegs must have been the first to detect Svyatoslav's troops passing through their land. Svyatoslav was not aware of what was happening behind him as he and his troops moved forward. An envoy from Kiev came to Pereyaslavets (Preslav), while he was occupying it, told him what had happened, and rebuked him. "You, Prince, seek foreign lands and neglect your own, for the Pechenegs nearly overtook us, your mother and your children. If you do not come soon and defend us they will overrun us. Do you not care for your homeland, your old mother and children?" Of course, Svyatoslav heeded the call and drove the nomads into the "field" (the steppe), but this did not eliminate the danger. Communication to the Black Sea Coast passed through the very steppes where one nomadic wave swept through after another and which represented the most vulnerable link in the communication system — a constant headache for the Kievan princes. This geo-military weakness was one of the major reasons why the Russians left the Balkans and why the Tmutorakan' principality (at Taman' and the Crimea) perished.

It was also the cause of Svyatoslav's death.

When he headed back to Rus', the prince must have left at least a few garrisons in some of the conquered places, to maintain his control over the region. Whether or not the Bulgarians had a hand in the Pecheneg attack against Kiev, they definitely would not miss a chance to take back what they had lost and to liberate themselves from this new Russian suzerainty. According to V. N. Tatishchev, they laid siege to the center of the new Rus' possessions, at Pereyaslavets.

It was defended by Voivode (military governor) Volk. The besieged soon felt the "dearth of victuals". And their intelligence informed them that some of the townsfolk had established contacts with the Bulgarians, who were up to no good. As we will see, Voivode Volk managed to scuttle their plans.

First, Volk decided to leave Pereyaslavets and march to meet Svyatoslav. But all the routes away from the stronghold, and the waterway down the Danube, were blocked by Bulgarian forces. Then the voivode decided to make good use of the presence of Bulgarian eyes and ears in the city of Pereyaslavets and to create a false impression about his plans and intentions. He spread rumors to the effect that he was going to defend Pereyaslavets until Svyatoslav came or "to the last man"; he ordered all the horses and cattle to be slaughtered, and the meat to be salted and dried. At the same time, his men secretly prepared boats at the Danube riverside. One night, Volk's men set fire to the stronghold in several places. The Bulgarians apparently thought it was a signal from their allies and stormed the city. Volk, at that time, with his host, servants and hoi polloi, boarded the boats and left the city. On the opposite bank of the Danube, he towed away all of the Bulgarian boats, thus eliminating any chance for the enemy to pursue him. ("The Bulgarians could not stop him, for all their boats had been confiscated.") That was a typical example of deceiving the enemy by disseminating false information. If only this entire description represents a true story!

We can only add that later on, Prince Vladimir had in his service a voivode called Volchiy Khvost (Wolf's Tail); he may well have been an offspring of Tatishchev's Volk.

2. Calokir's Scheme and Svyatoslav's New Plans. War with Byzantium

Despite Volk's success, the actions of Svyatoslav's secret services hardly merit applause. According to Byzantine chronicles, at least, during the second advance of the Russian troops into the Balkans (969-971) there were more failures than successes. And there are two reasons for that, according to my thinking.

First there was a general delay in the institutionalization of the secret services in pagan Rus' compared to its more advanced neighbors. Second was the personality of Svyatoslav himself. One chronicler depicts him thus: "When Svyatoslav grew up and matured, many brave men came to his service. He moved lightly, like a leopard, and fought many a war. He never surrounded himself or his host with a convoy, he never stewed nor boiled meat, but having cut it into small pieces he broiled it over the charcoal. He did not have a tent; he slept on the ground with his head on a saddle. The same did all his men. When he intended to attack a people, he sent an envoy ahead to voice his intention: "I wish to march on you."

Nice picture of a soldier! And it must be true. For even his contemporary, the Byzantine chronicler Leo Diacon (in the 10th century), who is averse to lauding "Tauroscythians and Russes", calls Svyatoslav a "hot and brave man, charismatic and active". What soldier would not envy such a compliment? Or what commander, who thinks it his duty to set an example? But a military leader who, so affably, warns his enemy of the impending onslaught evidently may only count on the psychological impact but not on much else. And more often than not, psychological action alone is not enough but it should be supplemented by additional military deceptions, active reconnaissance, espionage, etc.. But whom could he trust with such a task if "all his men were like himself"? And one should not wonder that the very first competition in the art of deception between the Russians and the Greeks, described by the imperial chroniclers Leo Diacon and John Scylitzes (in the 11th century), was concluded in favor of the latter. This happened after the first, insincere, alliance between the two powers had come to an end.

It had to do with the succession to the Byzantine throne and, according to Leo Diacon, to the activity of the former emperor's ambassador to Svyatoslav. Diacon attributed Calokir's treason of the Empire to the time of his stay in Kiev. Calokir ("a man of rather short temper in all respects") "persuaded" Svyatoslav to enter the war in order to win the throne in Constantinople ("to help fight the Eastern Romans, in order to ascend the throne and gain possession of the Eastern Romans' power"). He also meant to acquire Bulgaria for himself ("to conquer and keep the country for his own sojourn"), a country that was worthy of the attention of the future Vasilevs ("huge, untold riches from the king's treasury"). Allegedly he even swore fraternity with the half-wild and avaricious barbarian. (Fraternizing with a foreigner was a crime in itself, according to the Byzantine laws.)

Scylitzes, for his part, states that Calokir tried to persuade the Russians that if he were to be proclaimed Emperor of the Eastern Romans, he would cede Bulgaria to them, conclude eternal union with them, enhance the nature of the gifts promised by the agreement, and be their ally and friend for life. Contrary to his predecessor, Scylitzes did not blame the haughty patrician for the horrors suffered by the Empire and the trials to come ("he deluded them with his crafty speech"); he hinted that the Russians had their own considerations in embarking on the new military campaign. "Astonished at the beautiful locality", explained Scylitzes, "they severed the treaty concluded with Emperor Nicephorus and deemed it best to stay in the country and possess it."

We will not dispute the Russians' motives, which seem so naive from the modern point of view. The main thing is — they acted, of course, according to their own perceived best interests. Svyatoslav's collusion with the claimant to the most venerable position in the Christian world took place because both parties were more than ready for such an arrangement. It turned the shaky alliance with Byzantium into open enmity. The Kievan prince and the new emperor, John Tzimisces, twice exchanged rather inflammatory messages. The Emperor started the quarrel and, according to Leo Diacon's story, demanded that the Russians, having already received the promised remuneration, retreat from "Moesia" to their lands and the Bosporus of Cimmeria" (the Kerch straits). But Svyatoslav, "who became arrogant and haughty", responded in an impertinent manner: "I shall leave this rich country only after I receive a huge monetary tribute and ransom for all captured cities and prisoners. If the Eastern Romans do not pay what I ask, then I demand they leave Europe — to which they have no right — at once, and go to Asia. Otherwise they can abandon hope for a peace with the Tauroscythians." That is, we are newcomers here. But don't forget that you are strangers here also. So what if you have lost Bulgaria? . . . Tzimisces replied: "If you do not leave the country, we will drive you out against your will. I suppose you have not forgotten the defeat of your father Igor, who violated a sworn treaty and came to our capital with a huge host. . . and went back to the Bosphorus of Cimmeria with a score of boats and became a herald of his own ill fortune. I will not go into details about his pitiful fate. . . I think that you, too, will not return to your fatherland if you provoke the Eastern Roman power to repel you. You shall find your end here with all your troops, and no torchbearer shall return to Scythia to break the news of your horrible fate."

"Enraged and carried away by his barbarian frenzy and madness", Svyatoslav responded in kind. He sent to Constantinople the message, "I do not see any necessity for the Emperor to hurry toward us; the Emperor should not trouble himself by traveling to this country. We shall make strong barriers around the city and if he dares to come to us, if he decides to suffer such a scourge, we will meet him bravely and show him that we are not mere craftsmen who earn their bread by toil of hand. We are men of blood, who defeat the enemy by the strength of our weapons. In vain, in his foolishness, the Emperor takes the Russians for frail ladies and tries to intimidate us by various threats. . . ." That is how the Byzantine scribes depicted the diplomatic conflict between the Eastern Christian Empire and Russia, after Calokir's successful intrigue to occupy the throne of Byzantium.

The Russian chronicler, who was unaware of the Kievan Prince's "crazy talk", "full of barbarian boasting," according to Scylitzes, narrates the events somewhat differently and most probably using the legends that came down to him in his time. According to his sources, an active exchange of ambassadors took place at the time when Svyatoslav, having come back to the Danube, dealt a new and severe defeat to the Bulgarians, recaptured Pereyaslavets and then sent his envoys to Tsargrad. "By nightfall, Svyatoslav took the city with his lance and sent his men to the Greeks, saying: 'I want to assault your city and take it, as I have done with this other one.'"

In the *History of Russia*, by Tatishchev, this major decision is explained as one-sided and mysterious. And he links it to the success of Russian counterintelligence. "Having learned that the Greeks instigated the Bulgarians to fight against him, he sent a messenger to Constantinople to declare war because of their tsar's wrongdoing." Indeed, it is quite probable that the Prince hurled such an accusation at the Greeks during vituperative talks — and Leo Diacon may have just forgotten about it. Or maybe he withheld the fact, in an effort to downplay the low moral policy of the empire. And maybe Svyatoslav himself took the initiative of exchanging compliments, if he had already decided what he wanted to do next. But maybe, too, Svyatoslav simply did not accept fraud and hypocrisy, for he was a straightforward and short-tempered man.

According to the Primary Chronicle (or *Tale of Bygone Years*), the Byzantines having received a formal declaration of war, responded: "We cannot withstand you; you may collect tribute for yourself and for your troops. Please tell us how large is your host, so that we can collect something for each of you." For those who miss the subterfuge, the chronicler explains that Constantinople used the opportunity to seek to assess the enemy's military potential. "Thus acted the Greeks, trying to deceive Rus' as they so slyly continue to try, up to this day".

Svyatoslav tried his cunning, too, and gave double the number of troops at his disposal (10,000). But in this way he only aggravated his situation, for the worried Eastern Romans paid no tribute; they raised 100,000 men against him. (Byzantine authors count the troops absolutely in reverse. Thus, according to Leo Diacon, at the battle near Arkadiopolis, the Tauroscythians and their allies had 30,000 and

Strategus Varda Sclir — 10,000. But according to Scylitzes, the Russians had nearly 308,000 [!] and the Greeks — 12,000.) In the dreadful battle that followed, whose location remains unknown (for Byzantine chroniclers "naturally" forgot it and our scribe did not make it clear), Svyatoslav scored the victory and marched on the Empire's capital, "fighting and conquering the cities en route, that are still vacant up to this day". Such events are circumstantially confirmed by some Byzantine sources. Leo Diacon has it that "mad speeches" by the Tauroscythian leader made the Emperor Tzimisces "prepare for war with all diligence in order to preclude the onslaught and block the way to the capital." Scylitzes tells us of an inscription on the tomb of Nicephorus Phocas, summoning the Emperor to "rise from the dead, for all the Russian weapons have come against us and Scythian tribes are ready to slaughter . . ." And again, on the pedestal of an equestrian statue on a plaza in Taur, are stories about the last days of the city when Russians were ready to destroy it. Probably the would-be clairvoyant was afraid of Svyatoslav, "who stopped short of Tsargrad" (Constantinople).

In the course of the panic in Constantinople, the Emperor gathered his noblemen for counsel and said: "What shall we do, if we cannot repel him?" They advised him to send gifts and try to trick him by offering gold and fabrics". Emperor Tzimisces agreed and sent a "wise man" with the instruction: "Look hard in his face and examine his expression, try to estimate his wit." But Svyatoslav did not pay any attention to the tribute and told his men to hide it away. The envoys came back to Constantinople with empty hands, leaving the tsar and his "boyars" with another problem. Then the wisest councilor rose to his feet and proposed to "tempt" Svyatoslav once again by offering him weapons. "The others agreed, and sent him a sword and other weapons. He accepted it, began to praise it, and thanked the tsar." This new report, with the results of the "personality test", caused the council to make a unanimous recommendation to the monarch. "The man is fierce and wild, he does not cherish riches but accepts weapons. You should consent to pay tribute". The emperor gave his consent and dispatched to the Russians another ambassador (the fourth one), accepting all the conditions laid down by Svyatoslav. That saved them from having him fix his shield on the Tsargrad gates. After that, the Kievan prince went back to Pereyaslavets, content with the tribute and happy to be able to recompense those who had perished, by sending some of it to their relatives.

This simple and somewhat naive tale, rendered in the poetic style of a folk legend, contains to my mind some extremely interesting and unique information that has not been fully appreciated until now — specifically, the "personality test" that Byzantine envoys performed on the leader of the Russian host.

Such methods are well-known and practiced in modern times, when they are available to intelligence services all over the world. They were less common in previous epochs. It is clear: the less complex the system, the greater the leader's influence on the system. And this was also known in medieval times; people were keenly aware of one person's significance (at least in the upper circles of the society) as well as of their learned offspring's. This conclusion certainly is valid for Byzantium — creator of one of the highest medieval civilizations. In the many extant Byzantine compositions of the 6th-11th centuries on military art, much attention is paid to intelligence and counterintelligence and considerable interest is shown in the enemy's military leaders.

According to the treatise *De velitatione bellica*, written by an unknown author who was close to Svyatoslav's ally, Emperor Nicephorus Phocas, intelligence on the military leaders of the enemy was considered the most important, along with news about their troops' numbers, the quantity of footmen and cavalry, places of billeting and direction of movement. Garrison chiefs at the frontier strongholds collected primary intelligence. Diplomacy played a significant role in amassing information about military and political leaders and was of major importance in the overall strategy of military campaigns. So if we focus on the content (and not the form) of the events in the chronicle, we have to admit that the old Russian scribe did not slander "the sly Greeks" who, in attaining their aims, used bribery and hoax ("if he falls for gold and fine cloth").

Naturally, neither the scribe nor those who told him about Svyatoslav's valiant deeds were present at the meetings in the emperor's palace. But their predecessors, who went with the prince to the Balkans, may have seen Byzantine ambassadors either in the Russian tents on the Danube riverbank, in a mountain valley, or in quiet chambers in one of the cities captured by Svyatoslav, and they may have drawn an appropriate conclusion that did not differ from those that the chronicler and his contemporaries drew from meetings in Kiev. For Greeks "have not changed in their customs till this day". And while the Russians may not have approved such practices, they could hardly help but adopt them themselves.

The chain of events in Byzantine and Russian chronicles hardly coincides, and it is rather difficult to reconstruct them. There are grounds to suppose that the Kievan prince had some initial success. He could not have "stopped short" of Constantinople, as the chronicle mentions, without active counteraction on the part of the Eastern Roman phalanxes, without at least one major battle. It seems quite probable that the expeditionary corps of stratopedarch (military camp chief) Peter was destroyed in the winter of 969-970 along with the corps of *stratilates* Varda Sclir, who came from Asia Minor and headed toward Thrace. According to Leo Diacon, both military leaders got orders from the Emperor to station their troops in lands adjacent to Moesia (Bulgaria), to train their soldiers there and to go about the country so that no harm would be inflicted on it from Scythian encroachments." And though the next actions of Varda Sclir are depicted in some detail, there is no further mention of Peter. Though Leo of Caloy tells us that once "during a Scythian assault on Thrace, Peter and his detachment fought them". He allegedly demolished the barbarian military leader during a man-to-man combat. But the chronicler never mentions the outcome of the battle itself. Scylitzes does not mention Peter at all, as if the latter did not even participate in the battle. Sometimes omissions are more expressive than words.

3. Intelligence Among the Byzantines and Russians

According to Leo Diacon, Emperor Tzimisces "instructed Varda Sclir and Peter to send, to the military camps and the regions occupied by the enemy, people clad in Scythian attire who speak both tongues in order to learn about enemy intentions and report them to the Emperor." Byzantium entered the war using all the military experience and art developed from antiquity to medieval times. The diversified system of imperial intelligence gathering did not limit itself to sending spies to enemy camps disguised as enemy warriors (*stratiote*) or peasants, merchants or local inhabitants. They also sent *traipsetes*, who were experts in military and reconnaissance matters. They were "listed separately" and were headed by chiefs (*archonts*) who, besides being brave and experienced in military affairs, also "knew the roads and the localities".

The main mission of such investigators-*traipsetes* was to "bring harm to the enemy lands and to terrorize the local population". If possible, they were supposed "to kidnap somebody and bring him to the *strategus* in order to find out the enemy's intentions and the routes of his movements" (V. V. Kuchma). Such instructions were given in the Byzantine military book *De velitatione bellica*, intended for the military leaders who fought the Arabs in Syria. But in essence these instructions were not much different from those intended for their northern counterparts. The more so that *patrician* and *stratopedarch* Peter, before his march to Thrace, became famous due to his success in fighting the Arabs and conquering Antiochia. Intelligence procured by the scouts was relayed to road guards and then was transmitted to stationary lookouts — *viglas*. The latter were established by *strategi* of frontier provinces and were deployed in several lines or rows.

Such lookouts were posted on high ground, a few miles apart, surveying the most dangerous directions in order to provide timely detection of the enemy. They not only relayed information but also gathered military data. They were manned by physically fit persons who knew the vicinity well; they were replaced every two weeks. From time to time, experienced archons were sent by strategi to check their performance. *Viglas* were stationary but mobile. In the opinion of Byzantine military experts, this enhanced their survival ratio in case of a surprise attack by enemy reconnaissance. Given that several rows of them were deployed, such tactical methods undoubtedly increased the security of the Byzantine frontier lands. Communication between the lines in the mountainous country was probably achieved with the help of bonfires, as was the custom many centuries before. They could convey not only the fact of an enemy's approach but his strength. In some cases, they probably used special envoys, if the information required specific detail. *Viglas* of the last row relayed intelligence on horseback to stations located even farther from the frontier. Those further conveyed the messages to a *strategus*, who informed Constantinople.

Russian hosts since the times of Askold and Oleg may have encountered such a sophisticated system of military reconnaissance whenever they engaged in war with the Empire. We do not know what means they used to counter it. About Svyatoslav, Leo Diacon tells us only that when he learned of the approach of Peter and Varda Sclir (probably from his own scouts), the "Tauroscythians detailed a part of their troops, added a great number of Huns and Moesians, and sent them against the Eastern Romans". The Byzantine historian pointed out a very important feature of Svyatoslav's activity as a statesman and military leader: his active secret diplomacy, which made it possible to become an ally not only of the subjugated Bulgarians headed by Tsar Boris but also of the Pechenegs and the Huns (Tatishchev suggests that Svyatoslav was married to a Hungarian princess) and maybe even the Poles. These alliances concluded in the late 960s made it possible for Svyatoslav to control the conquered lands and easily recover losses. And, it gave him a mobile reserve of cavalry that could be sent off on a distant raid upon a suddenly discovered enemy or to exploit a propitious situation.

The maneuverability of his troops was thus enhanced his position overall, since most Russian troops preferred to fight on foot. Maybe the late discovery of Varda Sclir's troops made the prince "detail" the most mobile portion of his host and supplement them with Bulgarians, Huns and Patzinaks (Pechenegs, as they are called by Scylitzes) and send them against the enemy. Thus he greatly reduced the might of his own forces. Maybe this circumstance played the fatal role in the further march of Russians onto Constantinople, and his reconnaissance was at fault for not detecting Varda Sclir in proper time.

It may have been that the success of Varda and the Byzantine commanders was based on their managing to outwit the "Tauroscythians" and scatter their troops. Dispersion of enemy troops was one of the most important features of the military strategy and tactics of the Empire. One cannot exclude the possibility that Varda Sclir (with the help of informants) assisted Russian scouts to detect his troops and, having spread false notions about his military strength, induced Svyatoslav to remove from the major forces as many of his troops as possible. The Kievan prince must have thought that he would be able to quickly restore the previous ratio of forces by annihilating the sudden flare-ups. But if we believe the Greek scribes, fate decided otherwise.

Stratilatis and *magister*, Varda Sclir was an experienced military leader; he used sophisticated deceptive tactics and psychological stratagems (and, according to Leo Diacon, he was fierce and valiant as well). Having expected the "Scythian" regiments (they may have been led by Sveneld or Volk) at Arcadiopolis, he decided to defeat the enemy by a military ruse and some artful deployment of mechanical equipment.

And so it happened. The Byzantine feigned cowardice, locked himself in the fortress, and bolted all the gates and doors. "He kept his troops within the walls, though the enemy, many a time, attempted to make them come out for a decisive battle. He stayed within, even when he saw them plundering the vicinity. So the competition in various deception maneuvers was won, as one may have expected, by the "sly Greeks", who not only withstood all deception but, what is more, managed to dupe the naive Scythians.

The Byzantines' behavior "caused the barbarians to despise them". They thought that Sclir had locked himself in the city because he feared them. They roamed the vicinity, became careless in their camp, drank at night, played flutes and cymbals, and danced barbarian dances; the guards lost their vigilance. Medieval historians (including the Byzantines) very often mingled reality with imagination and tried to present what they desired as real facts. But, by contrast to modern historians, most often they did not do so deliberately. Depicting the situation in the camp of the Slavs, the Hungarians and the Pechenegs, they did not stray far from the truth. At least one is inclined to believe them (especially Scylitzes), for even nowadays such carelessness and imprudence are still to be met in Russia.*

---

*In *Taras Bulba*, N. V. Gogol has a Tatar woman wandering through the camp of the Cossacks who were set to besiege a Polish town. The scene takes place near the tent of Bulba's son, Andriy, who is in love with the voivode's daughter. The Tartar is her servant:

The field was scattered with carts . . . full of loot from the enemy. Near the carts, or under them and farther away one could see Cossacks from Zaporozhie lying on the grass. They slept in strikingly picturesque poses: some lay their heads on sacks, others on hats, still others rested them on the bodies of their fellows . . . One could hear heavy snoring from the grass, echoed by the shrill neighing of horses indignant at their tethered feet. The bonfires were dying and the guards were nodding off after a good repast. Andriy wondered at such carelessness and thought: "It is a good thing that no strong enemy is nearby and there is no one to fear".

He went straight to his father's cart, but his sack was not there: Ostap had taken it and was snoring, across the field, with his head on it. Andriy grabbed the sack and pulled it out from under Ostap's head, which hit the ground. Ostap sat up and with his eyes still shut, yelled: "Stop the cursed Pole! His horse, grab his horse!" Andriy was about to hit him with the sack but said: "Keep your mouth shut or I will kill you!" But Ostap was already asleep and snored so that the grass near his head swayed from his breath. Andriy timidly looked around in case Ostap had woken anybody up. One head rose nearby and,

4. Defeat at Arkadiopolis

Real life is sometimes more eloquent than the most talented fiction. Careless guards let slip information that was worth more than several sacks of victuals. Such information gives the enemy an opportunity to estimate the troops' whereabouts, their strength, the direction of their movements, and their composition and to find out their intentions. As Leo Diacon tells us, Varda Sclir summoned Ioann Alacas and sent him on a mission to investigate the Scythian host. Ioann was to procure all this intelligence as quickly as possible so that the Byzantines could prepare their soldiers for battle.

Ioann went with his men on horseback near to the Scythian camp. The next day he sent a detail to the *magister* with a request to come as soon as possible for the Scythians were located quite nearby. In all, *patrician* Alacas spent about 24 hours on the mission and did a thorough job in spite of what the scribe tells us at the end of the story.

Night has always been a scout's ally. According to *De velitatione bellica*, great attention was paid to night-time *reconnaissance details*. That is, guards were stationed around the enemy camp after the *stratig* secretly approached it. There were four *details* consisting of four horsemen each, to be replaced once or twice during the night, and they reported to the *tourmarkh*, chief of one of the regiments of the province (*theme*) within their host. Their mission was to "use the terrain and the night, to determine the strength of the enemy group by noticing the

having glanced around wildly, fell onto the ground again. After waiting a couple of minutes, Andriy went on with his job. The Tartar woman still lay on the ground, hardly breathing.

"Get up! Let's go, don't worry! Can you carry at least some of the bread, if I cannot take all of it?"

He put the sack onto his shoulder and, passing another cart, he picked up another sack of flour; and with his hands full of the bread he wanted the Tartar to carry he marched on bravely among the sleeping Cossacks.

"Andriy," old Bulba called to him when he passed nearby.

His heart jumped. He stopped and, shaking all over, whispered: "What is it?"

"You got a woman with you. When I get up I'm going to give you a good thrashing! No good shall come of you mingling with them."

He propped his head on the elbow and stared at the Tartar, whose head was wrapped in a kerchief.

Andriy stood still and did not dare to look his father in the eye. When he raised his head he saw that old Bulba was again asleep, having placed his head on the palm of his hand.

size of the camp, the noise made by the soldiers, the neighing of horses and mules." The *details* were to use special signals for communication (shouting, whistling, etc.). After being decoded, the signals were passed to the *tourmarch*, who relayed them to the *strategus*.

Alacas probably acted some other way but he managed to obtain the required intelligence and to send it with special messengers to his superior. On the basis of that information, Varda Sclir arranged the battle disposition. Leo Diacon tells us that, "having received the information, Varda divided his *phalanges* into three parts. One was to follow him, two others were to hide in the woods at the side and join the battle as soon as they heard the horn calling them. Having given such orders to his *lokhags* (commanders), he headed toward the Scythians."

One more night passed. "Then Varda waited for a propitious moment and, having examined the enemy thoroughly, set the day and the hour, placed hidden detachments at night in the most convenient locations, and sent Ioann Alacas forward in order to observe the enemy and keep him informed of their whereabouts. Ioann was to get close to the barbarians, attack them and then fake a retreat. He was to retreat slowly, in good order, until he approached the troops in hiding. Only after that he had to disperse his men and flee however and wherever they could."

A fierce battle ensued, the outcome of which, for a long time, was uncertain. Suffice it to say that it ended in full accordance with the strategic providence and tactical methods of the Byzantine military, supplemented by the personal valor of the *magister* and *stratilatis* Varda Sclir and his brother Constantine. Otherwise, we may have not learned anything about it.

It could be described otherwise. Medieval Greek historians, who were in full command of totally "objective" and unadulterated statistics, presented their "view" of the battle." They say, Leo Diacon tells us, tongue in cheek, that 50 Eastern Romans perished in the battle, a great many were wounded, and horses were killed; and Scythian losses were over 20,000." So far, by his own information, the total number of Byzantines was 10,000 and the Russians with their allies were over 30,000 strong; then the overall ratio of irreparable losses is 1: 400.

Even Scylitzes thought such figures improbable and slandering to the honor of the . . . Eastern Roman army. According to him, the "Scythians" were ten times stronger and Greeks numbered 2,000 men.

"Out of such a great number of barbarians only a few managed to survive; as for the Eastern Romans — they had 25 men killed, but nearly all the rest were injured." If we assume that "nearly all" recovered and "a few" barbarians survived — 8000 (out of 30,000), then we get a ratio of 1: 2,000.

Whatever happened, for lack of alternative sources we have to assume that although the Arkadiopolis battle was not so important as the Byzantine authors pretend (for Svyatoslav was not present there), still it certainly was detrimental for the prince and led to the conclusion of an armistice between him and the Eastern Roman Vasilevs.

By disregarding intelligence gathering, or because of its failure, a much promising military march of the Slavs and their allies onto the Eastern Roman Empire ended in a disaster.

5. Svyatoslav's Agents at the Greek Camp. Tzimisces Crosses the Rhodope Mountains

Svyatoslav did not learn much from this miserable failure. In the spring of the following year, 971 AD, John Tzimisces, having disregarded their signed agreement, headed his troops to Bulgaria in order to drive out the Russians. Svyatoslav was not prepared for such a course of events, although his informants in Constantinople (most probably native Bulgarians, or Greeks from Chersonesus) managed to detect the amassing of troops and the military activity within the Empire, and passed along the intelligence to Svyatoslav. This can be deduced from the fact that as soon as Tzimisces reached the city of Redesto on the coast of the Sea of Marmara, they met the Kievan prince's ambassadors, who presented him with angry questions from their lord.

The Greeks must have taken these "ambassadors" for scouts — and they were at least half right in assuming that. For it would have been silly not to use the occasion to survey the forces of the advancing enemy.

Scylitzes describes the encounter in as follows: "When they began rebuking the Eastern Romans for bad faith, the Emperor, clearly seeing the cause of their arrival, invited them to go about the camp and see it for themselves. After that, they would be free to go back to their chief and tell him what a good army, in perfect order, the Emperor of Eastern Romans has and is ready to wage war with." A method of intimidating the enemy by demonstration of battle power is well known in military circles all over the world. One may only wonder why the Emperor was so sure of his overwhelming superiority over the "barbarians". It was understood that he would still have to negotiate the very dangerous abysses of the Rhodope, where a small but well trained detachment could play havoc with a strong and large army. He was probably counting upon the success of his strong fire-carrying fleet that he sent under the command of *drungariy* Leo to the Danube River via the Black Sea. Besides, he must have had grounds to believe that the "stars" were favorable to him.

After he saw off the envoys, the Emperor marched without delay to Adrianopolis, where he "learned from his scouts that the narrow passes leading to Moesia (called *clysuras* because they are closed from all slides) were not guarded by the Scythians" (Leo Diacon). Tzimisces, rather pleased with such a gift from the gods, gathered his commanders (*strategi, lokhags, taxiarches*) for a counsel and spoke to them to the effect that: "I thought, comrades in arms, that the Scythians, having expected our arrival, would have spared no effort to block us by building fences and ramparts in the most dangerous, narrow and difficult passes so that we could move only with the greatest difficulty. But they have been distracted by the impending Easter and have not blocked our path, they have not impeded our ways, thinking that we will not renounce celebrating the feast, wearing holiday clothes, conducting sermons and other festivities instead of standing up to the challenges of waging a costly war. It seems to me that we had better use the favorable circumstances and pass the most difficult portion of our route as quickly as we can, before the Tauroscythians learn of our arrival, and force us to fight in the mountains. If we manage to traverse the dangerous pass before the Scythians and make a surprise attack on them, then (and God help us) we may capture the city of Preslav, the Moesian capital, and then moving onwards we can easily curb the Rhoses' (Russian) madness."

That speech is worth translating in full, for it contains interesting information about the principles used by the competing parties. As it turned out, Tzimisces counted on crossing the Rhodope canyons before the Russians and their allies took them, so he left Redesto on the heels of Svyatoslav's envoys (Scylitzes wrote: "After he let the ambassadors go, he set forth immediately with some 5,000 footmen with light weapons and 4000 cavalrymen. The rest of his host was to follow him slowly under the command of *parachimomen* Vasily.")

He was right, as it turned out, in hoping that Russians would not count on the swiftness of his march, and confident that he would not leave Redesto until the end of the festivities. This time, "The Tauro-scythians fell victim not to carelessness but naivety. For the large part pagans and newly converted Christians, they were very particular in religious matters. The cynical attitude of the upper circles of the most 'advanced' civilization was strange, foreign and despised by them."

They may also have been taken in by the Bulgarians' treachery, given that their position was rather unstable and depended to a great extent on the success of their secret diplomacy. And their failure may also have been the fault of Sphenacle, who had not placed guards along the route of the imperial troops.

In any case, Tzimisces' suggestion to cross the Rhodope at once was not greeted with enthusiasm by the Byzantium military command-ers. (Leo Diacon wrote: "The *Strategi* and *taxiarches* thought his plan ill-considered and too bold, his proposal to lead the Eastern Roman army along the canyons and the steep slopes into a foreign land rash and pos-sibly foolish enterprise. They kept their silence for a long time . . .")

They probably thought that the "barbarians" had not blocked the canyons on purpose and wanted to lure Greeks into an ambush as soon as they came down from the mountains, when they would not have time to get ready and would not be free to maneuver.

In any case, the Byzantine commanders, being experienced in military affairs, were more inclined to fear an enemy's ruse than to as-sume his naivety and neglect. The last time Svyatoslav had marched on Constantinople, he left the military men with unpleasant recollections that is not reflected by the court historian. The emperor was angry but understood their feelings. "I am aware," he said, "that recklessness and willful actions during battles may bring danger and irreparable losses . . . But if our fate is now balanced on the sword's edge and the options we have may not allow us to act as we would prefer, then we should move decisively and use the circumstances to their full extent. I hope that you who are so experienced in the vicissitudes of military affairs will agree with me. If you believe that my advice is best, then we should use the opportunity while the Scythians are inactive and are not aware of our arrival. After we cross the mountain passes, victory is in store for us. But if we are discovered while passing through the mountains, and if they put their army in order against us, then great calamity befalls us and the situation will be hopeless. So, lift up your spirits. . . Follow me as quickly as you can."

According to Leo Diacon, not only his 9,000 troops went with him as Scylitzes said, but also the "immortal" phalanx of 15,000 of the elite *hoplites* and the 13,000 horsemen; they entered the Cydera Clysura (Rishbick Pass) on Palm Sunday, April, 9. On Tuesday, the Byzantines, "contrary to all premonitions, passed through the dangerous mountains" and on Wednesday with much ado attacked the enemy ("drums echoed in the mountains, weapons rattled, horses neighed and men shouted, encouraging each other as always happens before a battle").

"The Tauroscythians, seeing the well-organized army approaching, were taken unawares; they were shocked and frightened" (Leo Diacon). "The Scythians were desperate" (Scylitzes). "But despite their pitiful situation, they hastily took up their weapons, covered themselves with shields (that were very sturdy and covered even their feet), and mustered into battle order on the field before the city, whining like beasts and shouting at the Eastern Romans". After a long and fierce battle, they were defeated; they could not withstand the heavy Byzantine cavalry. On Great Thursday, when troops with siege equipment, headed by *proedr* Vasily, arrived, Tzimisces began the assault on Veliky Preslav where the Bulgarian king Boris and Calokir were hiding. The latter fled the city "in the dead of night" and went to Svyatoslav, who was with his host at Dorostol (Doristol, Dristra). (Scylitzes asserts that Calokir appeared at the Bulgarian capital by chance, having left for the Russian camp the day before the battle.) Preslav held for two days; when it fell, the Russians lost their last allies.

6. The Collapse of the Russian and Bulgarian Union

After the Arcadiopolis battle, Byzantine chroniclers cease mentioning the "Huns" ("Turks") and the "Patzinaks" alongside the Rhos. Evidently the long-standing Russian-Hungarian-Pecheneg union had disintegrated — and not without some help on the part of the Empire's secret diplomacy, which was now supplemented by military success. Scylitzes, speaking about the events of the late summer period, noted: "So the war was not favorable to the barbarians, and they could not hope for aid from any quarter. Their own tribes were far away, and the nearby nations feared the Eastern Romans and refused to help the Russians."

After Preslav's fall, most of the Bulgarians changed their mind. During the capital's defense, they had sided with the Russians ("During the battle, many Moesians who fought against the Eastern Romans perished along with the enemy, who were to blame for the Scythian attack on them," — noted Leo Diacon), but now the situation was changed drastically. "On the way from Preslav to Dorostol, he [the Emperor] conquered Pliskouva, Dinim and many other cities that had refused to recognize Scythian rule and pledged allegiance to the Eastern Romans. After the emperor's phalanges turned out near Dorostol, "ambassadors from Constantine and other strongholds beyond the Istre (Danube) came to Tzimisces, pleading forgiveness for all their evil deeds and pledging their cities' allegiance to him. He received them graciously, and sent his troops to their strongholds in order to protect them."

That testimony suggests either that the Russian intelligence and protection system crumbled altogether, or Svyatoslav's troops were so exhausted that they could not control the key points of the conquered lands. Moreover, they seem to have stood by passively or allowed the Byzantines to corner them.

One cannot even tell whether the prince and his retinue suspected the fate that the Eastern Roman commander had in store for him. But the "Bulgarian issue" was of great concern to Svyatoslav, according to Leo Diacon. He wrote: "Svyatoslav saw that the Moesians had refused alliance to him and had gone over to the Emperor's side. Having considered the matter, he understood that this meant a profound turn for the worse for him. He therefore assembled some 300 of the most influential and noble men among the Bulgarians and slaughtered them with inhuman bestiality. Many of them were beheaded, others were put in fetters and thrown into jail."

During the Battle near Dorostol the Russians, according to Byzantine historians, put their best foot forward. "The Rhos, who had the glory of constant victories among the neighboring states, thought it would be a calamity if they should suffer a shameful defeat at the hands of the Eastern Romans. They closed ranks, squeezing their shields and lances together, and met the enemy's assault with great sang-froid.

Then they rushed the Eastern Romans, roaring like the possessed, for they were innately wild and mad". Thus wrote Leo Diacon. If only they had had, in addition to their fighting qualities, at least 60,000 of the 330,000 troops thousand asserted by Leo of Caloy. But they did not have even half that.

After the defeat, Svyatoslav locked himself up in Dorostol. Tzimisces set up camp near the city and the next day he laid siege. At the same time, Eastern Roman boats carrying fire weapons, food and supplies came up the Istre (Danube) River.

The Eastern Romans rejoiced greatly, while the Scythians were in horror — for they had heard of the liquid-fire weapon. They had heard from old men that the Eastern Romans, "wielding the Midian fire, had burned Igor's huge fleet at the Euscin Sea." So they quickly gathered their boats, and brought them close to the city wall, where the Istre makes a bend near Dorostol. But the fire-bearing boats were expecting the Scythians from all sides, so they could not escape to land. Scylitzes thought that the arrival of the boats was the signal for the siege. The emperor "did not start the assault, fearing that the Rhos could escape along the river, as it was not guarded by anyone. So he waited for the arrival of the Eastern Roman fleet. Upon its arrival, he started the siege . . ."

It does not matter which of the medieval historians was right; the fact remains that Tzimisces' strategic plan worked and the Russian army was encircled.

That was another setback for Svyatoslav's military reconnaissance, both at sea and along the river. He might not have wanted to quit the Balkans at all, even in an unfavorable situation. The prince and his voivodes must have understood what calamities the future would bring if they did not manage to break the tight land blockade. That explains the fierce battles near Dorostol. Both sides suffered severe losses, and their best soldiers perished there. The Russians lost their giant Sphenacle, who had yielded to none but Svyatoslav. The Byzantines lost "a relative of their lord," *magister* John Courkouas, who rushed forward to save "the Eastern Roman military machines". Because of his rich golden attire, the Russians took him for the Vasilevs himself.

Scylitzes, whose imagination was so rich, relates that in one of the battles the Greeks routed the Russians, drove them against the city wall and slaughtered a great many of them, destroying most of the Russian cavalry — but lost themselves only three horses.

7. "The Storm Was Raging, the Rain Was Heavy…" The Night Raid of June, 28, 971

Thanks to Scylitzes, we also have a story about one of Svyatoslav's successes, without any oblique comments, as unique as it is unsophisticated. It is the story of his last military success. It was a night raid, far away from the impoverished Dorostol, and was led by the indomitable soldier seeking to provide his men with food.

Scylitzes' text is so emphatic (he did not have to invent anything) that we quote it here without comment.

> Many of his soldiers were suffering from wounds, and hunger was at their door, for the food supply was coming to an end due to the Eastern Romans' siege. Svyatoslav took some 2,000 of his men, put them in boats, and set out in search of food. It was a dark, moonless night, it was raining furiously, and even hail slashed down with awful flashes of lightning and thunderbolts. They gathered whatever bread, grain and other victuals they could find and went back by river to Dorostol. Along the way, they spotted many convoys of soldiers along the riverbank, watering horses or gathering firewood. The barbarians disembarked, passed stealthily through the forest, and made a surprise attack; they massacred many and scattered the rest in the underbrush. Then they got back into their boats and sped to Dorostol, with a propitious wind. The emperor was enraged when he learned about this, and threatened his commanders with death.

One should also bear in mind that the Russian prince and the overwhelming majority of his soldiers were pagans. Their principal god was Perun — the god of war, storm, thunder and lightning. Thus Svyatoslav and his priests may have taken the evident signs of his presence in nature as a token of benevolence and grace, which prompted the Russian soldiers to act. "The storm was raging, the rain was heavy, lightning flashed in the darkness." I do not know whether these words from a popular Russian song about Yermak, the later conqueror of Siberia, will make an impression on an American reader, but they are dear to a Russian heart and are vividly reminiscent of the heroic deeds of Svyatoslav and his host. If one takes a sober look at the operation itself, one cannot but acknowledge that it was well planned and enjoyed one hundred percent effectiveness.

Having counted on surprise (so far, there were adverse weather conditions and no subversive actions on the Danube), Svyatoslav managed to catch the enemy off-guard. His soldiers evaded the Byzantine river guards and fulfilled their task unimpeded. On their way back, they were the first to detect the Eastern Romans' convoy troops (that is, soldiers on the lookout) and managed to take them unawares. Evidently the point of the action was not so much to inflict casualties on the enemy but to ensure a safe return to the city by cutting off and scattering the enemy messengers. They killed a good number of horses, which was important in view of the future battles. The Byzantines were dominant in heavy cavalry, and were armed with long lances; they were mainly used for breaching the otherwise impregnable Russian "wall". The cavalry losses may have been what pained the Emperor most.

Afterwards, at any event, both banks of the river were diligently guarded and Tzimisces resolved to shut up the Scythians in the city for good. He ordered trenches to be dug across the roads, and guards were placed everywhere; nobody could get out of the city to scavenge for food (Scylitzes).

According to Scylitzes, the night raid took place on June 28, 971. Another Byzantine chronicler, Ioann Zonaza, attributes it to June 23.

Both sides, and their leaders above all, were clearly nervous. Svyatoslav was evidently convinced that everything would change for the better and was expecting some favorable shift. Is that why he did not take the opportunity to get at least some of his troops out of the city on that stormy night? He probably blamed his setbacks on the wrath of the Slavic gods — and on treason.

8. Ikmor's Death. Sacrifice to Perun

In the course of the three weeks that followed, Svyatoslav repeatedly made vigorous efforts to liberate Dorostol. Both sides suffered heavy casualties. The Russians lost their third-ranking military leader — Sphenakl — a valiant and gigantic man, fearless in battle. The Greeks, for their part, lost master Ioann Kourkouas, a relative of the emperor. On the 20th of July, the day of the most important pagan holiday, the Slavic regiments were led into battle by Ikmor, the warrior they idolized. Like Sphenakl, he too was killed, and that determined the outcome of the battle.

Needless to say, the Byzantine chroniclers attribute the death of both Russian warriors to the valiance of the Byzantine soldiers who overpowered the enemy in combat. This view has generally been accepted, since there is no objective means to verify what in fact happened. However, it is worth reading more carefully Leo Diacon's account of Ikmor's death, and thereby dimming somewhat the halo that adorns the virtuous Byzantine knights.

> There was amongst the Scythians (he writes) Ikmor, the brave man, hugely built, [first] after Sfendoslav leader of the army, whom the [Scythians] honored in dignity second only to him amongst them. Surrounded by a detachment of his loyal soldiers, he fiercely rushed against the "Romeans" (Eastern Romans) and brought down many of them. On seeing this, one of the emperor's bodyguards, Animas, son of the arhigh of Crete, aflame with passionate valor, drew his sword, spurred his horse to a gallop and flung himself at Ikmor; having caught up with him, he struck him in the neck — and the Scythian head, sliced off together with the right arm, tumbled to the ground. As soon as [Ikmor] was dead, the Scythians gave up a cry (mixed with groans), and the Romeans swooped down on them. The Scythians, profoundly dispirited by the death of their leader, threw their shields over their backs and started to retreat towards the city.

"Because of this feat (says Skilitsa, practically repeating his predecessor's version verbatim), a great noise erupted, for the Romeans shouted with joy, celebrating their victory, while the Scythians wailed in dismay and lost all heart".

But did this feat really take place? For unless Animas was left-handed (and the Byzantine chroniclers do not record any individual features of the emperor's bodyguard), having come face to face with Ikmor (whether he was fighting on horseback or on foot), Animas could only have delivered a powerful blow from left to right. That is, he could have cut off not Ikmor's right, but his left arm. In order to cut off his right arm, Animas must have attacked from behind!

Given the context, it appears that that is what happened. For Leo says that Animas caught up with Ikmor — hence the latter wasn't coming towards him, but was moving away. Then it becomes understand-able why Ikmor was not able to defend himself — he was struck from behind. Finally, it is quite possible that Ikmor wasn't wearing any de-fensive armor (such audacity and contempt for danger were still popu-lar in the "barbarian" world). Otherwise Animas would not have been able to achieve anything (as was shown in his subsequent encounter with Svyatoslav). So much for the courageous and honorable heir of Crete's emir.

Leo Diacon gives us a description of a night after the battle, on July 20, 971, when the Russian hero Ikmor perished. In his words, the Russians gathered the bodies of the dead warriors, "piled them up at the city wall, made many fires and burned them. They also slaughtered many men and women taken prisoner. Having performed the bloody sacrifices, they also strangled several babies, and bantams, and drowned them in the Istre River."

This vivid description is the only mention by a Byzantine histo-rian of sacrifices among the Kievan army. It may signify the revival of pagan worship under extreme circumstances. It can be compared with events in the "Joachim Chronicle" quoted by V. N. Tatishchev. "After Olga's death, Svyatoslav stayed at Preslav on the Danube", as we read in *The History of Russia.* "He fought the Khazars, the Bulgars and the Greeks with the help of his father-in-law, the prince of the Ungrians, and the Polish prince, but he did not defeat any of them. At last, he had lost all his troops beyond the Danube near a long wall (I could not find any other mention of the wall anywhere). Then the Devil took the hearts of his retinue and they began slandering the Christians who were among their troops. They alleged that their failures were because of the Chris-tians, who angered their false gods. Svyatoslav became so fierce that he did not spare his own brother Gleb, and killed him after torture. The Christians endured the tortures with joy and received the halo of mar-tyrs. Seeing their stubborn attitude, Svyatoslav became angry with the priests for they were charming his men and strengthening the faithful. So he sent people to Kiev in order to destroy the Christian cathedrals and soon went behind them in order to slaughter all Christians."

"The long wall" is obviously Dorostol. The battle, where most of his army perished, is probably the one in which Ikmor was killed; he was the principal Russian hero. This battle was not the ultimate but the penultimate, though they took place just one day apart.

Ikmor was very popular among the rank and file Scythians, due to his physical strength and his courage. He was not of the nobility and did not belong to the prince's retinue. Thus, one may understand that he was not at the pinnacle of Slavic society and was, rather, close to the ordinary warriors. Ikmor's death had a disastrous effect on the army's morale — and Svyatoslav's, too. The demise of such an invincible hero, who had been the mainstay of the army, could have happened only at the will of an angered or discontented Perun. Leo Diacon described the event, as it made such a deep impression on him: Ikmor was killed on July 20. That was "Perun's Day", the greatest day for all Russians who bore weapons at the time. It was wartime and Ikmor's death as well that of so many other men caused a shift in the general mood. Scylitzes wrote about the night as follows: The "Scythians hid from danger behind the walls and began lamenting Ikmor's death."

The prince took part in the funeral feast; and some of his priests and zealots of the pagan faith drew his attention to the attitude of those among his troops who were Christians. Leo Diacon confirms the fact that Christian persecution began this very night. One can hardly say what may have been the accusations against the religion (that was mostly alien to the Russian society at the time) and how well substantiated they may have been. But if Svyatoslav did not spare his own brother, this confessional conflict was rather acute and may have involved other reasons as well.

Christianity was adopted in Russia only during the rule of Svyatoslav's son, Vladimir, and the attitude of Christians fighting in the Russian army was rather ambivalent for they had to fight against their own belief. The more so since the first Russians to become Christian did it voluntarily; they were ardent adherents of the faith. It was hard for them to bear rebukes of their own tribesmen, or to fight against other troops under Christian banners. However, there is no mention of a single act of treason on the part of the Russian Christians. But still, treason did take place in the camp of the Russian prince, and many an enemy spy was active among his troops.

9. Byzantine Ears at Svyatoslav's War Council. Investigation and Castigation

"The next day at dawn," according to Leo Diacon, "Svyatoslav convened a noblemen's council. When they assembled, he asked them what should be done. Some said it would be best to take their boats at night and try to escape, for there was no use to fight horsemen clad in armor, when they had already lost their best warriors — the core of the army and essential for their morale. Others reasoned they had to make peace with Eastern Romans by swearing a solemn oath, and thus spare the rest of the troops.

It would be rather difficult to slip away unnoticed, the more so as the enemy had fire-bearing boats along both sides of the river and they could burn the Russian boats as soon as they appeared. So, Svyatoslav sighed and made a bitter summary: "Thus we lose the glory of the Russian army. We easily conquered the neighboring lands and subjugated nations without bloodshed; now we miserably retreat before the Eastern Romans. Let us better gather our courage, remember the glory of our forefathers, and let us remember that up to now Russian might has been irresistible; and let us fight for our lives. It is not becoming of us to go back to the motherland in disgrace. We shall either win and remain alive, or we shall die gloriously, in deeds worthy of valiant men". Such was Svyatoslav's opinion. Having heard their chief, the Rhos willingly agreed to a perilous fight for their own salvation and swore to valiantly withstand the might of the Eastern Romans . . ."

With this kindly exposition made available to us by the Byzantine historian, we have just visited the Russian war council (or at least read the minutes of the main speeches). One may wonder how he came to be so well-informed. Maybe it was just the imagination of the scribe, and in that case it is not worth a tuppence.

But the story is also confirmed by Scylitzes, who disagrees with Leo on some points and on the precise dates of the events. He wrote: "When they gathered for a council, some gave advice to secretly flee at night, others were in favor of concluding a peace with the Eastern Romans and asking them for a pledge of safe return, for there was no other way to get back. Some were of the opinion that other measures should be taken according to the circumstances — but everybody agreed that the war should be ended. Svyatoslav, however, convinced them to risk one more battle and vanquish the Eastern Romans by stout-hearted fighting, or in case of defeat, die in glory rather than leading a shameful and dreary life. For how could they go on living after saving themselves in flight? They would be despised by the neighboring states who had feared them before. Svyatoslav's opinion was found to have merit, and everybody agreed jointly to face the lifetime danger."

Only a few words differ in those two descriptions, while the essence of the war council of July 20 or 21, 971 is related in identical terms, with none of the fantastic imaginings that would characterize a person who was alien to military affairs. (Leo was a cleric by origin, first a deacon with the Patriarch, then with the imperial court.)

The respected Russian scholar A. A. Shakhmatov thought that the similarity must be due to reliance on one common source, perhaps Bulgarian. ("I think there may have been some Bulgarian chronicle relating Svyatoslav's deeds, one that was concurrent with the Byzantines'.") But such an idea seems rather doubtful, because there is little resemblance between the two descriptions of the war council, though both descriptions are quite close in content (which is more important):

Svyatoslav began thinking it over with his host and said, "If we do not make peace with the king, he will keep us shut in the city since we are so few. The Russian land is faraway; we are at war with the Pechenegs; so who will help us? If we make peace with the king, we can even promise to pay tribute, and perhaps that would be enough. If he should demand it, we could come back later from Russia to Tsargrad in greater force." Of course, the host liked that speech very much. And it does not contradict the issues raised here.

So it seems quite plausible and one can hardly argue the point made by such a scholar as N. Ikonomidis that the Byzantines were informed about Svyatoslav's war council by local Bulgarian agents.

Some Bulgarian historians (N. P. Blagoev) are inclined to emphasize the significance of the military and spying services that their ancestors rendered to the empire during the Russo-Byzantine war, from the passage through the Rhodope clysura to the ceding of Preslav (Great Preslav) and support in the battle at Dorostol. There is no discrepancy with the data provided by Scylitzes.

One can hardly imagine that any Byzantine spies were present in person at the secret meeting, even in the guise of servants bringing food and drink. But one can never exclude the possibility that those who were prominent at such a council, either through careless banter or through intent, divulged the information to Tzimisces' spies. We do not know their names, but we can make a guess at two of them — voivode Sveneld and Svyatoslav's brother Ouleb (Gleb). At least, they must have been present at such a meeting.

Maybe Gleb's persecution, soon after, had something to do with the information leak; he soon turned up dead (presumably executed). Did the Kievan prince blame his brother, who was Christian, for the leak, which may have become evident during the battle? According to the chronicle, Svyatoslav had long been haunted by the thought of possible treason or deceit. ("He saw that he had few troops and said to himself: 'What if they betray us and annihilate my host and myself . . .'")

10. The Last Battle. The Dorostol Peace

The last battle (according to Scylitzes, it took place the day after the war council, at dawn, July 21, and according to Leo Diacon at sunset on July 24) began like this:

Russians exited Dorostol and shut the gates behind them (Scylitzes), determined to fight to the last man. Their attack was so fierce that by midday the Byzantines, "clad in heavy armor, thirsty under the scourging sun", gave way and began to retreat. The emperor introduced a fresh phalanx and brought water and wine to the exhausted men. The Stratiots launched a new assault at the enemy but it was no good. Then Tzimisces understood that "the battlefield is too small", and that that was the reason why the Scythians were prevailing over the Eastern Romans, who could not conveniently maneuver and fight.

He ordered his *strategi* to feign a retreat so that the Russians would come to a more open field, where they could be outflanked; and he had his troops re-align their ranks to resemble a wall. (The glory of the "wall" battle formation survived until the 19th century. Napoleon's generals recognized, as M. Y. Lermontov mentioned, in describing the Battle of Borodino, that the Russians deployed their troops as Svyatoslav's did, advancing like a wall.)

The Russians fell victim to the Greeks' favorite ploy, and went after them. That was a blunder. Despite the fact that the Byzantines had introduced fresh forces, fortune was still not on their side and the sun was blazing hard. ("When the Eastern Romans reached the assigned place, they turned about and attacked the enemy again. A fierce battle ensued.") Strategus Theodore from Misphia was nearly taken prisoner. Then both sides were exhausted and stopped fighting for a while, to recover their breath. ("Though the outcome of the battle was not certain, both armies stopped fighting).

Tzimisces, confronted by the stubborn Russian resistance, decided to take an unprecedented step. He challenged the Slav chief to fight man-to-man. According to Scylitzes, "Seeing that the Scythians were fighting more ardently than ever, the emperor felt sorry for his soldiers suffering in the cruel struggle. So he sent envoys to Svyatoslav and proposed a man-to-man fight. They should settle the outcome with the death of one warrior and not risk the fate of nations. The one who won would be the ruler of all." But Svyatoslav "did not accept the proposal".

Both Leo Diacon and Scylitzes note that, at one point during the fighting, Svyatoslav fell to the ground from his horse. He may have been attacked, like Ikmor.

One of the Basilian bodyguards, the Crete emir's son Abd El Aziz Al Nu Man (Anemas), came from behind and struck Svyatoslav on the left shoulder. The prince survived only because of his coat of mail and the shield that he held in his left hand. From this point onward, the chroniclers differ.

Scylitzes asserts that this took place after the proposal of a man-to-man fight; Diacon says that it was during the first half of the battle. The reader may ponder the following points. For Anemas, a warrior unsurpassed in his deeds, this episode became his last. Svyatoslav's men killed him on the spot.

Scylitzes then writes that after the refusal to fight one-on-one, the emperor tried by every means to prevent the barbarians from retreating to the city. He assigned the mission to *magister* Varda Sclir. At the same time, *patrician* Roman and *stratopedarch* Peter were to strike at the Russians from other directions. But the renewed fighting did not go as planned by the Basilians (vasilevs). The Scythians resisted stubbornly. For a long time the struggle was equal and many changes took place. Then came Anemas' turn. As the emperor's personal bodyguard, he may have acted at his own discretion. As he had done the day before, Tzimisces tried by every means, honest or otherwise, to bring down the greatest warrior and the Eastern Romans' chief enemy, whose will dominated all of his troops. If he could not do it himself, he would send the best of his knights. But Anemas failed to attain his goal. Svyatoslav went on fighting. And the bodyguard's death nearly caused the defeat of the Byzantine army.

The Russians were so encouraged by Anemas' death that they began pushing the Eastern Romans back with wild shouting. The latter began retreating under the awesome Scythian onslaught. The emperor saw that his phalanx was stepping back and had to join the fighting in person, leading his personal guard. The *stratioti* were ashamed and resumed their attack on the Russians.

But neither Leo nor Scylitzes nor any other Greek chronicler regarded the emperor's actions as decisive. Instead they speak of the "heavenly aid" that the Eastern Romans received at this junction.

"All of a sudden," wrote Leo Diacon, "a hurricane struck." Heavy rain fell and obscured the enemy, and dust flew and blocked the Russians' vision. They say that a knight appeared on a white horse, leading the Eastern Romans and urging them to scatter the Russian ranks. Nobody had seen the horseman before; the emperor ordered to find him so that he could thank him for his performance. But the search was fruitless. Later on, they were convinced that he was the martyr Theodore, to whom the emperor had prayed. He had asked him to be his patron and savior in battles.

Scylitzes wrote: "The Eastern Romans are said to have received heavenly assistance. For the storm picked up behind them and struck in the face of the Scythians. All the Eastern Roman army saw a man fighting on a white horse, driving back the enemy and scattering them. Nobody had seen him either before or after and they took him for Theodore, one of the heavenly martyrs."

Encircled by *magister* Varda, nicknamed Sclir, who approached them from the rear with many troops, they fled. Svyatoslav, "injured by arrows, bled profusely and was close to being taken prisoner. Only nightfall saved him from imminent death".

But Scylitzes also mentions that the storm prevented the Scythians from "implementing what had been conceived for the battle". Did Tzimisces know what was discussed at the war council the day before? We can only make a wild guess. We can only assert (with some reservations) that Svyatoslav suffered his last and tragic defeat, which was disastrous for the whole Balkan campaign, only after the Byzantine intelligence service took the upper hand.

This failure undermined the Russian army's morale. The prince sent his ambassadors to "the emperor John and sued for peace" on the following conditions. The Tauroscythians would cede Dorostol to the Eastern Romans, leave Moesia, and go back to their country. The

Eastern Romans should let them sail off unimpeded.

Svyatoslav put forward one more condition (either at once, or later when he met the emperor). Understanding that it would be hard to pass through the Pechenegs' land, he asked Tzimisces to sent an embassy to the steppe and provide for his safe passage.

The emperor believed in peace more than in war, for he knew that peace preserves nations and war destroys them; he accepted the Russian proposals, concluded a treaty with them and gave them sustenance. Scylitzes confirms that Tzimisces agreed to the terms and says that "the Eastern Romans are in the habit of prevailing over the enemy by good deeds and not by weapons."

11. Landscape with Oarsmen and Horsemen. Death at the Dnieper Rapids. Who is to Blame?

Then Leo Diacon writes: "After concluding the peace agreement, Svyatoslav asked the emperor for an audience". It took place — but not according to court etiquette. "The emperor agreed and came to the Istre riverbank clad in gold armor, with a large number of armed horsemen accompanying him. Svyatoslav appeared in a Scythian boat; he sat at the oar and pulled, like his subordinates, without any distinction. He was of medium height, neither very tall nor very short, he had bushy eyebrows, light blue eyes, and a snub nose. He did not wear a beard, but wore a very long mustache. His head was shaven but at one side there was a long strip of hair — testimony of his noble family. His neck was thick, his chest broad, and all in all he was well proportioned. But he looked harsh and wild. In one ear he had a gold ring decorated with two pearls. His clothes were white and were much cleaner than those of his retinue. Sitting on the oarsman's bench, he had a short conversation with the emperor about the peace conditions, and then left".

In the other side, "John, the emperor, looked like this: he had a fair face of healthy complexion; his hair was light, and rather thin over the brow, and he had blue eyes with a sharp glance. His nose was thin and well-shaped. His auburn beard was trimmed in a tapering flow. He was small of stature but his chest and back were wide; he seemed very powerful, and his arms were extremely agile and strong. His soul of a hero was fearless and displayed a valiant nature that was surprising for such a small body."

The following events are described in the Russian annals. "Having concluded peace with the Greeks, Svyatoslav came in his boats to the rapids. Then voivode Sveneld told him to continue further on horseback, for the rapids were blocked by the Pechenegs. The prince did not heed the advice and used boats instead. He sent envoys to the Pechenegs with the following words: 'Here comes Svyatoslav on his way to Russia, he has a lot of goods from the Greeks and his host is not large'. The Pechenegs then blocked the rapids. He and his troops had to spend the winter there, and food was scarce."

It is quite probable that part of the Russian army, after leaving Dorostol, went by boat down the Danube. And the cavalry (with horses for the oarsmen), headed by Sveneld, went alongside the river as had been the custom under Oleg. They most probably met at the mouth of the Dnieper, where the prince had to take some rest after crossing the sea.

By that time, Sveneld would have been able to get news of the situation at the rapids and report it to the prince.

But Svyatoslav did not heed the warning. Why not?

Scylitzes relates the events as follows: "On Svyatoslav's request, the emperor sent an embassy to the Patzinaks with an offer to become friends and allies." He asked them not to cross the Istre, not to plunder Bulgaria, and to allow the Russians to pass peacefully on their way home. Tzimisces had his own reasons for negotiations with the nomads, but he presented it as an indulgence for his "friend," the barbarian. The bishop Theophilus, who had taken part in concluding the peace treaty between Byzantium and Russia, headed the emissary.

The Pechenegs received the embassy and concluded peace on the stipulated conditions, but refused passage to the Russians. At least, they did not hide their intentions and then attack the Russians by surprise. Theophilus managed to safeguard the Byzantine interest, but did he insist on the Russian issue?

We do not know whether the bishop arranged the Pecheneg attack against the Russians — in other words, was Svyatoslav's death paid for with Byzantine gold? One may argue that Byzantium was interested in union with Russia, and that is correct. But they were interested in a force that would be obedient to them, that could be controlled by the empire. Svyatoslav was not such a person. The emperor Nicephorus Phocas might have made a blunder and Tzimisces had to deal with the consequences. The Byzantines were never particular about the means they used.

There is ample ground to suspect the emperor and his retinue for the demise of Svyatoslav and of his host the next spring; we can suspect as well the Bulgarian nobility, that was in alliance with him, in the next year. The maneuvers at the Russian war council in Dorostol on June 21 must not have been forgotten. The empire's secret services scored the decisive blow over Svyatoslav.

What happened next? Having spotted an ambush, Svyatoslav retreated to Beloberezhie and stayed there for the winter. Famine ensued; they lost their horses, and their fighting capability was decimated. In the spring of 972, Svyatoslav had to enter the rapids. "On the way," relates Leo Diacon, "the Patzinaks laid an ambush and slaughtered nearly all the Russians, including Svyatoslav, and only a few persons from the huge Russian army returned home".

Scylitzes wrote: "When Svyatoslav was on his way home, he passed through the Patzinaks' lands. They had arranged an ambush and were waiting for him. He was attacked and nearly all his host was annihilated. The Patzinaks were angry that he had concluded a treaty with the Eastern Romans." That does not ring true, since they might have severed relations with the Russians without any actions on the part of Byzantine secret diplomacy. "With the onset of the spring of 6480 (either March of 972 or February of 973), Svyatoslav went to the rapids. The Pecheneg khan Kouria attacked him, cut off his head, made a chalice out of the skull and drank from it. Sveneld went on to Kiev to Yaropolk. So Svyatoslav had ruled eight and twenty years altogether".

As has been said, Svyatoslav had no choice. He was weakened by hunger, and his army was only a shadow of its former force. He saw that his fellow soldiers were no longer holding up their swords and lances but rather using them as crutches. The Pechenegs saw that, too.

12. The Skull Chalice. Valediction to the Great Prince Svyatoslav Igorevich

Thus perished Svyatoslav. Leo Diacon called him a reckless, brave, militant and powerful leader. He could not cheat and deceive, even when necessary. He was the soldier who has been credited with the words that still resonate in Russian hearts centuries later: "We shall not disgrace the Russian land but shall die, for the dead cannot be ashamed. If we flee we shall be disgraced. So we shall not flee; we shall stand steadfast— and I shall go with you."

The legend of the chalice that his enemies made out of Svyatoslav's skull was much entertained by later Russian medieval historians. The Yermolin, Lvov and certain other chronicles say that the following words were carved upon the chalice: "Looking for strangers, lost your own". One of the annals appears to give meaning to that cryptic inscription. "The chalice is still kept, even now, in the Pecheneg treasury. Princes and princesses drink from it during marriage festivities, and recite the words: 'As was this man, here is his brow, so will be the one born of us'. Some of the soldiers also made chalices from skulls and ornamented them with silver, and drank from them." This commentary, though, only reflects old tradition and acknowledges the enemy's assets. But the inscription may have been invented later by the Russian scribes, according to their own fancy and their image of Svyatoslav.

Judging from "The Primary Chronicle", even some of Svyatoslav's contemporaries did not understand him. Maybe they were influenced by the Kievans' comments about the inscription on the chalice. "You, Prince, are looking after foreign lands and neglect your own." The following generations, who were Christians, could not be in sympathy with a pagan prince who had not adhered to the Biblical canons of peace and neighborliness. More recently, N.M. Karamzin cited Svyatoslav as a "great soldier" but not as a "great statesman", for he prized the glory of victory more than the good of the state. Another great scholar, S.M. Soloviev, wrote that "Svyatoslav's deeds, starting with the first Balkan war march, were of little concern for Russian history", for the prince with his host had left the Russian land for "deeds that were glorious for him and useless for his own land". Only during the Soviet era were Svyatoslav's foreign campaigns reconsidered, in light of the internal requirements of the developing Russian state. To my mind, even they missed the fundamental fact that the state was in many respects still in the nascent stage, that is, the process of formation of its own territory had not been completed.

What was Kiev for Svyatoslav? It was the city that his father, coming down from Novgorod, conquered with the help of Oleg. He did not consider the southward thrust begun by his ancestors to be finished. Thus he told his mother and the boyars, "I do not like to stay here in Kiev. I would like to live in Pereyaslavets on the Danube, for that is the heart of my land. All goods converge there: gold, fabrics, wine and various fruits; from the Greeks, silver and precious stones; from the Czechs and Huns, fur, honey and wax; and population from Russia". Svyatoslav kept on constructing the larger Slavic state begun by his predecessors, and he pondered its future shape. What might have happened if the Russians had managed to keep hold of the lower reaches of the Danube? Despite Svyatoslav's failure, he left his mark.

Chapter III.

THE SECRET WARS OF PRINCE VLADIMIR'S TIMES

*1. A Hunting Accident and the Beginning of the Power Struggle among Svya-
toslav's Heirs (the Svyatoslavichi)*

Secret agents became essential again during the strife between the
three heirs of Svyatoslav Igorevich, who was killed at the Dnieper Rapids by the Pechenegs in AD 972 (other sources say 970). The strife was
touched off, according to the chronicle, by the murder of Lute, son on
the chief voivode Sveneld (who had served the princely house of their
father and even their grandfather Igor and who now served the eldest of
the brothers, Yaropolk). Lute was killed by the Drevlian prince, Oleg.

Young Prince Oleg was hunting. Bursting through the underbrush
he spotted not a wild beast but a proud horseman, in rich attire. Oleg
blinked. "Who is that?" One of his men recognized him: "Lute, son of
Sveneld!" Bad luck had brought Lute to this hunting ground. He was
seeking game in the Drevlian woods, where his father had once sought
tribute.

Oleg had become a full-fledged lord only recently and had begun
to enjoy the awful appeal of a new sport: disposing of people's lives at
will. "He came up from behind and killed Lute", recounts the chronicler. As the artist of the Radzivill chronicle depicted the scene, Oleg
approaches the victim from behind, and spears him with a lance. The
victim has only enough time to look back to meet his assailant's eye.
Both enraged horsemen wear hats. Lute reaches out toward Oleg in an
expression of wonder, pain, and an appeal for mercy. The crime takes

place between two trees in a forest, on a hill. At the right side a great stag is halfway turned towards them. That is the beast that Lute had been chasing, a symbol of shifting fortune.

The motives for the crime seem rather feeble, if we are to believe the chronicle alone. Oleg killed Lute because such was his disposition. Tatishchev provides some further elucidation. Oleg was surprised by the sudden appearance of Lute and a quarrel ensued over hunting rights. The prince felt offended by young Lute and acted on impulse. S. M. Soloviev, for his part, thinks that it would have been far more natural to let the nobleman go without harm; since that was not what happened, there must have been more to the story. That is, Lute's murder was a political act, and was premeditated. It seems to have been the first shot in what became a full-blown war.

It remains unknown who started the conflict. Old Sveneld, at Yaropolk's side, was eager for revenge. "Go against your brother and take his land", he advised, as the scribe tells us. Vladimir, the younger Svyatoslavich (decendant of Svyatoslav), was supported by his uncle Dobrynia (his mother's brother). All those "uncles" and "tutors" had exerted great psychological influence since the princes were orphaned, and there were three rival factions of uncles (in Kiev, Ovruch and Novgorod) — a time bomb.

Yaropolk's court wanted him to be ruler. Oleg's and Vladimir's councilors countered by hatching separatist plans. Maybe Oleg's men deemed it time to throw down the gauntlet.

War broke out at last in AD 977. Yaropolk marched onto the Drevlian land. In the battle near Uruchiy (Ouruch), Oleg's forces were destroyed and he himself was forced to seek shelter behind the city walls. During the commotion at the bridge, he fell into the moat and drowned. Yaropolk took over the Drevlian territory.

When Vladimir, in Novgorod, learned of the incident, he was alarmed and fled. Yaropolk sent his men to Novgorod and he became ruler of Russia. Vladimir was quite right to fear him. His uncle, Dobrynia, the first recognizable chief of security services in Russia, certainly assisted him with news about his elder brothers' conflict — he had agents in Oleg's entourage. Yaropolk's actions testify that there was good reason for that!

Some historians think that Vladimir's maternal grandfather, by the name of Malk of Liubech, was the ill-fated bridegroom of Princess

Olga and the ruler of the Drevlians. In that case, the alleged collusion between Vladimir and Oleg by way of their "uncles'" voivodes may have had ample grounds. Uncle Dobrynia could get back his motherland (which might well have come to pass, had Oleg made it to the throne in Kiev).

This sojourn abroad was good for the impressionable Vladimir. He came back to Novgorod a year or so later, and drove away Yaropolk's boyars with the words of the legendary Svyatoslav: "Vladimir is upon you, get ready to fight". The miracle chemical that expelled them was the Varangian host he brought back with him.

Having asserted his militancy, Vladimir soon displayed a newly acquired quality — discretion. Vladimir sent some of his men to Polotsk with a marriage proposal for Rogneda, the daughter of the local ruler, Rogvold. Rogvold "presented Vladimir's envoys to Rogneda", but she declared that she was not disposed to marry "the son of a mother who was a prince's slave," but that she "wished" to marry Yaropolk.

Vladimir was offended, and decided with Dobrynia on "Plan B". Their Novgorod and Varangian troops invaded Polotsk; Rogvold was defeated and later murdered, together with his sons. And Rogneda, who had been about to depart for Kiev, became Vladimir's wife in spite of herself. Not that Vladimir could much help expect from Polotsk — but, at least, now Yaropolk couldn't either. So Vladimir's first diplomatic and military foray was a success.

But the real struggle still loomed ahead. Yaropolk was strong and the Novgorod prince and his charismatic and enterprising uncle, having learned their lessons, prepared themselves meticulously for the decisive encounter.

On the basis of the text by Joachim of Korsun, Tatishchev in his *The History of Russia* relates the events after Vladimir thrashed Polotsk: "Yaropolk, having learned what had happened, became enraged". He sent envoys to his brother. He also sent troops to the land of the Krivichi. Vladimir was intimidated and wanted to flee to Novgorod, but his uncle Dobrynia (having seen that Yaropolk was unpopular with the people because of his attitude toward the Christians) stopped Vladimir; he sent gifts to Yaropolk's voivodes and brought them to visit Vladimir."

Yaropolk's cavalry came to the Radimich and Krivich lands. Dobrynia repeated the trick of the prophetic Oleg and infiltrated the military camp with his agents, in the guise of "guests" (merchants), bearing gifts. The Joachim chronicle describes Dobrynia as an able man who effectively controlled the prince's intelligence services. Pondering the most effective means of recruitment, he decided to use a two-pronged approach, revealing a great understanding of human nature and an ability to play on both the high and the low strings. Dobrynia sought to procure not only paid informers and stooges but also volunteers, like-minded persons — especially among the "uncles-voivodes." And his hopes were fulfilled. "Some of them, not serving Yaropolk faithfully, decided to hand over their regiments to Vladimir. Then Dobrynia with Vladimir went to Yaropolk's troops and won — not through Vladimir's might and bravery but with the help of Yaropolk's treasonous voivodes" (Tatishchev).

2. *A Tale about the First Renegade*

A traitor, in old Russia, was called a *perevetnik* (renegade). This was understood to mean someone "communicating with the enemy, going over to his side — betraying his own people". That word was not yet coined when the Kiev chronicler was writing, but he depicted Blyud and his like in the harshest terms available, calling them "allies of Satan".

There were no written laws in Rus' at the time. *The Justice of Yaroslav*, an ancient portion of the *Justice in Rus'* (*Pravda Russkaya*), appeared nearly fifty years later; neither it nor the *Justice of the Yaroslavichi* or other 12th-century laws mentioned crimes of this nature. The first such "article" (judging by documents extant) appeared in the *Pskov Law* (*Pskovskaya Sudnaya Gramota*) that was written during 13th-15th centuries.

If there were no written laws, how could one pronounce judgment? Curses from historians, after the fact, would be meaningless. May that was Blyud's view, as he carefully listened to the words of the secret agents who came to see him in Kiev, agents whom the chronicler called ambassadors (the jargon of the secret services being rather primitive at the time). And the words of these "ambassadors" were alluring indeed.

"Be friendly with me," said Vladimir (or his voivode, on his behalf), "and I will treat you like my father and you will be greatly honored; for it was not I who set out to thrash my brother, but he. I felt threatened and was obliged to raise arms against him." There was certain a logic to such reasoning. Blyud soon accepted it — and the tempting offers.

In fact, it seems that Blyud had been recruited somewhat earlier, for he had received such proposals before. And he was not alone in this business, but had accomplices. As to the latter, the very delicate nature of the assignment made them indispensable. Dobrynia's envoys could hardly establish reliable contacts without collaboration from Blyud's people. During the siege, as testified the scribe, Blyud often sent his men to Vladimir. It was not by accident that the scribe used the plural when he castigated the faithless ones "who betrayed their own prince". That means not only servants, but also some people of higher rank. Are they the same people mentioned in the Joachim chronicle? Was it not during the military march on Smolensk and Polotsk that the Kiev voivode fell into Dobrynia's net? All that is quite probable, for the Nikon chronicle also tells us that Blyud was in favor with Vladimir long before Novgorodian horses started grazing on the Dnieper meadows. According to the Nikon chronicle, he would have been recruited at the time when both were sitting in their respective capitals and sharpening their swords. That is quite clear, for the historian of the 16th century did not know anything about the march by Yaropolk's troops on Krivich lands.

So Dobrynia's agents had to get to Kiev from Novgorod. Tatishchev gives more detail. Vladimir, having taken some troops from Polotsk and Krivich, that is, having attained one of the aims of his proposal to Rogneda, "went on to Kiev to take revenge for Oleg's murder and his own insult". The historian evidently relates these events in accordance with one of the documents that came to his hand: the "Khrushchev manuscript", that confirms a liaison between Vladimir and Oleg, and sets forth a new reason for strife between Novgorod and Kiev. Maybe the insult and offence consisted in Yaropolk setting his men to control Novgorod.

"Being fully cognizant of his brother Yaropolk's courage and might, Vladimir decided to win over Yaropolk's principal voivode, Blyud. Vladimir sent his men to Blyud with great promises in order to secretly tempt him to help overthrow Yaropolk. Blyud gave Vladimir his promise". In this account, the thought of recruiting Blyud occurs to Vladimir and Dobrynia at the start of the march on Kiev. And they emphasize Blyud's exclusive position at the Kiev court. He probably was Dobrynia's counterpart. Both chiefs of the secret services had known each other since Svyatoslav's times; they probably were buddies and had spent time together drinking mead (honey) and other hard drinks. It is no wonder they soon found a common language, and one of them started working for the other. It did not take long to persuade Blyud to stray, for he only recently had attained a major position with Yaropolk.

The reader may remember that as far back as 977, the young Kievan prince had been tutored by Sveneld. After the Battle of Ovruch, there is no more mention of him in the chronicles. Perhaps Yaropolk was so stunned by the death of his brother that he did not forgive Sveneld ("Oh, woe to me," grieved Yaropolk over the body of his brother — according to Tatishchev, "I should have died instead of seeing you so, as I was instigated by the slanderer!" And then he supposedly says to Sveneld: "Look what you have done! what shall I do with you now?"). Sveneld was fairly old at the time (for he had also served Igor), or he may have died in the interim.

Blyud had only recently been promoted. According to the Chronicle, Vladimir laid siege to Kiev in 980 and, according to "Hail and Remembrance to Vladimir" (*Pamyat' i pokhvala*), by Yakov, a monk, two years earlier. Blyud apparently could not have taken all advantages of his new position. And maybe his name (which means "to stray, to wander; to be duped or deceived) testifies to certain features of his character. And Dobrynia managed to recruit Blyud not because he was a pagan (as is sometimes claimed) but with a promise of greener pastures at the new court. Blyud's recruitment must have taken place at the time when Yaropolk's men were chased out of Novgorod. Dobrynia and Vladimir sent with them haughty words from the former fugitive to Kiev's prince. But maybe they also took word to Blyud, concerning treachery?

Why, then, the necessity to seduce Blyud in Kiev once again if everything had been settled beforehand? Maybe he had been bought on a "retail" and not a "wholesale" basis. Maybe he was first recruited at the Drouch or at the Dnieper, and then his compliance was verified and the conditions made more precise. In any case, a mission to the enemy military leader of a besieged city, bringing fairly transparent proposals, would have been far too risky without any preliminary probing.

But let us return to the events in Kiev. Blyud affably received the

Novgorod prince's "ambassadors" and told them to convey to Vladimir his "love and friendship". Then he began to distract the "doubtful" Yaropolk, who had started preparing his troops for the war march. "My prince, why should you take the trouble? (said Blyud). For I know for sure that Vladimir's troops despise him as the son of a slave-woman (*robichich*). When his troops see you, they will come over to your side without fighting. You do not have to meet him halfway; just wait for him in Kiev." Thus Tatishchev renders Blyud's "sly" speech, thereby confirming that "Yaropolk's favorite voivode" was the head of the Kiev intelligence service. In the same words, he reported new information to his prince. According to the Nikon chronicle, Blyud said it somewhat differently: "Your younger brother Vladimir cannot oppose you anymore than a chickadee can fight an eagle. So do not trouble yourself over it, and do not amass your army." At the same time he kept on sending his officers and scouts to the Novgorod camp. One might have supposed he was trying to dig out new information about the enemy, but in fact he was only exchanging news with his future "son", to help coordinate his own actions. The cover was perfect. And so, "The secret agent began acting".

Soon Dobrynia and Vladimir learned that the renegade voivode was ready to take the promised action. The chronicler tells us, "Blyud closeted himself with Yaropolk, flattering him, and at the same time sent many messages to Vladimir, telling him to come to Kiev and attack. He harbored the thought of murdering Yaropolk."

Some 500 years later, Baron Sigizmund Herbershtein — the Ambassador of the Emperor of the Holy Roman Empire to the Great Prince Vasily III in Moscow and a man who had carefully studied the Russian chronicles — describes the event as follows. "Having laid siege on Kiev, Vladimir secretly sent a messenger to Blyud, Yaropolk's intimate councilor . . . to how ask about destroying his brother. Blyud responded, and promised to kill his master, and told Vladimir to storm the stronghold." According to Tatishchev, "Blyud often secretly sent his envoys to Vladimir and showed him various ways to eliminate Yaropolk." That is, he presented his new patron with several means to implement the action. But the collusion failed, and the political assassination had to be postponed. Blyud was somehow hampered in his actions by the citizens ("because of the town folk, it was not possible to kill him secretly or openly"). The voivode did not despair, of course, and tried to dissuade

Yaropolk (who was "a brave man") from launching any sorties. "Blyud was pondering other ways of perpetrating the crime and tried to prevent Yaropolk from going outside the city to fight openly."

One may think that Blyud wanted to preclude any possible defeat of Vladimir's troops in open battle, for that could upset the whole enterprise. But Tatishchev explains the intentions of the servant of two enemies, "the protégé" of the Kiev prince and "the friend" of the Novgorod prince, in somewhat different terms. "Blyud, in his perfidy, thought to destroy Yaropolk by other means. He gave advice not to let the troops go outside of town, though some wise men insisted on a battle in the open field. But Yaropolk heeded his sly confidant. Yaropolk's army, seeing that, secretly began crossing over to Vladimir, and Blyud urged Vladimir to attack the city."

So Blyud instigated the troops that Yaropolk had gathered from various lands; they were vexed by their futile sojourn within the stronghold, they were uncomfortable with the idleness and long absences from home, and they smelled treason. If the historian is telling us the truth, then Blyud served Vladimir rightly. He constantly hampered his opponent his actions took him by his arms and legs (so to say), trying to enhance the chances of the attacking party. One may suppose that Blyud's men disseminated some derogatory information among Yaropolk's troops. They also tried to stir up the citizens, who were not happy having so many idle troops stationed there. Blyud was planning to surrender the city. Once, he reported to the nervous Yaropolk (as the chief of his secret service): "Some Kievans are leaning towards Vladimir and say, 'Come to the city and we shall betray Yaropolk.' I think you should flee the city." Tatishchev says much the same thing: "Today I have learned . . . " So the crafty Blyud presented his own thoughts as the intentions of the citizens and tried to pass off his agents or the soldiers who fled from Yaropolk as renegades. But the discouraged prince believed him. "Leave the city", his councilor whispered to him. And this time, the wise men kept silence. Yaropolk did as he was told. He went to the town of Roden' with his "faithful voivode". After that, Vladimir easily entered the city, as no one was there to stop him.

Blyud was still whispering in Yaropolk's ear. "Look how many troops your brother has. We cannot possibly counter such force; we'd better make peace with him." "We"! — He was trying to show that he was still heroically defending prince. The chronicler later noted that

Blyud was double-crossing his master, but since his master had no opportunity to consult the chronicle, he took Blyud at his word. He went along with the counsel once again. Blyud was very content and sent a message to Vladimir: "Your dreams came true, for I am going to bring Yaropolk to you and you can arrange his murder." In other words, during the exchange of information, the mission was altered. The victim was to be delivered alive.

In anticipation of a quick end, Vladimir came to the same palace court where in Olga's day the boat with the Drevlians had been heaved into a pit and buried. Blyud, at the time, was working on Yaropolk — who was as soft as wax: "Go to your brother and tell him, 'whatever you have in store for me (instead of the Kiev throne — *auth.*) — I accept." In vain Variazhko, one of Yaropolk's wise and faithful men, tried to talk him out of taking such a fatal step. "Do not go there, my prince, you shall be murdered"; and he advised Yaropolk to take refuge among the Pechenegs (who were their allies at the time) and amass a new army there. But Yaropolk had lost all will to resist. Blyud was still there, interfering. According to the Nikon chroniclers, Blyud said to Variazhko: "I am here as a counselor (*milostnik*) to the prince". That is, 'I am the prince's favorite'. Blyud thus intimated that his advice would prevail and warned Variazhko to watch his step. But Variazhko responded with an insult and a veiled threat: "Every *milostnik* is like a snake in the bosom!"

One may imagine how Blyud liked that. Was he undone, at the last moment? But judging by later events, he managed to control himself. He did not draw his sword, with his bejeweled hand, nor did he look around for a way to escape. Variazhko had no proof of his suspicions that the "favorite" was a traitor. And Yaropolk did not believe his warnings. He presented himself at court in Kiev. Hardly had he stepped inside the gate when two Varangians, with swords, grabbed him under the arms and took him away. Vladimir had brought his troops along for good reason: a verdict was promptly pronounced, and the execution took place at once. Blyud shut the doors (and "did not let his men follow him [Yaropolk]"; for he was unwilling to be present at the scene. The action was carried out flawlessly.. Everything must have been thought through in detail (for example, Blyud had to detach Yaropolk from his retinue at a crucial moment) and agents must have maintained contact without failure till the very end.

Thus took place the second state revolt in Kievan Rus'. You may recollect that the first had erupted nearly 100 years earlier under the prophetic Oleg. The chronicler left Oleg's actions without commentary, and Vladimir was denounced, though not directly but via his agent, the renegade recruited by him.

We have only to mention the strange position taken by the artist of the Radziwill chronicle when he presented Blyud. He painted five miniature pictures illustrating Vladimir's war with Yaropolk. But much as I tried, I could not identify our hero in any of them. In one image, for instance, Yaropolk with his host flees to Roden'. Blyud must certainly be there, someplace. But all the soldiers look alike. Any one of them could be the voivode. True, there is a small figure on the Roden' walls, pointing out a "prophetic bird" flapping its wings in a tree and crying: "Here he, is the traitor!". In another, we see Vladimir with his army and Dobrynia waiting in the palace yard. To the right, Yaropolk and his men ponder what to do. But the young man standing before him, with a round, tall hat on his head, is not Blyud but Variazhko. In another scene, at last, is the scene of Yaropolk's murder. The poor prince is being strangled in the gateway and stabbed by the swords of two severe-looking men. Vladimir sits on the throne, as if monitoring the proceedings. Nearby stands a young man with his arms raised to the heavens, profoundly moved by what he sees. But that is most probably the personification of the artist's own shock and not Blyud's, for he, after all, chose to remain behind closed doors.

So it turns out that one of the major heroes of the event, without whom the enterprise would have failed completely, is left out of the picture. To be sure, he was painted once, but that was during the events of 1018 that we shall come to later on. On that occasion, Blyud is so inconspicuous that he can be identified only by his gesture, when he delivers his witty speech about the Polish Prince Boleslav. And the most interesting point is that Blyud is shown there as an ordinary military commander. The artist was not interested to depict him in his primary role as the head of Vladimir's intelligence service. Or perhaps he did not wish to present him as such. Why not? Mediaeval artists had few means to depict the psychology and spiritual attitude of people. Artists could show specific people as "good" or "bad"; but characters with a mixed or ambiguous history represented a challenge. Blyud was, on the one hand, a traitor and a renegade; but on the other hand he served the future creator of the Russian Orthodox State, the Baptizer of Russia. The artist's Christian sensibilities and his perception of the historic values of his fatherland came in conflict, here, and precluded Blyud's appearance in the chronicle pictures.

Indeed, from what standpoint can we assess the morality of Blyud's actions? As an undercover agent in Vladimir's secret service, he rendered his master an immeasurable service: he handed him the Kiev principality on a silver platter. Thus, the intelligence professional may take pride in the fact that the second state revolt in the history of Kievan Rus' (like the first one, under Oleg) was performed exclusively with the help of secret agents.

Blyud's toil was not in vain. Vladimir did not forget his good services — though he had no compunctions about overlooking his own promises. Blyud did not become "a second father" to Vladimir (one may promise anything while fighting for power, but not all such promises are meant to be kept). Traitors are always considered useful, though they are never held in esteem. It was not by accident that the chronicler mentioned Vladimir's ambassadors, who arrived in Kiev "with sly intentions". Who knows what dishonorable actions lay behind these words: seduction, corruption, fraud, wit or perfidy? But Yaropolk's former *milostnik* acquired "much honor" with Vladimir — though the attitude was ambivalent. Tatishchev relates that Blyud was showered with honors for three days. And on the fourth day, Vladimir gave orders to kill him, explaining to the astonished celebrity: "I have honored you as a friend, and am judging you as a mutineer and the murderer of a prince."

Many historians hold Tatishchev's version of the events in doubt. In a later chronicle and chronograph collection there is an entry that is not quite clear: "Vladimir went to Kiev and murdered his brother Yaropolk, [and?] the sly lord-killing Blyud". Most probably, rumors about the death sentence carried out on the glorious Kievan voivode crept into the record later on due to the corruption of manuscripts by scribes, or it may be because of Blyud's eventual fate (which is reflected in the "Primary Chronicle"[9]). While some of the chronicles (for instance the Troitskaya) mention Blyud in 1018 as a tutor and voivode of one of Vladimir's numerous sons, one by the name of Yaroslav (though it is not clear if he was the same person of the past times and not his namesake), some others (Lavrientiev, Radziwill) call the tutor of the new Kievan prince "Boudy". That is why Blyud's personality and his fate have become a topic for many legends. Tatishchev provides some later sources according to which Blyud is Sveneld's (!) son. He is called Blewet, Bloume, Blote and even Lutre, that is, Lute. But the reader knows that Lute Sveneldich perished as far back as 911. It may well be that one of the old Russian scribes, moved by moral values, decided to make it quite clear that the sentence imposed by history was in accord with traditional understanding of the quick and just judgment of God. Such speculations appeared on the pages of the chronicles that Tatishchev worked from; and while there is some plausibility to the event as related in *The History of Russia,* I am more inclined to trust *The Tver' Collection,* compiled in the 16th century. That writer (either foreseeing the predicament of future historians or debating the various contemporary notions about the death of the first renegade) deemed it necessary to specify that Yaroslav's tutor was "the old tutor and voivode Blyud, who had served under Vladimir". So he retained for Blyud his right to go on with his laborious toil for the fatherland later on.

Supposing this version to be true and that Blyud, as a secret agent, had several nicknames, we shall see how he used the opportunity to add some more laurels to his crown under the name of Boudy. It seems that Blyud, having provided for his needs in old age, no longer cared much about glory (that is, he appears to have been more interested in wealth). Or maybe he did not find any more suitable opportunities? In the end, he became a laughing stock.

That happened, as mentioned above, in 1018. The usurper of the Kiev throne, Svyatopolk the Accursed, having been defeated by Yaroslav at the Dnieper River, came back with Polish support. The armies met at the Bug River in the Volyn' land. Nobody knows why Blyud started harassing Prince Boleslav the Brave (who was such a stout man that a horse could hardly carry him). He threatened to "prick his fat belly with a lance". Boleslav flew into a rage. But while he and the Zaporozhtsi were ready for a fight and provoked the enemy on purpose, Yaroslav did not have a chance to prepare properly, and was defeated (which means that Blyud had not lived up to his foremost duty as a voivode). Thus, the encounter ended in a farce. At first glance, the event does not seem to be directly relevant to our story, but the early writer deemed it necessary to divulge every trait of Blyud's biography and even of his appearance, and we wouldn't want to miss a telling scene. Since his biography comes to an end at this episode ("And here was killed Yaroslav's voivode, Blyud", the Nikon chronicle says), this was the end of the "snake in the bosom": not by execution, which he merited, but by his own folly.

3. Vladimir's War March on Korsun (Chersonesus Taurica)

Perhaps this was not "just good luck"; the excellent results of his secret service, headed by Dobrynia, were largely due to the work of good agents. In any case, the intelligence service soon scored another point and brought to the prince one more city, this time overseas.

Late in the 980s, the Russian troops laid siege to a Byzantine city on the Black Sea, Korsun. Most historians agree that the Kievan troops marched on Korsun because of the reluctance of the Greeks to make good on the support Vladimir had provided in suppressing the mutiny of the chief Varda Phocas. Judging by Byzantine and Arab sources, it was thought that the main obligation of the emperors Basil and Constantine consisted in marrying their sister Anna to the Slavic prince. (As a pagan, Vladimir was free to accumulate wives.) The Russian chronicler, however, claims that Vladimir put forward his demand concerning Anna only after capturing Korsun.

The Russian chronicler clearly saw the true aim of the march: capturing Korsun, with its possessions, and other Crimean lands. One version of the Ipatiev chronicle describing Vladimir's march ends with the words: "He took the Greek city of Korsun (in the Crimea) and the whole island of Taurica." As to his vanquishing the whole "island", that is surely an exaggeration; but one Western historian notes that after this march for the "bride", the list of Byzantine possessions in the Crimea does lack Cimmerian Bosporus (i.e. Kerch/Korsun), the "town" (*theme*) established after the war between John Tzimisces and Svyatoslav. It was restored only a century later. Vladimir's military expansion is surprising if one bears in mind that the agreements between Igor and Svyatoslav and the Greeks stipulated that the Russians were obliged to restrain themselves from the obvious temptation to attack Korsun and other cities. But the Kievan princes evidently did not place much importance on those agreements. So, entering Taurica, Vladimir spread his troops over the Crimean Peninsula, as if by the historic force of inertia.

The chronicles do not divulge what route Vladimir took or how strong his troops were. Historians' opinions are divided on these points. Some, along with N. M. Karamzin, think that the Russian host went down the Dnieper River and then took the shortest way to the Taurida coast, by sea. Others support the idea of a land march. I, and Academician B. D. Grekov, think that Vladimir (like Oleg and Igor, before him) went as far as Tsargrad (Constantinople), then traveled to the Crimea both "on horseback and by boat", that is by land and sea, for either of the versions may be true.

Cavalry was essential for bringing up the food supplies, for laying siege, and for mounting raids throughout the Chersonesus and Bosporus regions up to the Kerch Strait. The presence of nomadic troops (Black Bulgars) confirms that this would have been a consideration.

The fleet was necessary both for blockading the city by sea and for launching operations along the coast, even as far as Constantinople. But its availability was predicated on having favorable weather conditions, which would be likely only if the Russians arrived near Korsun during the summer season (most researchers set the events in July or August). Their small boats could safely navigate the Black Sea only from mid-May to mid-September.

Vladimir's host (including Black Bulgars, Varangians, Krivich and Slavs, i.e. Smolensk and Novgorod troops) according to A. L. Berthier-Delagard, did not exceed 6,000 to 8,000 or maybe not even 5,000 to 6,000 men. But to lay siege to a city with a population of not more than 10,000, even that number would have been far too many. Apparently, Vladimir had mobilized this host not for the siege of Korsun but to support the Vasilevs' (emperors') troops against Varda Phocas. He had to delay the siege because of Anna's failure to arrive.

Vladimir was also eager to see the surroundings of Kerch, where another Russian principality, Tmutorakan', was being established. Though the population of the city was less than the figure cited by Berthier-Delagard, it was still 6,000 to 7,000 (which is a good number for a medieval town). That means that the city could provide for its defense at the most 1,000 men: fishermen, seamen, small and large merchants, various craftsmen such as blacksmiths, potters, builders, goldsmiths, etc. It may have also been protected by a Byzantine garrison headed by a military-administrative chief — the *strategus*, whose rank at the court was high — or a *protospapharius*. Besides, Korsun itself was a first-class fortress, one of the best in the Byzantine Empire.

A stone rampart — a *proteikhisma* — reinforced the key areas of the defense. More than twenty towers (round and rectangular) were erected along the perimeter of the stronghold. There was also a citadel inside the city. The Goths and Turks, Khazars and Pechenegs had attacked the city, but none of them had managed to overcome the wisdom of the Byzantine builders and the valor of its defenders. So the inhabitants of the 1500-year old city were sure that the barbarians would be repelled this time again.

Summing up various testimonies, one may conclude that Vladimir dropped anchor at the distance of an arrow's flight from Korsun. An arrow sent by a good archer can go as far as 100 meters, but the average is more like 60 to 70 meters. So the Russians must have stopped either at the Round or at the Quarantine Bay.

Having surrounded the city, Vladimir could hardly have expected its inhabitants to surrender peacefully. Perhaps he tried to find out what was the temperament of the besieged. Eventually, arrows started flying, and stones were thrown from the walls. One can see such a scene depicted in the Radziwill chronicle. Last but not least, one cannot exclude the possibility that some brave men climbed the ladders and established personal contact. The men of Korsun must have repelled them. That is how I understand the sentence from the chronicle and from *The Life of Vladimir*: "They fought hard from within the city". Though Berthier-Delagard thought this was a reference to sorties organized by the besieged and their attempts to break through by sending messengers and spies.

After a first setback, Vladimir started a full-scale siege, assigning various "regiments" of Varangians, Slavs, Krivich and Black Bulgars to various portions of the wall. He also sent a message to the "citizens": "If you don't surrender, I am going to stay here for three years". But "they did not heed his warnings". Then, according to the chronicler, the prince ordered his men to pile up rocks and earth near the walls so as to make a platform for storming the stronghold. That is extremely hard work, especially given the stony soil of the Crimea — so we may conjecture that the prince gave this command only when his patience had come to an end.

Events did not take the expected turn. "The Korsun men dug under the wall, and carried the piled-up earth into the city. Vladimir persisted, though the besieged managed to take away most of what was brought up". He was vexed at the enemy stealing the fruit of his toil. We will never know how it all would have turned out if things had gone on this way for many months.

Then, one day, an arrow flew over the Russians' heads and landed somewhere inside their camp. A piece of parchment was wrapped around it, with a bit of writing — a secret message that determined the city's fate.

Using arrows or other propellants to send messages (let us call them arrowgrams) was a common practice in the olden days, with writing on the arrow shaft or on a parchment wrapper. Participants in the Trojan War used them. The Persians, Langobards and Scandinavians knew them. Russian epic bogatyrs (heroes) such as Ilya Muromets, Duk Stepanovich, Vasily Buslayev, and Mikhalka, communicated by arrowgram. Ilya sent his arrows to Duk and received his responses via a falcon that picked up the arrows in the field. Even Vasily used arrows, if only to "mail" messages. (When fighting, he preferred fists or a wooden pole, at least a cart shaft.) One bylina has it as follows:

> He began making arrows,
> With an inscription on them:
> Those who want good food and drink
> Come to Vas'ka's wide yard
> To the wide yard and the honest feast!

This form of data transmission had certain deficiencies. The distance had to be kept short, since one can never hire enough heroic archers. Besides, one must be careful not to hit the client in his head (or elsewhere). And if the arrow went astray, it could be lost altogether, or fall into the wrong hands — unless you had a top-notch domesticated falcon at hand.

Another bylina about Vasily Buslaev suggests a messenger service was used.

> Vasily sat in his writing chair,
> Dashing off letters sparkling with flair.
> The letters were written in wisdom and care:

'Those who wish free drink and good fare,
Come to Vasily's broad grounds
For the best food and drink anywhere around;
Free clothes and other gifts too may be found.'
He sent the letters with his servants
Along the wide streets
And narrow by-lanes in and near town.

4. Anastasius' Story in the Chronicles

Arrows were in great demand during war, and everything that could be used again was picked up and saved. The arrow with the secret message was not lost. It was taken to the prince.

The impression the message had on the prince was tremendous. An unknown friend offered him the keys to the city. The prince was so moved that, "raising his eyes to the sky," he vowed to have himself baptized if the prediction came true. And so, the chronicler asserts, the prince was baptized right there, on the Black Sea Coast, and not as others claim, in Kiev or in Vasilev at an earlier time. It may well be that the Russian lord said something of the sort, overwhelmed by emotion and in anticipation of a sharp turn in the nation's course. Naturally, he took the advice, and some time later entered the subjugated city.

Let's imagine the scene. Here along the straight main street of the city come Varangian, Slav, Krivich and Black Bulgar troops stretching nearly for a mile. They wonder at the beauty of ideally straight streets, magnificent squares paved with antique slabs, huge basilicas and other public buildings, statues on pedestals and fountains (now void of water) at the crossroads. The prince is eager to find the one to whom he owes the triumph. This conclusion may be drawn from the Nikon chronicle, where the man says: "I am Anastasius, and what I say is true, Vladimir . . ."

This chain of logic is true however only if Anastasius' message was a surprise for Vladimir; it does not hold together if this was, instead, a long-awaited report from a secret agent. One cannot exclude the possibility that the Prince's secret service, headed by Dobrynia (which may have included Blyud as one of its chiefs), might have gotten someone into the stronghold with a special mission to discover the source of the city's water supply, and that he managed to find a local citizen as a helper.

Let's try to imagine how the Russian intelligence was organized at Korsun, what mission it was charged with and to whom it was entrusted.

Did Dobrynia follow Vladimir as before, or did he stay behind in Kiev? Most likely, he joined Vladimir's campaign. Very active in the 970s and 980s, Dobrynia was still mentioned as the Kievan prince's right arm at the time of his baptism.

The Korsun campaign was an important and difficult affair. There cannot be any doubt that Dobrynia was one of its authors. And he could hardly have left his nephew alone during such an important mission, the more so that he had assisted him in all his previous campaigns.

I shall invoke here an epic story, the bylina of bogatyr Dunai, who went to the Liakh (or Lithuanian) king with a marriage proposal for his daughter Opraxa, on behalf of Vladimir. His friend and assistant on such an important state mission was Dobrynia Nikitich who, in the popular lore, is the uncle of Vladimir. Researchers have identified this folkloric hero with the episode from *The Life of Vladimir*, during the prince's approaches to Rogneda and Anna. In fact, in the *Life of Vladimir*, the voivodes Oleg and Zhdebern went to Constantinople on such a mission, but the situations are quite similar so that Dobrynia may have been at Korsun, and not Liakh, at the time.

Blyud, his chief assistant, most probably was in Kiev at the time, for he was the tutor of Yaroslav (then a teenager) and was also in charge of Kiev's defense. But the above-mentioned voivode Oleg most probably was one of his subordinates. As seen in the case of Dobrynia and Blyud, voivode Oleg also must have been responsible for intelligence and counterintelligence services. Oleg probably was the commander of a Varangian regiment, the elite corps of the Russian army. So he was sent to the Byzantine tsars, together with the Varangian Zhdebern, who distinguished himself during the siege. They might not compare themselves with Dunai but they must have been among the most influential people in Vladimir's entourage. Still, if Dobrynia did not go south during the campaign, then Oleg may have been in charge of Vladimir's reconnaissance.

If there are directors, then there must be a service to be directed. Berthier-Delagard did not doubt that and wrote about the efficient reconnaissance work performed during the preparations and execution of the march. He thinks that for such a job, "some were probably selected from among the merchants, skilled warriors, or common renegades picked up along the way". In other places, he writes about "snoops, scouts, tradesmen, freelance warriors, and adventurers". Here one can see the plausible composition of the agent corps that was under the command of a small cadre of professional reconnaissance officers.

What could have been the tasks of Dobrynia's service during the Korsun campaign? Academician Grekov considered one of the major tasks of the Russian troops to have been the establishment of an Eastern link "with some procurement bases in the Crimea or even on the continent"; for instance, making an alliance with the Goths, based on their former relations with Svyatoslav. The intelligence service was to reestablish or arrange such a link. It could also have acquired all sorts of information on the Korsun-Tmutorakan' union, which most probably was an operational aim of Vladimir. And at Korsun itself, besides dealing with enemy spies, Vladimir had to send his own spies into the city and maintain reliable contact with them. That does not seem to have been too hard task, owing to the wide use of "arrowgrams".

Berthier-Delagard wrote: "It was not a great effort to send an arrow from Korsun. All sort of messages were sent by arrows, the more so during a siege. Each day proposals, instructions, news (either real or false), suggestions, pledges or curses, threats, even flaming arrows and other evil things were exchanged. That sort of weapon was convenient, for the flight of an arrow was clearly visible, as was the place it landed. One could send not only a message containing secrets about the water supply, but also complete information about all the military secrets of Korsun, about its military leaders, the attitude of the population, which people were "not averse to the Russians, with whom one could establish useful relationships", etc.

The point is, did Dobrynia's men manage to get into the city and find people there who were willing to cooperate?

The example of Anastasius shows that such people could be found. Berthier-Delagard had no doubt that the archer mentioned in the chronicle was "a clever man, who headed the party willing to surrender the city; and he could not have been working alone." Grekov agreed with him on that, and wrote that "Vladimir, in assaulting Korsun, did not rely only on the might of his weaponry" and "it is no wonder that among the besieged there was a group of persons who favored surrender to Vladimir."

Chersonesus in fact was not an ethnically homogeneous city. Besides the Greeks, there were a lot of Sarmats and Alans, even Goths and Slavs — among whom there were kinsmen of the assailants. On the squares and in the streets of the maritime city, in the mansions of white stone (two-storied, in the wealthy area) one could hear Khazar, Pecheneg and Armenian tongues. Fate brought there many a foreigner and it was an obligatory anchorage. It would be naive to think that the multifarious population of Korsun was enthralled by feelings of imperial patriotism. The more so as the Greeks themselves, as witnessed by Constantine Porphyrogenitus, were not much captivated by it. And for good reason.

Chersonesus had long cherished its autonomy and the Vasilevs kept encroaching upon it. After the 9th century, they began appointing military governors to the city, *strategi*, people trusted by Byzantium. Their duties included taking the political pulse of the Taurica population, that is: keeping an ear and an eye out for traitorous talk and seditious activities. And sometimes they killed people for that (and not only for that). The metropolis was worried, particularly as Chersonesus was a recognized center for political and religious outcasts. In the 1st century, the Roman Pope Clement was sent there and sentenced to death, only to be sanctified later on. At the end of the 7th century, even the dethroned emperor Flavius Justinian II Hypomet turned up there. He tried to use the city in his struggle for power, but he did not attract enough support. That is why, when he did manage to regain his throne, he sent the imperial fleet to Chersonesus twice. The first time, the city was plundered by the emperor's troops, but the second time the local garrison and the citizens rose in revolt, with the help of the Khazars, and thus saved Chersonesus. In the 8th and 9th centuries, iconoclasts of the original iconoclasm flocked there to evade religious persecution.

The major Byzantine stronghold in Taurica fomented anti-empire feelings. That was further stimulated by the difficult international situation. In the 8th and 9th centuries, Chersonesus had to bow to Kharas Kagan (in the 8th century the city was even under Khazar protection), and in the 10th century to the Russian prince. This led to the formation of competing parties of interests followed and, inevitably, strife among them.

In this connection, we should bear in mind the following: It is quite probable that the *protevon* (mayor) of Chersonesus in that period was Calokir — the same Calokir who, two decades earlier, had been awarded the title of *patrician* by Nicephorus Phocas and had been sent as ambassador to Kiev's prince Svyatoslav, in order to induce the latter to march on the Danube. There he made friends and even fraternized with Svyatoslav, becoming his ally and councilor during the Russo-Byzantine war. His actions could be explained not only by his personal plans and ambitions but also by the designs of the Chersonesus elite to revise their relations with the empire. Calokir had spent enough time in Kiev to get acquainted with the children and retinue of Svyatoslav, including Dobrynia and the young Vladimir. Now he could be reminded about the friendship that had started at the Dnieper banks. Had he not headed the pro-Russian party to which Anastasius also belonged? Hadn't Vladimir counted on him during the Korsun campaign? They may have established preliminary communications.

But that may be only one of many possible variants.

Certainly, it is one thing to help the Russians (with one's own interest in mind) against the empire during clashes over the Balkans, but quite another to allow the Russians to take over one's own city. We do not know for sure who was the *protevon* at the time. A. Poppais' assumption, however, is that "the party that favored surrender of the city to Vladimir" was not anti- but pro-empire, that is anti-Chersonesus. So it should have been headed not by the *protevon*, but by the *strategus*. There does not seem to be much doubt that such a party existed. There is an indication in the *Life of Vladimir* about differences of view between the two heads of the city. After Chersonesus' surrender, the "Korsun prince" (and his family) were executed, that is either the *protevon* or the *strategus*, but not both. Archaeological evidence seems to suggest the same thing. Excavations at Chersonesus show that the city was greatly plundered by the Russian host. Its western section suffered the most. It was inhabited by fishermen and handicraftsmen and occupied one third of its territory (117,000 square meters). Life ceased to flourish there and a vast deserted area replaced the densely populated quarters. By contrast, the houses and the streets of the local nobility and merchants, located in the northeast part of the city, fared better. One can conclude with some certainty that the "traitors' party" in Korsun, or so to say "the party favoring surrender to Vladimir", consisted predominantly of those who "also cry the most" (the wealthy).

So if Vladimir's intelligence services represented market demand, there was certainly supply offered by from some segment of the Korsun population. Regretfully, we do not know whether Dobrynia's agents managed to establish contact with those people. We can only insist that such attempts must have taken place both in the form of directly hunting for chinks in the city's stone walls and in the form of arrows shot over the parapets, with suggestions of surrender, which did not anger everyone in equal measure. One may present the outward circumstances of Anastasius' treason in many ways, but one should also exercise one's powers of imagination and conjecture in trying to reconstruct the most probable scenarios.

5. Anastasius. A Quick Portrait

Who was this Anastasius?

Historians seem to be unanimous in thinking he was a Greek. It may well be so. But this is just a logical conclusion from the assumption that Korsun was a Greek city and it is valid only with certain qualifications.

The writer Ladinsky thinks he was a Russian. Whoever was, he must have spoken Russian, for if his message had been composed in Greek, it might have gone unheeded.

Some think he was a spiritual leader and doubt that he was personally involved in the mechanics of communication. Few priests are champion archers. Berthier-Delagard surmised that Anastasius might have masterminded the "operation", while the arrow was sent by a common soldier who may not even have known what he was doing. Ladinsky speaks of an accomplice.

But early scribes do not tell us anything about such matters. Only in the later version of the *First Novgorod Chronicle*, passed on to us in copies from the 15th century, Anastasius is identified as a priest — but even then only in connection with events some three years after the story, when Vladimir placed him in charge of a newly built church of Our Lady.

Later on, annalists of the 15th and 16th centuries mention Anastasius' priesthood in the same context. In the *Book of Degrees* (Stepennaya kniga) and certain other compositions, Anastasius is called archpriest. Only the 16th century Polish historian Stryikovskiy accords the Byzantine man this title from the very beginning. In two editions of the *Life of*

Vladimir (from the 16th century), Anastasius is given an even higher rank and is presented as the "Korsun Bishop". It is clear that the price of the archer's shares rose over time, in the imagination of the Middle Age bookmen.

Anyway, we doubt he was a priest at the time of the siege. He may not have been a cleric at all. Did he ever don a cassock? The idea of a clergy familiar with the Korsun public utilities seems unlikely. But we shall come to that later.

We know that Vladimir returned to Kiev with some "Korsun priests". Their mission was certainly noble — to bring a great country onto the path of the true faith. It may be that Vladimir had promised them to help spread to the north the cult of the martyr Clement and other Korsun saints. But if they agreed to cooperate with the person who brought so many calamities onto their parishioners, the Chersonesus priests put themselves into a rather dubious position, unbecoming to prelates (a possibility that cannot be totally excluded). One of the Russian popular compositions from the Middle Ages, *A Conversation of Three Prelates* (Beseda trech svyatiteley), has such a description the priest's life: "The surplice is the truth, and the cassock is justice; the truth comes from heaven and dons justice, so a priest should not separate a surplice from a cassock".

Vasily Nikitich Tatishchev could not reconcile himself with the thought that the baptism of Russia was conducted using the services of an obscure person. So he made an attempt to exonerate the Byzantine who sought political refuge with the Russians by inventing an "honest" biography for him. This is what he wrote: "We know he betrayed his city, but we also know that he had been associated with Olga and Vladimir long before, and that he induced Vladimir to become baptized; thus, since according to St. Paul's teaching the crime followed by repentance presumes innocence, so he became a traitor without blame." It is really hard to accept that an obscure and immoral individual was the helping hand that instigated the baptism of Russia. One would prefer an honest and noble fellow. One would prefer an Anastasius deserving of the Order of the "Honest Criminal and the Blameless Renegade".

The chronicler is terse in describing the social status of this future protégé of the Kievan prince — "a man from Korsun". In Old Russia, a *man* was a free person, a person of certain property and social status. Those who, besides personal liberty, had any position, wealth or nobility were called "first", "great", "distinguished" or "best" men. Since Anastasius was not favored with any of these qualifiers, he can be considered a common citizen that had gone over to the other side; with other honest people whose conscience was not quite clean.

The fact that he knew the sources of the city water supply — certainly a state secret! — but was not part of the establishment may lead one to infer that he was rather close to the local security services. Korsun, by virtue of the city's location, an outpost of Byzantium far to the north of the imperial capital (irrespective of its relations with the empire), must have had such an essential corps. Imperial diplomats would go from here to the Khazars, the Pechenegs or to Russia on various missions, acting within a larger network of intrigues. Korsun merchants gathered military intelligence from those countries, and fishermen at the mouth of the Dnieper noted the movements of Russian boats; sailors notified Constantinople about anything out of the ordinary. So people in Korsun must have been involved in intelligence, first-hand, and must have been aware of the value of information.

Documented history does not give us much to go on, when assessing the personality of Anastasius and his motives. The "Korsun man" who became Vladimir's secret agent must have known one of the basic rules of his profession — keep your mouth shut.

6. Zhdebern

As we have mentioned above, some historians doubt that it was Anastasius who sent the arrow. In *The Life of Vladimir*, another person is credited with this accomplishment, and that is Zhdebern (also Zhbern, or Izhbern, from the Scandinavian Skibiorn or Sigbjorn), supposed to have been one of the Varangians sent by the perfidious Vladimir to the Greeks several years before.

After Vladimir conquered Kiev and killed Yaropolk, with the Varangians' help, their demand for pay forced Vladimir to promise to consider rewarding their labors. They waited for a month, and then charged the prince with cheating. They decided to "go to the Greeks". Vladimir selected some of them who were "kind, clever and brave", gave them a few towns as compensation, and let the rest go to Tsargrad. His ambassadors were warned, however, to convey a message to the emperor, saying: "The Varangians are coming to you; do not keep them in town, for they may do you harm as they have done here. Send them to different towns but do not let anyone come back here".

It is quite probable that Constantinople heeded the friendly advice and the soldiers of fortune were sent either to Korsun, Cimmerian Bosporus or Trabzon and other provinces of the empire and were left there for the remainder of their lives. Some may have been angry, but then some might have sized up the situation and decided to make the best of it. One of them may have settled in Korsun, clinking the gold coins from Dobrynia and awaiting instructions.

A Varangian would be a good candidate for sending a crucial "arrow" at a crucial moment.

The Life of Vladimir tells the following story about Zhdebern. "Vladimir laid siege to Korsun for a long time but failed to starve the city. In the city, at the time, there was a Varangian by the name of Izhbern, who wrote a letter, attached it to an arrow and sent it to one of Vladimir's regiments with the words, "Great Prince Vladimir! Your slave the Varangian Izhbern is very much attached to you. I shall tell you how things stand. You may stay here two or three years (he must have heard about Vladimir's threat) and you will not be able to starve the city, for you are not aware that ships come here with food and drink". As one can see, in *The Life of Vladimir* changes not only the author of the letter but also its contents, though the text of the letter varies from copy to copy. In another version, it says, " To my Lord, Prince Vladimir! Your friend Izhbern writes to you... People from boats come to the city, by land, and bring here food and drink". According to this version, victuals were brought to the besieged city not directly from the boats but were hauled over the land. It also mentions that he sent the arrow not straight to Vladimir's camp but to the Varangians, who were stationed near the city walls. He is also supposed to have hailed them, calling, "Heads up! Take this letter to the Prince!" Shakhmatov thinks, however, that there is not much difference between these hypothetical letters and to his mind the original text must have said, essentially, "Prince Vladimir! Your friend Zhdebern is still devoted to you. I have to inform you about the following. You may stay here for two or three years and you won't be able to take the city by exhausting its supplies. People from boats come here by way of land and bring food and drink. Their route lies to the east." (The last sentence is taken from the tale of Vladimir's baptism after the conquest of Korsun).

I hope the reader understands the authors' attempts to probe into the contents of the Varangian letter to his Russian "friend". Here we have one of the first early Russian intelligence reports. One may imagine Vladimir's thoughts as he read it with the greatest attention! So we shall go on.

Shakhmatov's reconstruction of both versions leave many questions. The first version has little to say about any "land route": just a suggestion from Zhdebern to block the access of Greek ships to the city port. But why did Vladimir give an order "to dig the route across" soon after receiving the letter? One can dig across a land route, but not the sea. Maybe he ordered the construction of a dike? That may explain why the city surrendered only three months after Zhdebern's report was received. Building a dike is a laborious task, but, still, it was possible.

The sense of the words can hardly be deciphered, even if we prefer the version suggesting people carrying sacks across the steppe, from ships, on a dark night, along some backwoods path (this is the version that has attracted the attention of most scholars). What did the Varangian, by the name of Jzhbern (Zhdebern), mean when he sent a message from the city about a "land way"? And why did Vladimir give an order to "dig across the route" when he learned about it from a Varangian?

Berthier-Delagard thought that the letter referred to deliveries from the east shore of Quarantine Bay. "Victuals could be delivered to the city only by sea, as indicated in *The Life of Vladimir*", he wrote. Sailors also took part, but they could not deliver the goods directly. The Korsun harbor and port were controlled by the enemy; they could not get to the city from the north since the steep shores made it impossible to land safely or to safely unload any goods, the more so in the bad weather that prevailed during the autumn and the winter of the siege." The ships came at night to the large bay (which is now the Sevastopol roadstead), moored in the shallow coves and hid from bad weather and enemy inspection until the moment was right. Loopholes in Vladimir's security service helped the sailors take the goods to the cape, and then the townsfolk delivered everything in small boats across the mouth of the bay to the city. This entire route was from the east, as specified in *The Life of Vladimir*. In the end, Vladimir stopped the delivery by stationing a regiment on the cape; they may have dug holes and trenches there, a mile away from the camp.

One can understand the words "to dig across" as to setting up an interim outpost there. Otherwise any digging would have been of no use there, since the place is wide and open and could not be easily interrupted by a series of ditches.

The solution presented by Berthier-Delagard is quite plausible but it presupposes a total lack of patrols on the part of the Russian army. Grekov finds that doubtful; he thinks that the attacking forces must have detected any deliveries before the besieged could have used them. Nights in the Crimea are very dark in summertime, and porters led by an experienced guide could have reached the city even if they had to bypass some Russian outposts. One or two such operations might have been successful — but the city could hardly have been sustained that way for long. It would have been difficult not to stray from the safe route, and to maintain silence during the unloading of the goods from the ships to the smaller boats and then to land, and all along the route to the city itself.

Yet, the most puzzling thing here is: why did Vladimir have to dig in any place in order to block the traffic? He could have laid an ambush to the "life trail" of Korsun for the benefit of his own troops. The explanation of Berthier-Delagard is somewhat far fetched. Later on he offered another one.

Grekov offered another solution to the issue of the sailors' "mysterious" path. He thought there might have been an underground tunnel, unknown to Vladimir. It is not very difficult to imagine such a construction since "there are many graves and underground premises cut into the stone in different parts of the city." It is plausible that such an underground path could evade discovery by ordinary means; and it could not be ambushed and could be only be breached by "digging it across".

It's worth mentioning the description given in the bylina about the founding of Korsun by prince Gleb Vladimirovic that:

"Underground passages there / lead to the bread store rooms."

N. V. Piatysheva joins Grekov in his argument against Berthier-Delagard but opposes the idea of an underground passage when considering the geologic and the topographic properties of the land east and southeast of the city, where there is a deep and marshy ravine. Grekov makes no mention of where the underground passage might have been. But he may have been inspired by Shakhmatov, who wrote in his *Story of Vladimir's Baptism*, that the "ground path" was located to the east of the Russian troops. Shakhmatov himself took it from the story about Anastasius and the water supply main. But one may also consider that such an underground pass might have been in place west of the city, leading to the seacoast.

(One may wonder how Vladimir and Dobrynia could solve such a puzzle, if we cannot do so even now. But we should also remember that Zhdebern's letter came to us in a much-distorted condition).

According to Piatysheva, the city outskirts on the southeast were rather marshy, sometimes flooding to become a lake. Piatysheva thinks that what Zhdebern meant by the "ground path" or land route was an artificial road to the center of Chersonesus, south of the city wall, near the main gate. The Russians encircled the city from the southwest, from Round Bay to the main gate tower under which the water mains would have been located. Further on to the south, the walls mounted a steep hill and stopped at the marsh, which was itself impregnable. Only on the southeast was there a weak section in the wall, especially near the 20th shutter and the 17th and 18th towers (the Zenon or Siagre tower and the Kentinarisiyskaya). Vladimir seemed to have controlled that zone because his camp was at Archers' Bay. The season for "the secret enterprise was rather propitious" —from September until February, when the nights were dark and it often rained.

Between the Russian troops to the west and their outposts to the east there was a large territory through which the sailors passed. They followed the path leading from Quarantine Bay (the probable place of disembarkment) to the center of the marshy gorge. The road here was in the form of a dike capped with stones and was up to two meters high and three meters wide. It may have been camouflaged "for strategic purposes". During the winter and spring-time the level of water in the gorge rose, and only people who knew the place well could use it. Sailors must have known the way also. Piatysheva is sure that it was this "ground way," east of Vladimir's camp, which they dug across at Zhdebern's advice. That would be an effective measure to curb the delivery of foodstuffs and munitions. Some ancient freshwater wells were discovered near the road, in 1896. Cutting off such an essential artery did, indeed, lead to the city's collapse, as presented in *The Life of Vladimir*. This might have been the first stage of the assault; the second was the breaching of the water pipes.

This version is rather interesting and shows Vladimir's siege of Korsun from a new perspective. However, a few questions arise. Is it possible that the Russians allowed so many enemies to pass near their own camp without hindrance? How could the Greek sailors arrange a regular supply of goods during that season, so unpropitious for sailing?

Berthier-Delagard thought that the goods came, for the most part, from Taurica, "the nearby coast, mostly from today's Eupatoria, long under the influence of Korsun." But we have no definite evidence of that. Why, then, should the Russians have dug across the dike and its approaches, if one could easier lay an ambush at the source? Only Grekov's version offers a way out of the logical dead end. But so far, archaeologists have not found any trace of an underground pass connecting Chersonesus with the seacoast and one cannot be sure it ever existed.

In that case, one may prefer the chronicled version (it is known as *Life story* and *The tale about Vladimir's baptism*) whose author, supposedly, is Anastasius himself. In his version, the advice to dig across the earth seems most rational since it refers to the water supply pipes.

Does it mean that the annals' story about Anastasius, the archer, is more credible and that the tale about Zhdebern from the *Life of Vladimir* was written later, and is a lore version? I do not think so, as many investigators beginning with N. I. Kostomarov are inclined to take as folklore the story of Anastasius. Shakhmatov preferred the *Life story* version as the earliest though he thought both of them rather lore inventions. What did bring him to such a conclusion? To his mind, the character of Zhdebern was taken either from the *Tale of Vladimir's Baptism* or from a "Korsun legend" written in the 11ᵗʰ century and that has not survived in the original. The author of that legend, a Greek who may have been a descendant of one of the priests who came with the prince from Chersonesus, served at the Tithe church built in Kiev afterwards. In this view, the Zhdebern story about Vladimir's march on the Greek city was just a bit of lore created after his abortive attempt to marry the local princess.

According to Shakhmatov, the scribe who copied the story must have left out "nearly everything that emanated from the original tale", because it does not reflect any historical truth. Specifically, Shakhmatov says, the scribe replaced Zhdebern by Anastasius due to an odd analytical process.

First, according to Shakhmatov, Zhdebern seems like a character from "an ancient bylina". Second, the Varangian in the story was accompanied by the voivode Oleg, and we all know that Oleg had been Igor's voivode (or at least his contemporary and not Vladimir's). "The circumstances preclude our considering Zhdebern as an authentic historical person, a contemporary of Vladimir, so his name should be excluded from the story. But who should be substituted for him?" — reasoned the scribe, according to this scholar.

The original chronicle tells us that Zhdebern was one of Vladimir's favorites, after the capture of Korsun. The scribe also knew of favors bestowed on Anastasius; he was taken from Korsun, along with other clerics, to Kiev. On the other hand, Anastasius was reputed to be a traitor who later on served Boleslav (more on that to come). These two factors prompted the scribe to assert that Vladimir took over Korsun because of Anastasius' treason and that it was Zhdebern who had sent the arrow to Vladimir.

I doubt it. Whatever the history of the "Korsun legend" (some think it originated in Tmutorakan') and whatever its relation to the chronicle and *The Life of Vladimir*, one cannot conclude that both of the Black Sea archers were fictional. The early scribes introduced many improbable details into the annals but they never mixed fantasy with facts taken from other sources. In any case, the chronicle version of an archer who used his knowledge of the city's water supply for his own profit does not raise any doubts.

Then, is it credible that Zhdebern is a fictional character who crept into the "Korsun legend" from some folk bylina, as Shakhmatov believes?

It is hard to believe in the authenticity of the bylina, despite its picturesque and detailed descriptions; even less, to believe that Shakhmatov's scribe composed "the life story" using the methods described by the scholar. If the ancient scribes served as fiction writers combining real facts and real personages with elements from their own imagination, then the entire history would have been phony; but that is not the case with the chronicles and the annals. The philologist Shakhmatov sometimes lacked a sense of history.

I do not doubt the authenticity of the bylina when it describes Vladimir's march to Byzantium, but I am skeptical that it refers to Zhdebern. Folk memory is rather indifferent to foreigners and usually does not retain their names. Not a single Scandinavian has left an essential trace in Russian folklore. Most probably the Zhdebern item was incorporated into one of the versions of the "Korsun legend" and life stories either from the heroic epics (for there were always many Scandinavians among the troops) or some other source. His deed might have been written down by some cleric and that has preserved his name from oblivion.

I do not consider Zhdebern a legendary personality, a feeble counterpart of Anastasius. Like Berthier-Delagard and Grekov, I consider him a historical figure, and not even a pretender claiming the laurels rightfully earned by the Greek. The text of the archer's message, in both the chronicle and the life story, is rendered rather liberally and approximately, which raises issues of incompatibility regarding its content and the interpretation of these secret reports.

In Anastasius' message, the water supply source is inaccurately sited to the east of Vladimir's camp (it was to the south rather than the east). In the *Life Story of Vladimir*, the prince's order to dig across the "ground way" so as to prevent "sailors" from getting into the city makes little sense. This latter stipulation raises doubts about the authenticity of the Varangian legend. I would rather agree with Berthier-Delagard, who thinks it to be a common borrowing taken from the end of the Anastasius story, placed in the wrong context since "digging across a water course is not quite natural or feasible." All of the above-mentioned reasons do not deprive the original 10th century documents (of which we only have indirect knowledge) of their authenticity, each probably describing an important act in the success of the Russian war campaign.

Still, the Varangian, first and foremost, brought starvation to the Korsun folk, though Delagard asserts that Chersonesus had enough supplies to last for at least half a year —although there are no actual data to that effect. During archaeological excavations several cement or stone-lined holes in the ground have been found; they would have been used for storing grain or salted fish. Bread and not very choice fish were the townsfolk's staples during hard times, and one can only imagine the quantity of water needed for a population of 6,000 to 7,000 when they had been eating salted fish for three months. Anyway, Zhdebern distinguished himself and like Anastasius he was granted many favors.

A. A. Shakhmatov called Zhdebern's shot "a traitor's arrow", putting the Varangian on the same footing with the "man from Korsun", hardly doing him justice. Anastasius was a traitor, but Zhdebern rightly deserves the status of an intelligence officer. He was, most probably, one of those Varangians that had been sent away to Byzantium by the ungrateful Vladimir with a dubious recommendation. Some of the features of Zhdebern's address to the Russian leader give grounds for such speculation. "My lord, Prince Vladimir! This is your friend Zhdebern writing to you!" — we can read in one version of the *Life Story.* "Great Prince Vladimir! Your slave Izhbern is greatly devoted to you" — says another. Here one may detect the reverence accorded by a subject to his suzerain that is absent in Anastasius' letter. "Slave" is from the same system of relations. "Friend" is not just a well-wisher's greeting but an acknowledgement of familiarity with the prince, a reminder of former contacts.

Zhdebern must not have been an ordinary mercenary but a member of the Varangian nobility, in order to have known Vladimir personally. In one version of the *Life Story* it is said that Vladimir, having taken the city, married a Korsun princess to the boyar Zhdebern, gave them a good dowry and made him the city's deputy. It is not quite clear whether Zhdebern received the boyar title before or after he fired his lucky arrow. It is hardly probable that the prince sent into exile a person to whom he had accorded such honors.

But it may be that "the boyar" had never been to Byzantium, for there is some mention that his mother called him not Zhdebern . . . but Dobrynia! Yes, that's right, our old friend. Such a juxtaposition of identities was tendered by none other than the well-known pre-Revolutionary researcher of ancient Russia's life stories, N. Serebrianskiy. Some eight decades ago, he wrote the following: "Some may accuse me of a groundless and risky assumption but I would venture to put forward such a thought. Maybe the name Izhbern/Zhdebern is just a corruption of the Russian name Dobrynia? Was he not the main person who played a momentous role in the taking of Korsun?" In Serebrianskiy's opinion, some other chronicles "attribute to the Zhdebern biography some traits in common with Dobrynia". But even his conclusion is rather unexpected: "Voivode Zhdebern is a collective name for two historic personalities — voivode Zhdebern and Anastasius of Korsun."

7. Anastasius' Star, or the First Agent Who Defected to the West

While Zhdebern reaped the laurels of success and sank into obliv-ion, Anastasius enjoyed a different fate. He did not become the hero of a bylina. But he probably did not regret that, since he did not toil for glory's sake. The chronicle relates that after the described events, a lucky star shone for a long time upon the clever Black Sea dweller who felt aversion to the diet of salted fish. Vladimir took him to Kiev along with the "tsarevna", who arrived at last from Tsargrad, along with "Korsun priests", and the relics of Saints Clement and Phoebus, and church utensils, icons and other treasures. The Nikon chronicle enu-merates them: "Anastasius, who wrote on the arrow", two copper idols, four copper horses and three copper lions. That looks like a description of loot in the prince's treasury: one Anastasius, two idols, four horses . . . Such a trivial account! Then it goes on: "And Anastasius was given to his father metropolitan Mikhail" (according to the chronicle he was made metropolitan of Russia at the time). Together with Metro-politan Mikhail, the Byzantine bishops and Dobrynia, Anastasius went in 990 AD to Novgorod "to destroy idols and baptize the citizens; the next summer he went to Rostov".

Soon after the Korsun campaign and the baptism of the people of Kiev, Vladimir laid the foundations of a cathedral in Kiev — the Church of Our Lady, also known as the Tithe (Dessyatinnaya) Church for he gave one tenth of all his profits to the church. The nickname of Tithe was also given to Anastasius, who was charged with the collection and disposition of duties. Some later sources called him a priest. But I am inclined to think that Anastasius was not a cleric, as many researchers suppose, but a sort of administrator who later became *metropolitan boyar*. We think that it is his image in the small picture illustrating the conse-cration of the Tithe Church in the Radzivill chronicle. He is the first man standing behind Vladimir among the group of nobles; a man with golden hair and beard in a yellow garment with a greenish overcoat. His face is pious, a fairly ordinary nobleman of the 10th century. Or could be that he is the man standing behind?

Another picture confirms the first guess; it is next to the text recounting the tithe donation to the Church of Our Lady. "Anastasius of Korsun" is entrusted with the custody of the church revenue (he was obliged to be present here by virtue of his office). The Prince is standing, head uncovered, beside the greatest cathedral of Russia. Behind him stand two officers (their faces are extremely pious). The first of them, clad in a typical Russian garment of the epoch, holds the prince's hat in his hands. One of those remarkable persons undoubtedly is Anastasius.

The two images seem to be the only existing pictorial testimonies of the brave archer and custodian of the church funds. That means that the painter treated him the same as Blyud and did not depict the major deed of his life. What a colorful picture it could have been: the archer standing at the wall of the fortress pulls the string of a bow; the arrow takes flight, bearing an important message to the Russian camp. Vladimir, greatly moved, grasps it in his hands and immediately gives the order: "Look for it! Start digging!"

But the artist who painted the Radzivill chronicle failed to include him. He painted three small pictures dedicated to the siege and the storming of Korsun. In all three pictures the citizens are battling the attackers. Only the last of them shows the crucial action. But how? On the left side, the troops are advancing onto toward the stronghold. On the right, two brave men with long curly hair and short shirts, spades in hand, are implementing Vladimir's order to "dig". And that is all. So the previous supposition, on the absence of Blyud's images, may be confirmed. The artist's focus was not in the complexity of the person but on the psychology of the main character in such circumstances.

The pious and reverend attitude was typical of the former Korsun resident, now the Tithe, until the very end of Vladimir's rule. But when Svyatopolk and Yaroslav started fighting and the Polish troops entered Kiev, something happened to Anastasius. When the people of Kiev and other cities started harassing the unwelcome guest, Boleslav the Brave, he "fled Kiev" taking along with him the possessions of Yaroslav, his sister, the boyars and many other people. He also took along the "treasure of the Tithe church". "And Anastasius was in charge of the Tithe property", writes the chronicler. It is hard to say who was deceived by whom. The Korsun man who had betrayed the Greeks in exchange for the Russians' reward, now left his new homeland with the convoy of its enemy. The treasures of the principal Orthodox sanctuary of the Russian capital was now taken away! He may have sent another "arrow" to Boleslav as before. And hit the bull's eye again.

N. M. Karamzin is straightforward in his opinion of the Korsun archer. He wrote: "Sly Anastasius, formerly Vladimir's favorite, managed to gain the trust of the Polish king and became the caretaker of his treasury (looted from the Russian land) and left Kiev having betrayed his first and second homelands for his own personal greed". "The knave —" agreed S. M. Soloviev. "An adventurer, renegade and traitor, there were many like him in 11th century Byzantine history" — added one Soviet researchers.

If Zhdebern was partially rewarded for his deeds by some mention in the epic memory of the people, Anastasius certainly deserves a monument erected either at the Korsun ruins, in Kiev or at least in Moscow. He was the progenitor of all renegade agents of international caliber (as opposed to Blyud), for he betrayed not only the princes but also his own peoples and nations.

8. Russian Strategic Intelligence in the South

The formation of a great newly-enlightened eastern Slav state, and its interests in domestic stability and foreign security, required a solid knowledge of the outer world and information about the way of life overseas. One may consider the Nikon chronicle, relating events before the year 1001 AD. "In that year, Vladimir sent his 'guests' (that is, merchants) as emissaries to Rome, Jerusalem, Egypt and Babylon to learn about their customs and ways of life." That brief record is rather cryptic. Why were merchants chosen as scouts and not somebody from the prince's host (boyars, men, officers etc.) who were accustomed to such missions, the more so as they were still employed by Dobrynia? Why were these cities chosen, and not some others? What was the specific task of the emissaries? The answer to the first question is more difficult. But when Tatishchev describes it the other way around — "Ambassadors were sent under the disguise of merchants," that seems to be closer to the truth. Diplomats and scouts were both sent under the disguise of merchants (and maybe they took along a merchant or two). Such practices have been in wide use since times immemorial and still are, today. The readers of this book may recollect the first appearance of Prince Oleg in Kiev.

One should bear in mind that in ancient and medieval times merchants often served (voluntarily or otherwise) as scouts; because they saw much and heard even more. They certainly attracted the attention of the special services, who gladly established contacts with them: "Hallo, guests and merchants! Had a long trip? Rough sailing?" etc. It is not possible to ascertain who went where: either ambassadors under the guise of merchants (we know that at the time scouts were called ambassadors) or merchants with "diplomatic passports".

It all depended on the tasks involved. Tatishchev gives more detail: "They were sent to gather descriptions of lands, cities and other things and the rule of law that prevailed in each of them". The historian adds, significantly, that "Vladimir's queries about conditions in such faraway countries is quite laudable. One may judge that he also had sufficient descriptions of conditions in his own state and neighboring lands, though nothing of those reports has survived. Such investigation require not only proper intention, but also a skillful observer. In addition to knowing what is needed for the good of the country, for example, one must also be able to draw a good map. Information about magnificent buildings, the law and the customs of other lands, the system of rewards and the punishments, military matters, trades and crafts, the ways and means of making profits, all are important targets of investigation — and such are the information to be obtained during such travels."

Tatishchev's instruction to Vladimir's "writers/travelers" clearly shows the mentality of a rational reformer of the 18th century. But on the whole, it fits the description of the classical "investigators into other lands and customs". Kievan spies must have practiced something similar. Indeed, the necessity to expand Kievan Russia's trade and economic relations to the East and the West was predetermined by the natural course of the social and economic development of societies at the time; and by the effort to occupy a new, more worthy, place in the world community, an aspiration that Vladimir apparently shared with his closest entourage.

Russian envoys might not have traveled as far as Babylon for that purpose — they must have meant here the New Babylon, i.e. Cairo, for the old Babylon had been in ruins for many centuries by then — but Russian merchant convoys did become familiar with the routes to the lands of the Arab khalifats since the 8th to 9th centuries. Jerusalem and

Egypt were evidently very little known to them, as was Rome.

Yet, the Kievan court was concerned with seeking potential allies at its western and southern borders, in a rather complex situation for Russia; clerical and political relations with Byzantium were rather tense.

The visit to Rome becomes understandable if one reads the paragraph in the Nikon chronicle about the envoys "from the Greek kings with peace proposals" ("seeking love") in 990 AD and in the next paragraph we read: "there came to Vladimir envoys from the Pope of Rome with love and honor". It is quite clear that the Pope's "Foreign Office" carefully monitored relations between Kiev and Constantinople, and tried to use any pretext in order to take revenge against the baptism under the Orthodox rite that had taken place in Russia. Vladimir, for his part, considered his contacts with Rome a good means of bringing pressure to bear on his relatives from Byzantium whose character was terse and unyielding. Tatishchev writes about the arrival of the Pope's ambassadors: "Vladimir received them with love and honor and sent his own envoy to the Pope." Of course, soon after that, the Tsargrad Metropolitan's reaction inevitably follows, in a letter to the Kievan prince wherein he explains why "the Roman faith is not good" and admonishes him not to listen to the Pope. "Do not fall prey to their evil faith and their teaching, but, considering their deceit and deviousness you should refrain from carrying on any further correspondence with them".

Vladimir did not refrain from extending his reach to the "evil" Rome, and we know that in 994 his envoys were coming back from another visit to the Pope; although, in Tatishchev's words, they came back without any tangible results ("having done nothing"). Maybe the new voyage to the "eternal city" had as one of its aims the restoration of talks interrupted seven years before; understandably, the newly converted Christians paid attention to the "Jerusalem of the Western world," the center of Western ecumenism.

Behind the shifting reasons, aims and interests of the young state that was gathering force, there loomed the Russian need to comprehend the world (not unlike Ilya Muromets, or "Ilya from Murom", the hero who climbs high upon a mountaintop, looks around as far as he can see, and prepares himself for the next adventure). Tatishchev thinks that such an extension of the scope of military and diplomatic intelligence gathering went hand-in-hand with the expansion of the Russians' ever-widening reach in trade, travel and migration at the time. After the story described in the *Bertine Annals* and commentaries about the travels of the Kievan prince's emissaries in quest of a "faith to choose", we have the first recorded case of a Russian strategic intelligence mission: a simultaneous mission to all three continents at once. Unfortunately, no details about the undertaking or its results, and no information about travelers themselves, have survived. Maybe it was because no state had yet proclaimed the world an exclusive abode of its vital interests.

9. Folk Wits

"Disinformation" was also effectively used by the Russians and we have at least one example from the times of Prince Vladimir. It happened in 997. That year, Vladimir went to Novgorod to gather some troops to fight the Pechenegs. Pecheneg intelligence reported the prince's departure, and they also knew that there were no spare troops in the south of Russia at the time (the Kievan state was hard-pressed to contain the encroaching nomads). Soon, the steppe cavalry invaded the Russian lands and focused its attacks against the city of Belgorod (now, a suburb of Kiev). The town was dear to Vladimir's heart, as it had become prosperous and densely populated under his reign.

The siege was severe. When the starvation became unbearable, the citizens called for a *veche* (town meeting). All the speakers were of one mind. If there is no help from the prince, why should we all starve to death? Shouldn't we rather surrender?" An "old man" was absent from the meeting for one reason or another. Afterwards, he asked what was discussed at the *veche*, and they told him. The old man got angry and sent for the town elders. He may not have been all that "old" and he probably was not an entirely ordinary person. "I understand you are going to surrender the city to the Pechenegs?" — he asked angrily. They offered lame excuses: "The people cannot stand the hunger any longer". But he would not listen to that. "Look here," he interrupted them, "you wait for three days. But before you surrender, do what I tell you". The aldermen "gladly complied".

The self-appointed voivode ordered them to search for and find at least a sack full of oats, wheat or barley. And they managed to find some. The old man told some women to prepare a barrel (one in which they usually cooked *kissel*); then a well was to be dug, the barrel was placed in it and was filled up to the brim with oats and barley. Then they took another barrel and dug another well, one just like the first, and went out to look for some mead (a fermented honey-based drink). And they managed to find some, in a local "prince's cellar" (one can imagine that it was not quite empty). The mead was diluted with water and poured into the barrels. The next morning, the wise man from Belgorod told his men to bring some Pechenegs into the town, "so they could see for themselves what was going on in this city". The Pechenegs rejoiced, thinking that the city was going to surrender and, having taken some hostages, sent "their best men" inside. But the curious envoys were embarrassed to hear the following: "Why are you so reckless? Do you really hope to exhaust us? You can lay siege here for ten years, it will be of no avail. For we have wells full of grub. You may see them for yourselves." The Pechenegs were taken to the barrels and several bucketsful were drawn up. The Russians drank *kissel* themselves and gave some to the envoys. The astonished nomads asked for some to take along with them as a token of proof. The happy citizens (most likely, those who guarded the prince's cellar) complied with the request and some days later the nomads disappeared beyond the steppes. Such was the end of an operation named "Kissel from Belgorod".

Well, the chronicler may have taken this tale from the popular culture and some readers may consider it a myth. The name of the main character of the story remains unknown. The scribe must have thought that doing good is selfless. Still, one might try to reconstruct the portrait of the Belgorod wizard.

Historian I. Y. Froyanov called the Belgorod wise man "an angel from the heavens". The man most probably belonged to the noble circles that came to the prince's service and tackled important state affairs. These noblemen were probably newcomers to the town — it had been built only some six years before the events described here. The chronicler says that: "He constructed several towns and brought many people to them, for he was very much in love with towns." That means that the prince knew many of the people who came to settle there, since Belgorod was not only one of the prince's favorite residences but also a major stronghold on the western and southwestern approaches to Kiev. (It was located on the high banks of the Irpen' River and had a well-protected castle with a *kremlin* inside, where Russian troops were stationed). The prince often visited it and most probably he knew personally the old man who had the Pechenegs drink kissel. Though he might not have been one of the prince's officers and might not have belonged to the local authorities; we cannot consider him the chief of Vladimir's secret services in the city. The man must have been a member of the people's (self-appointed) "counterintelligence forces." The only name under which he is remembered is "the Old Man".

The artist of the Radzivill chronicle painted three pictures on the topic of the "Belgorod kissel". In the first, a great many people are present at a meeting on the city square near a tower of the town wall (the scene may have taken place near the kremlin). The expression on their faces and their gestures seem to indicate that the artist did not approve of their intention to surrender. Near the tower, we can see a person who may be of interest to us. This is a respected God-fearing old man who stands half-turned and spreads his arms as if perplexed by the proceedings. He is the only person who evidently does not like what he sees and hears. If there is any doubt as to what this picture represents, the next one is absolutely clear.

In the center of the city, near a tower, a young-looking man, his hand raised, calls for action, while the older countrymen, some bald, some gray-bearded, are applauding and pointing at him with enthusiasm. A girl and a young lad are pouring honey into a barrel, according to the authoritative instructions. Here we see the "master picture" known to every Russian who is well-schooled in Russia's history.

The last picture, the "deception of the century", presents the epilogue. Two Pechenegs, with jugs in their hands, are waiting for a young man to boil some kissel for them at the fire. The Pecheneg prince is eating with gusto the gift presented by the citizens of Belgorod (he is literally being fed false information).

10. Vladimir's Domestic Law-and-Order Philosophy

The chronicle tells us that under Vladimir, not only the military power and the international cachet of Kievan Russia increased, but that criminal activity, highway robbery, and brigandage became more common. We should recollect some folk songs (bylinas) about Ilya Muromets and Solovey-the-Brigand, describing the danger of traveling to Kiev.

> The straight way has been abandoned,
> It is pitted and covered with grass.
> For the last three score years
> No one has used it on horseback
> No one has trod it on foot.
> Not a bird flies that way now,
> Not a beast scurries along it.

The custom of the time was to fine criminals, for the benefit of the prince or, at best, of the victim. No harsh penalties were meted out, no prison time or death sentences were known. Finally, when crime became widespread and out of control, the Greek bishops (brought up under a different legal system) started a campaign, asking the prince, "Why don't you punish them?" Prince Vladimir responded: "I am afraid of such a sin". "You are God's servant and you must punish a villain when his guilt has been proven". Vladimir eventually complied.

We can see one such reprimand in the Radzivill pictures. A sturdy fellow is brought into the hands of the law enforcement officers, but he does not seem to be visibly sorry. A young executioner gracefully swings his huge sword. But then the "old men" start explaining. They remind the prince about the military demands, and the expenses they incur. They speak about profits that could be made and that now will be lost. Vladimir consents. The man is fined and set free.

In 1008, the Nikon chronicle tells us: "That year, a dreadful brigand by the name of Mogut was caught by crafty means". *Mogut* must be a nickname. The dictionary of the Old Russian Language (11th-14th centuries) has only one meaning for the word — ruler, lord. *Moguts* are also mentioned in the *Lay of Igor's Host* as part of the prince of Chernigov's troops, among them "Tatrans", "Shelbirs", "Topchaks", "Revuches" and "Olbers". (They brandished long knives as weapons against whole enemy regiments.) According to Academician B. A. Rybakov, they were probably Turkish-speaking warriors who had settled in Chernigov long ago. Turks or Bulgarians, they came from the Caucasus under Mstislav (the son of Vladimir who was the prince of Tmutorakan') early in the

11th century. But *moguts*, designated by a Slav word, were probably remarkable warriors, something like Solovey-the-Brigand.

> When he sang like a nightingale,
> When he howled like a dog,
> When he hissed like a snake
> The grass and flowers wilted,
> The leaves and stems perished,
> The men nearby fell down and died.

When, finally, according to the chronicle, Mogut was brought before the prince, he broke out crying, weeping and saying: "I promise, my Prince, I will never do evil again either against man or God; and I will always repent for what I have done!" This hardy highwayman was ready to become a suffering monk and lock himself up in a monastery!

Vladimir, who was just preparing to introduce a new penal system, was moved by the man's repentance. In the words of the chronicler, Vladimir had been leading a quiet life lately, was rather meek and placid, and prayed often, repeating: "Grace onto those who repent at the Judgment". He sent Mogut to the Metropolitan and ordered him not to stray. Mogut followed the instructions, "kept his word and lived an ascetic life, was always meek and placid, and then died as a God-fearing person". Such is the story of the first repentant Russian brigand.

Why do we remember him? Once a famous court case, Mogut stands as a role model and a proof of the power of repentance.

The next crime report comes from Novgorod. The episode is narrated in a saga about Olaf written by the monk named Od. When he was a child, the future King of Norway Olaf Truggvasson was sold as a slave with his tutor Torolf Lusakegg. Soon after, Olaf witnessed the murder of his tutor, Torolf, by his master, before his eyes. Luckily, Olaf's uncle, Sigurd, who was in the service of Prince Vladimir, saved the boy by buying his freedom and brought him to Novgorod, where the boy lived with his uncle for a while.

In *Land's Ring*, another saga attributed to Snorry Sturluson, we have the next episode of the story. "Olaf, Tryggve's son, once went to the marketplace (in Novgorod) and among many people there he saw Klerkon, who had killed his tutor. Olaf had a hatchet with him, so he struck Klerkon in the head, causing the man's death. He then ran to his uncle's place and told him what happened. Sigurd took the boy to Princess Allogia and asked her to help the boy." At the time, such crimes were punished in Holmgard (the Scandinavian name for Novgorod) by execution.

When the Novgorodians, according to their custom, went out looking for "the boy", they learned that he was hidden at the princess' court and that armed people were ready to defend him. The Novgorodians complained to Vladimir about this gross violation of the law. Vladimir came to his spouse's court with his own soldiers, but decided not to resort to fighting, but rather came to an agreement: "The prince settled the dispute by assigning a fine, and the princess paid it".

The moral of the story? As soon as the law was violated, the population rose up in arms for its protection. The *veche*, the self-government, not only allowed for but also impelled everyone to obey the law. As in this example, the *veche's* (one may say municipal) investigation will weigh in future disputes involving not only criminal but also political violations of the law, such as treason.

In this case, since foreigners of royal blood were involved, who were protected by the princess's Varangian guards, more diplomacy was required. The prince sided with the felon, but did not enter into conflict with his own people. In accordance with Old Russian law, a fine was deemed fair by everyone.

Chapter IV

Epic Heroes

1. History and the Heroic Epics

The story of the border guards is not based on contemporary material (for there is none) but is based on bylinas. If you read Russian folklore with an open mind, you soon find that its central message, distressingly, seems to encourage people to achieve their well-being and happiness by "a miracle," "free of toil", and to value laziness above all. Ilya Muromets, for instance, had been idle during his thirty best years, "until pilgrims came and 'cured' him". Vasily Buslaev, instead of increasing his fortune, invites various dubious people to his large court and tells them that they can eat and drink as much as they please, and dress themselves in his splendid clothing. Just think of the miraculous tablecloth that provides free food at your finger tips! In Honshu or Kyushu, in Bremen or Amsterdam, the morals of the folk tales seem to be somewhat different.

The reader may doubt the historic value of epic fables, especially as some folklore specialists share in their skepticism. I shall tell you my opinion. Folks really believed what they sang and what they recounted, and considered it all true. Here is a scene of bylina-telling in a northern village, over a hundred years ago, as related by a folklorist who was present there.

"It was a holiday and there were many people in the village. The room soon filled with visitors. . . . Outka, an old man, of medium height, sturdy and broad-shouldered, entered the room. He was a handsome man, with short and curly white hair over a large forehead; a sparse, pointed beard adorned a creased face with somewhat devious lips. He had large blue eyes. There was something simple-hearted, childish and helpless in his face . . . Outka threw back his head, looked over the assembled folk with a smile and, noting their impatience, he coughed once more, and began singing. His face changed bit by bit while he sang, and everything devious, childish and naive disappeared from it. Inspiration shone, his eyes dilated and sparkled, two small tears came forth, his swarthy cheeks became rosy and his neck was trembling nervously".

He lived the life of his favorite bogatyrs; he felt pity for the ailing Ilya Muromets, idle for 30 years, only to be elated, then, at his victory over Solovey the Brigand. Sometimes he would interpose on his own behalf. All those present also felt acutely the life of the hero. Sometimes an exclamation would burst out, other times a peal of laughter went through the audience. Some would wipe away a tear that hung on the lashes. Everybody gazed at the singer and caught every sound of the monotonous but wonderfully quiet melody. Outka finished and looked around the room with a triumphant expression. For a while silence reigned; then the talk started in all corners.

— That is a fine old man, he sings mightily . . . What a treat . . .

— It is probably just a fable, — someone said in doubt. Everybody began arguing.

— Why a fable? That was in olden times. Under the kind prince Vladimir.

— I'm thinking, what? How could a man be so powerful? Look what he did.

— He was a bogatyr, and you should remember that. He was not like you or me — he was a hero! What is impossible for us, for him it was easy, — they spoke from all sides.

That is how the Russian peasants treated the story, as told by Nikifor Prokhorov.

That may well be, a reader may retort, it's a wonderful scene, but belief in a tale's authenticity has nothing to do with the truth itself. I agree. But the collective memory of a people, while often mistaken in the detail, never erred in the main subject. History and its reflection in epic stories are certainly not identical. The bogatyrs' images are yet integral, although their actions are exaggerated to the scale of a national monument. The figures grew and were transformed into heroes. Still,

behind this wonderful collective poetic "yarn," behind excessive cos-
tumes and stylistic decorations, one may discern the outline of what
took place in real life.

2. Ilya Muromets and his Friends. "Heroic Outposts"

Who bore the burden of the bogatyrs' (border guards) hard service, at the outposts of Vladimir's kingdom? Fedosia Churkina, a story-
teller from Ust' Tsilma, claimed that she once remembered the entire
staff, so to say (namely, the "one and thirty bogatyrs"); however she
was able to name only eighteen of them.

> Old Cossack Ilya was the chieftain,
> Ilya Muromets and son of Ivan,
> Samson of Kolyvan was the second captain,
> As scribe lived Dobrynia, Nikita's son,
> Alyosha Popovich served as a cook,
> And Mishka the Hasty as a groom,
> And Vasiliy, Buslai's son, also lived here
> Then Vasen'ka Ignatievich,
> And Duke, the son of Stepan,
> Then Permya, Vasiliy's son,
> And Rodion the Tallest,
> Then Potaniushka, who limped when he ran,
> And Potyk Mikhailo, son of Ivan,
> Then Dunai Ivanovich dwelt here,
> And Churilo, Plenkov's offspring,
> Then Skopin, Ivan's son,
> And the sons of Pyotr, two brothers,
> Luka and Matvey, their blood being as one . . .

Well, this is of course a "general list", and for the most part it is
not authentic. For example, Vasiliy Buslaev was never known to guard
any frontier whatsoever, much less Novgorod's. Potanyushka the Cripple was only a participant in Vasiliy's brawls. Churilo Plenkovich — a
lady's man, a masher and a brigand — was never suited for frontier service. Mikhailo Skopin — he was a general in the times of Smuta.

In fact, there were only one or two bogatyrs from Kiev. To defend
the southern borders of Rus', bogatyrs came from Murom and Rostov,

Novgorod and Kolyvan, Golytsin (Galich) and the Volkhyn' lands, and from other places as well. Throughout the ages, it was natural for people to perceive Rus' as a united, inseparable empire, the capital of which (whether Kiev or Moscow) must be defended by all. The only persons who thought otherwise were the appanage princes, striving for power and money, and those fed by them. For the folk, the perception of Rus', the image presented in bylinas, coincides with the historic data.

Whom did Vladimir resettle to the border strongholds? Folks from the regions located to the north of Kiev: Slovens, Krivich, Chud', Viatich. "These words of the chronicle convey very interesting information about the orientation of the state's defense", comments B. A. Rybakov. "Vladimir managed to make the struggle against the Pechenegs a cause taken up by all of Rus' ". Indeed, men for the garrisons of the southern fortresses were recruited as far as Novgorod, Estonia (Chud'), Smolensk and the Moscow River basin, i.e. in lands that had never been reached by any lone Pecheneg. It was through Vladimir's effort that all the forested land of the North was made to serve the interests of defending the southern border that passed through the lands of the Polyan, Ulich and Severyan peoples".

The routine life and service at an outpost were simple and unpretentious enough: wake up early in the morning, and sweetly doze away the leisure days.

To reconnoiter the terrain or intercept a trespasser the bogatyrs rode out, usually alone — unlike in Vasnetsov's famous painting, familiar to and beloved by every Russian from childhood. The guards would press an ear to the damp earth, or use some similar technical means. A watch was kept in all four directions. Ilya Muromets even managed to look in five directions.

And for good reason; Kiev is known to have been placed under siege by the Pechenegs, during the rule of Svyatoslav; it was seized by the Polish prince Boleslav in 1018; and it was under threat of devastation from the Polovtsi at the end of the 11th century. Thus, the inventions of the folk songs were not inconsistent with the truth.

Sometimes when on duty, riding through the countryside, a bogatyr might come across some combatants banging swords together. Here are the "instructions" given by Ilya Muromets for such cases:

When two Russians are in combat — speak to them,
When a Russian and an Infidel fight — help the Russian,
When two Infidels confront each other — head for the hills.

If a "trespasser" was detected by the hoof mark of his horse, the main thing was not to find him but to "capture" him. But if the watchman encountered a stronger man, or a large gang, he should send word to an outpost.

> Shouted Yermak with all his lungs:
> "Hey, old Cossack, Ilya of Murom!
> Sleeping, idling, having fun,
> Ignoring the danger that toward you comes:
> Against our beautiful capital, glorious Kiev-grad
> Rides Kalin-tsar, the cur, seeking blood".
> Then said dear Ilya of Murom-grad:
> "Oh, Yermak, Timofei's lad!
> Climb that tall hill, with steep slopes of grass,
> Take a look through your spy-glass,
> Size up the host, the Tatar force:
> How many soldiers, how many horse?
> How many of our brave men must ride,
> Shall two or three men go astride,
> Or all the Russian bogatyrs with shoulders wide?"

News of danger was often sent directly to the capital, as was done by the twelve-year-old Mikhailo Danilovich: "Drink, eat, great prince, have a good time, as yet unaware of the sorrow to come." Here comes a young man from the open plains, riding into the court of the prince . . . He runs to the bright chamber, his hood still on his head. He addresses the prince: "Lord Vladimir, the Red Sun, Great Prince, in Kiev you hold the throne, you drink and eat and amuse your soul, not knowing about the threat coming to you: from the great Horde comes tsar Bakhmet, son of Tavrui". Messages from the watchmen were supplemented by suggestions of possible enemy attacks obtained from "agents".

Once Ilya Muromets happened to be in Kiev, naturally as a guest of Prince Vladimir.

> He, the old one, watched the people pass,
> Looking out through that crystal glass,
> Spotted a roaming mendicant at once.

The wanderer, appearing before the prince's palace, stood beneath the "small curved window" ("in the place of beggars"), and started to beg alms in a "deep-throated voice". Ilya then called Vladimir and, indicating the poor man, he gave the following directions:

Oh you, Vladimir-Prince-Sun,
Go outdoors, hurry, run,
Call that beggar who strays,
Greet the poor in honorable ways,
No matter how lowly his place.

It was unlikely that Vladimir understood the sense of those mysterious words, but

Here again the prince was quick not to mishear,
Out of the palace he sped like a spear,
He dashed to the steep-stairs porch at once,
Down the steep stairs he flew like a lance.

And bowing deeply, the prince asked the mendicant to be welcome "into the prince's palace, and to eat bread, and to drink mead". After waiting until the beggar was sated and "seated on a wooden bench", the commander of the prince's frontiersmen

. . . went on inquiring, everything about,
Went on asking and ferreting out:
"Where are you from, wanderer shy,
Where are you going, for how long, and why?
What, you went by road and saw nothing,
What, you went by road and heard nothing?"

At this moment the peripatetic finally admits that he came from the ice-cold sea, from Alatyr mountain to the Yelisei River, and that he had not "drunk" or "eaten" for three days and three nights, as he had "run across" the "black cloud" — "Hordes of pagans" led by the "cur Kudrevanko-tsar". The mendicant gave a detailed and comprehensive report on how many troops Kudrevanko had on his right and left hands, in front and behind him, how the tsar "talked" his army into action, who was his envoy on the way to Rus', what he looked like, what message he had to deliver to Prince Vladimir. In brief, a genuine dispatch from a professional and very effective scout. The bylina, by the way, reads the same:

> He told them all that he had scouted,
> And then began to take his leave,
> And off he went the way he came.

"Scout" is a very rare word in the vocabulary of the bylinas. One cannot help feeling that it was not the prince's alms that drew the mendicant to Kiev from the Yelisei River and directly to the palace of the prince, or that Ilya found himself in Kiev by chance just in time to notice the beggar. It is very likely that the chief came to a meeting with his agent that was planned in advance. Otherwise, Ilya must have had an extraordinary flair for spotting invaluable informers; although that too is proven by another event that took place in Kiev.

Once Ilya saw Alyosha and Dobrynia beating a mendicant with a club. He was quick to interfere:

> Oh, Russian bogatyrs, you are misled!
> Why do you beat the poor beggar's head?
> We need yet to ask if he has any news:
> What has he heard, what has he viewed?
> (i.e. "What the hell you are doing? He's one of ours!")

As a result, he learned about the advance of a "countless multitude" of forty tsars and young tsars, kings and young kings, each leading a host of "three tmas and three thousand warriors (if we believe the bylina, this army counted 5,280,000 men!).

As is known, the ball comes to the player. It appeared that the mendicant had just voluntarily served the Fatherland as a scout, and had "captured a prisoner" — bogatyr Turchenko. He seized him "by the yellow curls" just "amidst that pagan host" (with the help of our Lord, perhaps), did not hoist him onto his back but having tossed the captive against "the damp earth", interrogated him on the spot. After that he "rode" (not astride) to Kiev, announced himself (knocked off the "peaks" of the palace gables with his voice), and then took part in the destruction of the enemies in tandem with Ilya and Dobrynia. And again, folklore is true to life.

The names of the scouts remain unknown. Here is one portrait:

From the woods of birch and trees more rare,
From the dense young hazel-grove
Out stepped the cripple, on his long wayfare,
Roaming, dirt-poor, traveling much.

. . . .

Climbing, the wanderer scaled the heights,
Hiked above the standing trees,
Just below the floating cloud.
Then down went the beggar to the flatter quarters,
To fields, green meadows,
And the Pochai River's (Pochaina's) rolling waters. . .

The bogatyrs themselves went on reconnaissance missions "camouflaged" as mendicants, wearing Greek hats from Sorochin weighing thirty poods, bast shoes of seven silk colors "framed" with pure silver and decorated with red gold and semi-precious stones, and long sable coats. They also would take a heavy staff of forty poods, or a walking stick filled with Chebourets lead, or would turn into "elders" (monks or old men) with an appropriate hat or a walking stick. They did that in order to get more detailed on-site information about the enemy, to meet and appraise them or even to exchange some revealing banter, to look into their "pagan eye", and perhaps, make feathers fly.

When Ilya meets a bogatyr pilgrim plodding on his way from "holy places" or from "Tsargrad", he starts to fish military and political information out of him. Hearing that the pagan Idolische mocks Christians, yet the raconteur did not aid the Christians in trouble, Ilya becomes enraged:

Fool you are, great, strong Ivan!
Your strength is double mine.
But courage and wit you sorely lack;
You will never match me on that track. . .
Why then failed you to do a good deed
To rescue Constantine Bogoliubov, indeed?
Now hasten and take from your leaden feet
Your bast shoes woven of seven silks.

Put on my own morocco boots,
A roaming beggar's disguise I need.

The foe (Idolische) naturally does not guess who is in front of him (or at least is in doubt: "Judging by his clothes, this is an elder, and by his footstep — Ilya Muromets"). In his turn, he tries to get the necessary information in advance by asking the "Russian mendicant" what Ilya Muromets looks like, whether he is very fond of eating and drinking. Having received the answer: "Ilya is as strong as I am, eats as much as I do, drinks as much as I do", Idolische is filled with contempt towards his enemy.

3. An Epic Picture of Ilya Muromets

Ilya Muromets, folk commander of the frontiersmen-spies, is regarded by many people as the major defender of the Kiev empire, a watchful and reliable guard of state security. Replacing Dobrynia, in a way, in the chronicles, this folk bogatyr is of course a far brighter personage. He possesses the most attractive human and professional qualities. Being strong and brave, he is also wise, honest and not greedy. Once when he met some brigands who tried to buy themselves off with gold, brilliant clothing and good horses, he answered:

If I took your rich treasure of gold,
I would leave deep gullies behind,
If I took your colored clothes,
I would leave high mountains behind,
If I took you fleet-foot horses,
I would leave great herds running behind.

It is significant that Ilya is a "pure" (or almost "pure") scout (besides being, of course, a warrior), i.e. he tracks only foreign enemies. When meeting "kamyshnichki" or "stanichniki" (brigands), he either scared them off by splitting an oak with his arrow into "knife handles"), or beat them with his hat. He was always on the defense, not provoking any conflict or seeking to eradicate the brigands. The only brigand whose death he caused is Solovey, but that happened before his service and the reason was not an ordinary one. He did not conduct domestic investigations. People instinctively understood that such activities might cause personality changes, and thus people guarded the beloved hero against any rumor that could damage his reputation.

Later, Ilya and Dobrynia went to the Saracen land to rescue Mikhailo Potyk, who had gotten into trouble. Disguised as mendicants and accompanied by an old man whom they had met along the way and picked up out of courtesy, they went and stood under the window of the "handsome tsar" Ivan Okulievich and his wife, Maria the White Swan, that the tsar had lured away from Mikhailo Potyk. When the beggars shouted "at the top of their voices", Maria easily "deciphered" the bogatyrs, ordered they be given food and drink, and have their bags filled with gold and silver. Then the "mendicants" went away, forgetting the reason for their trip. Collecting their wits, they came back and asked Maria directly what she had done with their "brother-warrior". It appeared that her former husband had long been lying under the "white stone of sorrow". Their aged companion helped them find the place. Then that same old man, who turned to be Saint Mickola Mozhaisky ("Oh, Russian bogatyrs! I am Mickola Mozhaisky. I assist you in your struggle for the faith and the Fatherland") brought "Mikhailushka" back to life. But when the revivified bogatyr asked the "brethren" to assist him in getting his wife back, they contemptuously refused to hunt after "another's woman". Thus Potyk fell again into the nets of Maria, and was rescued only by the tsar's sister, Nastasia Okulievna.

People sculpted the figure of Ilya after their own image, creating a picture of Defender of the Fatherland stripped of any unnecessary features, and not making him a child of good fortune (Ilya is not married; in the lands far from Kiev he has a son and a daughter out of wedlock, and his meetings with them result in tragedy). In creating Ilya's image, people did not care about his good looks (as the bylinas narrate, Ilya is not a handsome young man but an "old Cossack" and a "seasoned old man"; the "Stanichniki" call him an "old graybeard", his son calls him an "old nag" and his daughter — an "old good-for-nothing"). His sober behavior matched his age; he never finds himself at a loss for sharp words, sometimes even four-letter words (that have never been printed, as far as his story has been told). That did not diminish his image, but made him closer to the grassroots, more real, more understandable, an ordinary man from the street (it is hard to find a Russian who doesn't like "people" — except those with sharp tongues).

4. Dounai

Among the bogatyrs who served with Ilya Muromets, special attention should be paid to Dounai, Dobrynia and Alyosha Popovich. However, we have nothing much to add to Dounai's characterization. From the point of view of those who chanted the bylinas, Dounai did not perform any heroic deeds worthy of attention. Maybe it was not by chance that he was sometimes called "quiet". But in his case, too, it should be noted that this is a personage with an unusual biography of the ordinary. He "set out" for Vladimir from service in the court of a different sovereign, as so often happened both in the 10th and 15th centuries. Here is how he described events to Ilya Muromets:

> Lived I, ere now, across the sea,
> Across the blue, the Aral Sea,
> Served I that prince Semion Likhovityi,
> Three long years with his horsemen,
> Three long years serving table,
> Three long years as courier to be,
> Thus passed nine years of the life of me...

(Readers should not be embarrassed that Semion Likhovityi (alias Mikoula Liakhovitsky, alias King Liakhovinsky or the "brave Lithuanian") lives beyond the Aral Sea. Geographical accuracy is insignificant for folk poetry. Another epic variant mentions the locale of "Czechs and Liakhs". Dounai's terms of service and positions are also at variance in different versions of the bylinas.) According to the king, Dounai served honestly, "with high loyalty", rendering "good services", and was well rewarded:

> Earned I all the crystal, and ducats,
> Rich I was with wine by the bucket,
> Earned I tubs of honey, sweet and good,
> And tables built of white oak wood,
> Then a tent of deep-hued velvet...

But then a wave of homesickness flowed over the young man, and he no longer wanted to stay in the town of Liakhov, getting rich:

Longed I then to go back to my land,
Back to my land, to my Fatherland. . .

Thus Dounai found himself in the open steppe at the Russian frontier. He put a "threatening" sign in front of his tent, naively believing that it would ensure the safety of his property. Dobrynia explained his mistake, but the prince put the guest into the dungeon in reply to his explanations. Still, Vladimir highly esteemed any person whose knowledge about how people lived "across the sea", whose understanding of their interests, was based on more than hearsay. Using some of his channels (the ears of counter-intelligence are always open), Dobrynia was able to determine that Semion (alias Mikoula) was not the only one to whom Dounai had served:

And saw Dounai all the lands under the sky,
All of the lands, and various towns,
And served Dounai all of the kings,
— All kinds of people he knows, that Dounai.

That's it: "knows all kinds of people". This is the way the chief of a secret service would report. Somehow, that was done too late (readers may remember that Dounai "served a term of imprisonment". By the time of the report, Vladimir suddenly remembered him and the luck that turned to him). The prince needed such seasoned "young men" of marked individuality — not so much at the outposts, but in Kiev and for "trips" abroad. And maybe it was not by chance that people retained in their memory only this "foreign service" of Dounai, where he showed his high skills as both a diplomat who was fairly knowledgeable about the situation in the country of his mission, and that of a scout or subversive agent. Folklore (I must repeat again) perceived the pulse of life very keenly. Really, what a romantic folk "biography", what a dramatic life story, what good fortune!

The man served abroad for a very long time, serving an alien country (or alien people). Then he came back to repay his debts to his Fatherland — and wound up in prison. He served his sentence, and then served his people. What happened next is related differently by various versions. According to one of them — after a trip abroad — Dounai got married, had a row with his wife and killed her (with an unborn child), and then committed suicide:

> Slew he Nastasia Mikoulichna,
> and burst out wailing:
> "Where a white swan falls,
> The bright falcon will also be failing!"

According to another version, Dounai set out with the pilgrims:

> And off went the travelers to the town of Jerusalem . . .
> And there were they met by Vladimir the Sun-Blest,
> Dismounted he at a distance before them,
> Dismounted from his steed, bowed from the waist:
> "Good health, Mikhailushko, son of Mikhailo!
> And to you, Dounai Ivanovich, greetings my best!
> Be healthy, Kosma, son of Ivan! . . .

5. Dobrynia Nikitich

On the other hand, Dobrynia Nikitich and Alyosha Popovich were Ilya Muromets's most active and heroic assistants at the border outposts. Dobrynia was known to have routed the Seven-Headed Serpent named Zmei Gorynich (alias Zmeiunische-Likhodeiuscho, Zhmeiadischo-Likhoradischo, etc), and to have rescued the daughter (or niece or sister) of Prince Vladimir, as well as his own aunt Maria Divovna (alias Avdotia Ivanovna, or Maria Elizastovna-Iziaslavna) from the "caves". He also freed "forty thousand" pilgrims, and "countless" tsars-kings, "great chiefs", king's sons and "young princes", priests and deacons , as well as "many plain folk".

> And now you are on your own, and free,
> Serve anyone, and go anywhere you wish to be.

— the liberator speaks his parting words to the exhausted prisoners.

The epic mentions more than once that Dobrynia had a long service record at the outpost, and the burden of the prince's errands sometimes made him gloomy. After another heroic deed — killing Nevezha, a black raven, Dobrynia broods:

> What shall I do in Kiev region?
> Will serve yet twelve years more,
> Then will not be needed anymore.

Dobrynia's mother (Ophimia Oleksandrovna, alias Amelpha Timofeievna, alias Stepanida Abramovna, or Veria Timofeievna), tries to keep him home, and allows him go neither to the open field and the "dreadful" Pochai River, nor to a feast for Prince Vladimir — she is afraid that the prince will notice her unfailing son and "yoke" him to a "great service".

> Oh, stay, Dobrynia by your family homestead,
> At your home, Dobrynia, your place of birth,
> Enjoying our plenty of salt and bread;
> Drink green wine and be filled with mirth,
> Live in gold treasures and family love.

Learning that her fears have come true, she reprimands him:

> Oh, didn't I tell you, in so many words,
> Neither foolish nor false nor bad;
> Don't go, my son, with the lords,
> Don't go with the boyars, my lad.

(Mothers will be mothers. And who can judge Ophimia Oleksandrovna for such words?). Once, in a fit of temper, Dobrynia reproached Zapava (Zabava) Putiatichna (alias Apraksia, Marfida Vseslavovna, Marfa Dmitrievna), whom he had rescued:

> Why, Zabava Putiatichna, are you so cold?
> Because of you I traveled and rode,
> Because of you with the Serpent I fought . . .

What else could he do — it was no joke on the prince's side, besides, his bogatyr's honor was at stake. And Dobrynia responded to the wailing of his old mother:

Oh my parent, my dear mother!
You will forgive me — for go I must,
You say no — but go I must.

But Dobrynia is not just a reliable watchman good only at swinging his sword, as the folktale narrator Leonty Gavrilovich Tupitsyn put
it. Nor he is a high-class frontier scout like Ilya Muromets. The way he
behaves and performs his epic deeds gives the impression of a highly-
skilled intelligence man, proficient in various fields, capable of acting
on the spur of the moment, where an immediate decision is needed.
Thus, when meeting the snake for the first time, he happens to be un-
armed:

And teenaged Dobryniushka, about in the land,
Had nothing available, nothing at hand,
To beat the Serpent, . . .

Still Dobrynia keeps a cool head, and in a fit of "that great spite"
routs the beast either with a lump of yellow sand, or his Greek hat, or
his black hat ornamented with golden stones which, following the advice of his far-seeing mother, he did not take off his head even when
bathing.

For nine long years Dobrynia tried in vain to "beat and slash" with
his bogatyr sword Baba Yaga (alias Baba Gorynishka or Latygorka), the
giant "Polish witch", until he drastically changed his tactics on the advice of Ilya Muromets ("Hit baba's tits, kick her in the butt" — mut-
tered his commander). Aided by his friends Vasilii Kazimirovich and
Alyosha Popovich, Dobrynia killed Tsar Batoui Kaimanov, as well. That
happened "at the bright palace, in the warm bedroom":

Then Vasily came alive,
Rushed he over to Dobrynia,
From Dobrynia to Alyosha,
Then Alyosha took his life.

Readers perhaps remember that when Dobrynia set out with
Dounai in connection with the bride for Prince Vladimir, Dobrynia, as a
bogatyr and diplomatic envoy, did not act in a proper way. He was
"planted" in the embassy incognito ("a great fellow of unknown ori-

gin" — according to the royal guard), with a subversive mission. He acted almost under the Polish king's eyes while Dounai was conducting talks in accordance with the diplomatic protocol. One version of the bylina about Dobrynia and the Snake relates that the young knight-errant sets out on a dangerous voyage to "endless backwaters" not to free a captive maiden or some other prisoners, but to acquire three precious stones for himself which he finally receives from the conquered enemy. Of course, that is not a heroic deed worthy of a bogatyr — defender of all Russian lands. It is significant that the snake tries to bribe Dobrynia with either towns surrounded by suburbs and villages, or a precious stone, colored clothes, pretty maidens (or goat leather boots, mittens, cotton shirts, a Greek hood). Facing such lavish offers, Dobrynia would either refuse ("I need nothing from you; say that again and I will flog you to death"), or accept the graft not like a famous Russian bogatyr but like some over-spent executive agent. The fact that the bogatyr's image is somewhat belittled speaks for itself.

There is also a version narrating that before the fight, having received no respite from the serpent, Dobrynia still manages to write a "yarlyk" (letter) to his own father Mikita Romanovich, and to the "holy fathers", notifying them that in spite of all favorable predictions of the latter he seemed to be getting into a real mess. Indeed, he seems to act like an eternal agent, obliged in the performance of his duties to send a dispatch even in the most critical situation.

The range of Dobrynia's travels, while in service, is too great and strange for an ordinary watchman, exceeding the distance from Kiev to any of the border outposts. Too often he finds himself at faraway locations: either at the sea, or across the sea, at Mount Ararat, or on the peak of Afon or Sion mountain.

He comes to a feast — a "wedding party" — with his homemade psaltery at which he is equal to Sadko, famous epic chanter.

> He played and sang about Tsargrad,
> Then sang Jerusalem in his chant,
> The third time he played the ballad
> Of all his life and escapade.

What "escapades" did Dobrynia have in life? There are various answers in the epics. In one song, the bogatyr would add new "holy Russian lands" to the state, in another he would collect tribute or fight off enemies. Some folk ballads describe him riding in the open field for no reason, or simply taking it "easy" just because he "wanted to look at the blue sea" (who will believe that!). Is something that is not known or that is purposely omitted from the epics? Anyhow, the greater the distance separating a bogatyr from his Motherland, the less likely he is a frontier guard, and the more likely — a scout.

These conclusions about Dobrynia's status, based on his folklore biography, are supported by his personal qualities. Dobrynia is a very good chess player (it's not just to kill time that he plays against himself a party of "gilded checkers" in the open field), at some very crucial moment he beats the best five players, selected out of the hundred best players of tsar Batei Bateievich (according to other versions, he beats the ruler himself). He has no equal in archery, is an excellent fighter in a "single-handed combat", and would not disgrace himself in playing "dice and cards". The man is so good in changing his appearance that his own mother does not recognize him, never mind pilgrim Ranzha or Prince Vladimir. And finally, he is notable for his fine manners, good breeding, and knowledge of customs and rules of behavior. One bylina characterizes him thus: "Dobrynia's manners are born and learnt" (i.e. acquired with birth and good breeding). Vasily Kazimirovich, his buddy, even sang kind of a paean in his honor:

> In God I trust and keep my hopes,
> I pray to the Virgin, our God's Mother,
> And I rely on that son of Mikita,
> Dobrynia, good fellow, my dear sworn brother.

It is plain that persons with such a range of talents have always been highly valued, especially by the secret services, because an agent had to play most different roles, change guises and make use of a wide stock of skills and tricks of the trade, just "at sight". We know nothing about Dobrynia's early years as a real, historic person, what experience he acquired in delicate matters, before being appointed to the post of Vladimir's military commander and head of the prince's secret service. But if he happened in his late years to listen to some wandering minstrels or mendicants chanting a bylina about his own "adventures", he would, to my mind, justly appreciate at least the physiognomic authenticity of his epic counterpart created by sharp-eyed folk chanters and tale-narrators.

6. Alyosha Popovich

Compared with the bright and almost always successful Do-brynia, Alyosha appears to be quite modest, though that does not mean that this personage is less expressive. But his expressiveness, as the readers will see, is of a special kind. Alyosha's major heroic deed was his duel with Tugarin Zmeievich, in which he demonstrated his great qualities as a warrior. There also exists a rare (only one is recorded) bylina that relates how Alyosha with the "brave host" liberated the Russian capital under siege by the "pagan force" commanded by Vasily the Fair. Before engaging in battle, Alyosha ardently addressed his troops, urging them to rescue "the beautiful Kiev-grad from trouble".

> Our service shall not be forgotten,
> Great glory shall spread from this deed,
> Our bogatyr honor shall be begotten,
> And old Muromets will dismount from his steed
> To greet us all when he learns of our feat.

In other epic situations, Alyosha either commits no outstanding deeds in his "bogatyr service", or stays in the background, playing secondary or tertiary roles. He is not always depicted as a man possessing the best human qualities, he lets down his comrades-at-arms, may do a friend an ill-turn, and sometimes makes a fool of himself. Readers remember how Ilya Muromets rejected Alyosha (set on silver and gold, and also too long-winded) as a candidate to intercept an unknown enemy bogatyr somewhere in the open plain, as well as how Alyosha was unable to control his tongue and temper and thus nearly foiled the bogatyrs' plans against Idolische. As a watchman Alyosha is not very skilled: applying his ear to the earth, he fails to hear what his commander Ilya Muromets hears perfectly well.

Nevertheless, as a frontiersman, Alyosha is depicted by the epic rather positively. He would either be shown riding along the open steppe, or climbing trees to find the best position for secret surveillance. And once:

Sitting atop the rain-soaked oak, descried Oliosha . . .

Alyosha "descried" not a Pecheneg, not a Tatar, nor any other pagan adversary, but his sworn brother Dobrynia fighting with the snake and then concluding a truce. And thus, in this episode he already stands out as a counter-intelligence man, but not an ordinary frontier watchman. In fact, Alyosha appears and behaves in the palaces of the prince not as a rank-and-file serviceman of the secret department, but as a higher position officer who has the right to give orders to the sovereign:

> Swaggers Alyosha about the palace,
> Word-by-word instructs the prince:
> — You, Vladimir, Prince of Kiev!
> Give the great mission to young Dobrynia,
> The mission to go to the far open field . . .
> The mission to find your beloved niece . . .

No questions asked, docile Vladimir goes to Dobrynia and repeats the above words:

> I entrust to you this greatest role,
> The mission to find my beloved niece . . .
> Bring her to my chambers white. . .

(It is significant that when Alyosha's place is taken by a certain Semion Karamyshevskiy, alias Ivan Karamyshevskiy, acting as a sleuth and advisor, the latter respectfully explains to the prince:

> O my lord, Vladimir-prince of Kiev proud!
> In the open plain I was lately by,
> I saw Dobrynia near the Pochai River —
> Against the Snake he fought with fever,
> For mercy begged that Serpent, . . .
> As a younger sister promised to be.
> Send Dobrynia to the mountains of Tougi
> For your daughter, tsarevna dear . . .)

Being in the frontier service, Dobrynia Nikitich and Alyosha Popovich were also involved in informative, investigative and subversive activities, and as such participated in many glorious actions of the sort, for instance, working to neutralize the attempts of pagan Idolische, Vasily of Turkey, King Gremin and the "great tsar Vakhrameische" to marry Prince Vladimir's niece or sister (Marfa Mitrevna, Anna Poutiatichna, Marfa Korolevichna). However, the counter-intelligence operation in all cases followed almost the same scenario.

Vladimir cared about his niece Marfa Mitrevna most of all, and kept her behind thirty-nine locks. He feared that word of her extraordinary beauty would spread around the world, and all kind of "non-Christian", "pagan" khans, kings and "idols" would come from everywhere to take her as bride (domestic "Christian" bridegrooms seemed to be in short supply). Apparently, Kiev at that time was not at the height of its power, and the prince wanted to avoid the wars that would be imminent should any offer be made and refused. Indeed, when the news of Marfa's beauty "spread out" all over the world and Idolische came by black boats to woo her, Vladimir vainly struggled to gain the support of the princes and boyars, as well as "all good people", whom he called to a mighty feast. The worried speech of the ruler of "Kiev-capital" touched nobody:

> Said to him all his good flocks,
> Simple peasants, Orthodox:
> "We shall not stand for your beloved niece —
> Our children shall not be orphaned for this."

In brief, people refused to place the defense of the princely relative on the same footing as the defense of their Fatherland. No escape! Marfa Mitrevna bade farewell to her sweet-tongued, white-necked uncle, and set off to travel. But there was a trick. She made an agreement with Idolische that she would sail on her own boats (to which his entry was yet denied); she loaded the boats with "strong beer" and "various sweet vodkas", and took Dobrynia and Alyosha as assistants (for some unknown reason, perhaps very important, the latter did not fight with the pagan "groom" in Kiev). When at sea, Marfa Mitrevna called the bogatyrs and disclosed to them her plan, which might make the seasoned counter-intelligence men blush with shame at their own slow wits. She said with a marked professional "slang":

Call you Idolische's boat tonight,
A good design I have in mind,
Invite this pagan to come to me, right . . .

When he came, Marfa Mitrevna explained, she would treat him
with Kievan "drinks":

You get the sailors dead drunk,
And one of you stay, near my bunk . . .

And if Idolische gets drunk and starts making passes:

You run to me and help me out . . .

What should be done after the help is rendered was not specified
by the beauty; she apparently assumed that even Alyosha's brains
would be enough to take the right direction. The plan turned out to be
fine, although judging by the narrative some last minute fine-tuning
was needed. Getting the sailors drunk was, naturally, took some doing.
The old sea dogs were seasoned drinkers, and began to nod off only after having "drunk the whole boat of strong beer". And finally:

Then all the sailors fell and dropped,
Dropped all the sailors, fell they dumb. . .

By the time Idolische also got "hard" drunk, and started to behave
improperly, apparently none of Marfa Mitrevna's assistants happened
to be by her doors. However, this was not necessary because Vladimir's
niece received her guest in a "crystal" cabin:

Oh! sees Dobrynia, Mikita's son,
Oh! sees Alyosha, Popovich's son,
To the crystal cabin they both at once run,
Seize they Idolische by his curls of black . . .
Oh, let their sharp swords fall on his neck . . .

After that, they dealt with the enemy crew, and returned home with trophies.

7. The Case of the Stolen Silver Chalice

It seems that Alyosha acted as head of the "secret affairs department" only in Dobrynia's absence. The above episodes, recounting their joint activities, prove beyond doubt Dobrynia's seniority or primacy. It should be recalled that it was also Dobrynia who "submitted" to the prince the "report" on the services of Dounai Ivanovich at "the overseas" kings' courts.

A bylina about the collision between Dobrynia and Alyosha relates that the former had three "prophetic birds" — "three full-fed ravens" that served him, and the birds brought bad news to the bogatyr that clouds were darkening over his head.

> Flew those ravens, making haste,
> Where Dobrynia slept in the open waste. . .
> One perched atop a tall green oak,
> Another roosted on the white tent's post,
> The third alighted on the earth, rain-soaked.

Then the ravens, one by one, started to "caw", and at the first signs of an earthquake, Dobrynia awoke "from the great drunken slumber" and realized at once: "It seems that misery hovers over our home".

Another proof of the commonly recognized fact that Dobrynia was a more skillful and experienced professional than Alyosha is found in the story of a "stolen" silver chalice. The story is told in the bylina named "Forty mendicants and one". No one is better-clothed than those mendicants, relates the bylina:

> Their dress is sort of poppy-color,
> Their handbags all have velvet covers,
> Their pouches are damask all over.

These pilgrims were traveling from the north, "from the freezing blue sea, from Masleyev Lake", and heading to the faraway "Jerusalemgrad".

To pray to Our Lord the mercy-giver,
To rest on purple loosestrife,
To bathe in the Jordan-river.

Before setting out on the pilgrimage, they assembled around the precious Levanidov cross, and took a vow to guard themselves against any sinful intentions and deeds, namely: not to steal, not to cheat, not to behave lecherously. And if any of them was found guilty, they would not seek justice at court but would "pass their own judgment upon such":

We shall dig a waist-deep hole
In the open plain, in the damp soil.
Tongue too long, strike the head,
Eyes too bright — prick them dead,
Heart too ardent — stab his chest,
Leave the punished in eternal rest.

Having protected themselves against sins in such a dreadful manner, the travelers set out, and on the second day of their march came across the prince. Vladimir treated the pilgrims with great respect:

Stopped he in the distance, seeing not a pilgrim,
Dismounted from his steed, bowed in esteem:
Welcome, you brave young fellows, never at rest . . .
Be healthy, Mikhailushko, son of Mikhailo!
And to you, Dounai Ivanovich, all my best!
Good health to you, Kosma, son of Ivan! . . .

It should be noted, however, that Vladimir did not have to dismount from his horse but actually stepped out of his carriage, with Alyosha standing at the footboard and Dobrynia serving as a "coachman". As was the custom, the prince traveled with a specific guard, disguised (in accordance with later traditions) as lackeys and coachmen.

After the exchange of greetings, Vladimir asked the mendicants to chant "The Verse of the Deer". I cannot tell for certain what that means — it could be an unknown or forgotten story from the wide collection of ecclesiastic verses (the chanter himself named his bylina "The Poem of the Deer"), or a piece of folklore permeated with the images of the Book of Psalms, as "glimpses" of deer appear very often throughout the elaborate poetic lines of the latter. Vladimir had been, until quite recently, a pagan believer; readers might remember the miniature painting depicting the battle between Oleg Svyatoslavich and Lute, son of Sveneld. What is the pagan symbol of the feudal hunting? A deer; although the bylina recounts that the prince went out to hunt geese, swans and ducks, also. Then there is the Biblical deer. The pilgrims described in the above epic situation might sing a song to Vladimir about deer that came to a water source to quench their thirst, or, say, a variation on the theme of Psalm 18:32-24:

> It is God that girdeth me with strength,
> and maketh my way perfect.
> He maketh my feet like hinds' feet,
> and setteth me upon my high places.
> He teacheth my hands to war,
> so that a bow of steel is broken by mine arms.

Hunting, in ancient Rus', was an indispensable attribute of any prince's leisure. Like war, hunting was an integral part of his state activities; it showed whether a ruler had valor and skills, i.e. whether he met the requirements of his post. That is why, though the Psalm's topic is not about hunting as such, the high style of the Old Testament lyrics, glorifying the strength of feet, arms ready for fighting, and powerful hand muscles, could hardly fail to flatter the sovereign on his way to "have some fun".

What happened next was this: the pilgrims complied with the request — anchored their walking sticks into the ground, "hooked" the bags on them, seated themselves in a circle and started to sing their song in just a half-tone. Mother Earth, damp (as usual) "quaked", water in the lakes "quivered", trees in the dark forest swayed. Finally, Vladimir begged the mendicants to stop singing, because he could not endure their chant even while lying at rest, not to mention while standing or sitting. Besides:

Fell Alyosha down from the foot board,
Clattered Dobrynia down across the coach rod.

Such great artistic effect was natural: Dounai was not the only bogatyr among the members of this singing team who had used to ride across the open field in search of an enemy. According to the taleteller, "prior to that, they were 41 bogatyrs, they fought, and then went to repent". Expressing warm gratitude to the now silent pilgrims, and not losing a moment in getting away while the getting was good, the prince invited the travelers to go to Kiev to enjoy the hospitality of his wife Oprakseia. The pilgrims accepted his invitation.

When the palace stoves "sagged" and dishes spilled because of their singing, the princess, lounging on the glazed stove (used to heat, not only to cook), invited the wanderers to stay and eat, with God's mercy. Bending "step after step" and at the risk of damaging the new entrance-hall, the pilgrims came into the palace. Just at that time the trouble came. While hungry guests were chowing down on white swan, darkness had fallen. The hostess offered them beds, and accompanied guests to their rooms. As to Mikhail, son of Mikhail, she took him to her "chamber", "laid him down onto the bed of yew", "and laid herself down upon the glazed stove".

Most readers have already understood that the events were going to repeat the famous story about Joseph and the wife of Potiphar. For those who do not know this story from the Holy Bible, I shall explain: too vigorous, Oprakseia tried to seduce Mikhailo in a nice and delicate way.

It happened at an early hour of night,
Princess Oprakseia came down into view
From that glazed stove glowing bright,
She went to that wooden bed of yew,
To that feather-bed, couch of down so light,
To those small pillows, and cushions, fluffy and new,
Under that blanket of falcon black-bright
(Not native, but falcon, exotic and few);
Flung her right arm on Mikhailushka,
Flung her right leg on Mikhailushka,
To her ardent heart pressed Mikhailushka:
"Oh, Mikhail's son, Mikhailushka dear!

> Fall in love with me, princess Oprakseia, here,
> Fall behind those roaming mendicants, dear,
> Hire out yourself to the service of Vladimir, here,
> We shall live with you together, dear
> And the treasury will be by your hand, ever near".

Mikhailushka appeared to be no less dignified than Joseph. He responded: "Leave me, princess Oprakseia", and explained that they had "taken the great oath". The angry princess climbed up back onto the stove, but tried again in an hour another attempt, whispering more vague insinuations. Mikhailushka again managed to fend her off. Then, at the start of the third hour of the night, seeing that Mikhailushka "had gone into the bogatyr's sleep", the princes for the third time

> Clambered down from the warm glazed dome . . .
> And took she that silver chalice so rich,
> That the prince drinks from whene'er he comes home,
> And took she the traveler's bag — which,
> Was unlaced, when it should have been done,
> Placed she the chalice into his bag,
> Laced she the bag as before it was stitched.

The next morning the pilgrims continued their way, and in a while the prince returned from hunting. He had scarce arrived "at the wide yard", when he demanded the princess to bring his favorite vessel (it is an appropriate moment to remind of Vladimir's words when choosing the state religion: "Rus' is merry drinking, we cannot be without that"). The princess promptly answered:

> Oh, my dear Vladimir, prince of Kiev right!
> Pilgrims stayed in our white palace last night,
> And they stole that chalice of silver so bright
> From which you sip on return from a ride.

The prince hailed Alyosha and ordered him to return with the stolen item ("Set out, Oliosha, ride down, overtake them and take away . . ."). Popovich mounted the most fleet-footed pacer, rushed like a meteor to the open field, climbed up a "steep gully", watched through the "spy-glass" in all four directions, and having detected the pilgrims, spurred forward towards them, "shouting and roaring" while galloping, in the best traditions of the worst representatives of the well-known department: Stop, thieves, give the chalice back! — However, the mendicants were not embarrassed. On the contrary, they became indignant and put up resistance to the "authorities", in a manner that the latter found very offensive:

> Great offense the pilgrims heard,
> Awaited Alyosha who toward them spurred,
> Flung Alyosha from his steed,
> Tore his pants off without a word,
> Whipped his arse as felt they need,
> Put Alyosha back on his steed,
> Tied Alyosha to the stirrup of gold,
> Hardly sits Alyosha in saddle of old
> And his horse with slow pace homeward leads.

Meanwhile, Vladimir was pacing the "balcony" in impatience, trying to locate Alyosha through his spyglass. On his return, the unfortunate detective told all, without holding back the truth.

As usual in such cases, Dobrynia was sent to rectify matters. The latter left the town in the same way as Alyosha, located the pilgrims in the open plain, but omitted flying at them with abuse. Instead, he bypassed the wayfarers by "by-roads" and made it appear that he met them by chance ("rides he towards the pilgrims from the opposite direction"). Before coming up to them, Dobrynia dismounted from his trotter, bowed from the waist, expressed his greetings, and politely inquired:

> In the town of Kiev you stayed overnight,
> At the palace of our Vladimir-prince right.
> Did a silver chalice come your way,
> The one the prince drinks of on homecoming day?

For one reason or another, the travelers were not surprised that the good man looking for the chalice rode not from Kiev, but towards Kiev. They promptly shook out the contents of their bags, and soon discovered the chalice, which Oprakseia, full of passion and "in anger", had put into the bag of Mikhailushka. The vessel was returned to Dobrynia.

Strictly speaking, this is the end of the story as far as our interest in proof of Dobrynia's high professional qualities in solving state crimes (the "missing chalice" should be regarded as such). True, the prince's "coachman" seemed to avoid asking how it had happened, and the prince remained ignorant as to Oprakseia's perfidy. Or perhaps Dobrynia understood everything and decided to keep it quiet. On that matter, the bylina remains discreet.

8. Dobrynia and Marinka

The passage dealing with the confrontation between the prince's favorite servant and the cunning Marinka has quite a different, partially satirical coloring. Contrary to the previous situations, Dobrynia herein had at least his ego at stake, if not his life.

> For three years Dobrynia waited at tables,
> For three years Dobrynia served the drinks,
> For three years Dobrynia guarded the gates.

Such was the usual beginning of the chanters' narration. We should note, first of all, that to serve the prince at table (not to mention "guarding the gates") has throughout the ages been a mark of distinction, a most important function granted to a sovereign's guards. Dobrynia's taking on Marinka is often presented in the epic as though it were a thoughtless action, since "There were many fine fellows and if any one of them went to her street, he would never return". Dobrynia's confrontation with that evil maiden, however, must have quite a different meaning. Hence, he did not follow the advice of his wise mother, who instructed him:

> Go you not to the prince's tavern,
> Drink you not that strong green wine,
> Go you not to those streets stone-paven,
> To those bystreets of Marinka maiden,
> Bitch and poisoner is this Marinka-kite
> Poisoned that Marinka nine good men,
> Nine strong men, all falcons bright,

And you, Dobrynia, will be number ten.

Dobrynia brushed aside his mother's advice:

Turned he to the prince's taverns,
Drank Dobrynia strong green wine,
Met he tarts and played he chess.

Was he obliged to do so, being a "guard"? Indeed, it is common knowledge that a wealth of information could be obtained in those haunts of vice. In many such places valuable information was acquired and submitted "upwards." Marinka of Ignaty (other names: princess Kaidalievna, princess and fairy, maiden Malinovka) was not just a whore or a witch, but a very dangerous domestic enemy. She was responsible for the death not of nine ordinary "good men", but nine "strong Russian bogatyrs" who were in the state's service. This act was an enormous offense to the state and placed Marinka under the investigative jurisdiction of the security department. However, the range of Marinka's crimes was far wider:

Many Russians she put to death,
Many princes and princely sons,
Many kings and kingly sons,
Nine strong Russian bogatyrs,
And common people we can't count here.

It might also be ascertained that Marinka entertained Tugarin the Serpent-Son, a well-known enemy of Rus' (or maybe Serpent the Flame-thrower, Idolische, The Immortal Kaschei or the Tatar) in her palace-tower.

Such was the situation when Dobrynia found himself in the streets of Marinka and the byways of Ignaty (or vice versa). He was walking down the street in Kiev with his bow on one shoulder, when he noticed two doves kissing each other at Marinka's window. Instead of being touched by such a picture of pastoral sweetness, the bogatyr on the contrary either got angry ("Dobrynia took offense at this, seeing it as a mockery of him"), or suspected something ("Maybe Dobrynia Mikitich saw a vision of male and female pigeons sitting side by side, nose to nose, mouth to mouth"), or, finally, had thought everything over beforehand ("Well, what a joke I will play on Marinka"). The knight-errant placed an arrow on his bow, pulled the silken bowstring and released the arrow.

However, that was a bad shot. "By ill-luck", either his foot slipped or his hand faltered, but the arrow knocked out the upper "silver lintel", broke the "window glass", and slew "Marinka's darling friend" right on the spot (another version claims that the "friend" was safe, but was indecently afraid and ran away). Anyway, Rus' now counted one enemy fewer.

Marinka was in grief, while Dobrynia was anxious to retrieve his arrow back. When he entered the richly decorated halls, Marinka either rushed to hide herself ("sits that whore behind the curtain"), or cursed, or offered herself as a mistress (different versions for every taste). But after Dobrynia left, she scraped off his "foot prints" with a knife, threw the shavings into the fire, and pronounced a love incantation. Dobrynia came back and was turned into a golden-horned bull, or a "golden-horned bull chieftain", or into a wild deer. And that is how another honorable citizen of Kiev disappeared.

We expect that the state would conduct a search for its missing servant, but the bylina provides no mention of that and informs us only about the efforts of his relatives — Avdotia Ivanovna and a certain very active old lady. Dobrynia was discovered under obscure circumstances. Some epic chanters claimed that Dobrynia, even when turned into a "golden-horned bull", did not drop his furious bogatyr habits, and started to savage the flocks of his dear aunt, who finally guessed the reason of her misfortunes.

> And said Avdotia Ivanovna,
> This is not a golden-horned bull,
> This is my beloved nephew,
> Young Dobryniushka Nikitich.
> Charmed he was by Marinka,
> That Marinka-witch, Kaidalievna.

Other taletellers recounted that once the daughters of his aunt went "berry-picking", and by chance "turned to" the field where forty bulls were grazing. A bull ran up to them and began to make up to them. Back home, the girls told their mother that awhile before there had been thirty-nine bulls running on that field, and "now forty bulls run about (sharp eyes must have run in the family!). And one bull ran up, fawned like a dog, and his eyes streamed tears". This came to pass after Dobrynia had been "missing in the town for six months already ".

In the mid 19ᵗʰ century Trophim Romanov, epic narrator from Pudozh, assured P. N. Rybnikov (an antiquarian specializing in folklore) that the course of events was quite the other way around, that Dobrynia was a Muscovite from the place named Vshyvaia Gorka (Lousy Hillock). When he got lost, the honest widow Ofimia Aleksandrovna somehow managed to find out what had happened to him, and rushed to hunt down a doctor in Moscow. Meeting with no success, she set out to Kiev to visit a certain old woman living somewhere in the back streets of the town.

And finally there is a version according to which Marinka herself leaked word. By that time she had already managed to find her way into the palace of the prince ("Played with the prince's children" — says the narrator.). At some feast she "got very drunk" and plunged into shameless boasting in front of Ofimia Aleksandrovna and "young Anna Ivanovna" ("that godmother of Dobrynia"):

Oh you all, princesses and boyars' wives,
In the glorious capital of Rus', Kiev rich,
No one is more smart and wise,
Nine good men did I bewitch,
As fawn bulls I charmed the good knights,
And the tenth was Dobrynia Nikitich,
He is the golden horned leader, with bulls he fights!

Hearing these words, the "young Anna Ivanovna" rode her down, and leaped trampling on the "white breast", saying:

Oh, what a bitch you are, heretic whore and tart!
You are, you say, more cunning than us, and smart. . .
I will turn you into a real bitch, we'll see how you like this art!

And so on, in the same vein. The women interested in Dobrynia usually addressed Marinka with such round oaths. Marinka was stricken with fear. She wanted to be neither a "pregnant bitch", nor a "stray dog" (as suggested by the more moderate mother of Dobrynia), nor even a magpie. Hence she turned herself into a grey martin or that same magpie, flew to the open plains or to the Turkish sea, perched upon the horns of the new chieftain of bulls, or on his shoulders, and promised that she would "turn him back" if he married her. Dobrynia's state allowed no options. If only he could become a man again, and then he would teach her! And he did teach her, after the marriage. The epic narrators provide various versions of the revenge. The simplest of all was related by Ivan Nikitich Remisov: "He tossed her up to the skies".

Seemingly, the only denouement that stands apart from the other bylinas is that of Trophim Romanov. This fairy-teller claims that Dobrynia resumed his human appearance with the assistance of an old granny, without Marinka's intervention. The granny instructed Ophimia Aleksandrovna to take her to "white-stone Moscow, to that Lousy Hillock". Once there, she ordered the "taut bow of Dobrynia" to be brought.

> Taut the old woman draws the bow,
> Sets she the arrow of tempered steel,
> Keeps she saying to that arrow:
> "Fly, dear arrow, to the plain now,
> Find, my arrow, Dobrynia,
> The wild deer in the open field:
> Let him run to white-stone Moscow,
> Let him hasten to our Lousy Hillock".

The old lady was apparently a good archer. The singer fails to inform us how it happened that the "dear arrow" from Moscow found the deer in the plains around Kiev, how the animal put two and two together and understood what was needed of him, etc.. The chanter briefly states that: "this elder made Dobrynia back into a good strong fellow". And she "converted" Marinka "into a dog", this time without Dobrynia's participation.

But such a variant derogated the role of Dobrynia too much, and besides, the punishment of Marinka was presented not as a lesson but as an ordinary thing. That is perhaps why this version did not become widespread. On the contrary, there was an attempt, though too late, to add more heroism to the image of Dobrynia using some passages from the bylina about Ilya Muromets. The Pudozh chanter Nikita Antonovich Remisov and his children related how the frightened "maiden Malinovka" handed Dobrynia the "bunch of keys" to the dark cellars where she kept her captives:

> How Dobrynia Nikitich opened those heavy doors,
> How the great crowd poured out from the dark,
> Priests, scribes and simple peasants . . .

By rights, the story is worthy of such a truly epic ending. But even without such a finale, the bylina is very impressive for its dramatic and ingenious recitation of events (leavened with a taste of humor). No matter how one treats the role of Dobrynia in that epic work — in the purely folkloric context, or with my corrections in accordance with chronicles — the essence is the same. In the essence of the heroic folk-lore, he saved the princedom of Kiev from a sly and clever enemy who was an apparent threat to the state security.

9. The Vicissitudes of Service (Intrigues, Conflicts, Dungeons, etc.)

Evgeny Dolmatovsky was very precise in saying: "Arguing with legends is a waste of time: you will not out-argue them. A legend is the same 'non-ductile thing' as facts. Folklore is hard-grained. Seemingly unsteady, it is granite-solid." People understood perfectly well that to serve a prince, even such as Vladimir the Red Sun, is no easy job and could not be performed under idyllic colors; they knew it was hard be-ing a bogatyr.

> When Vladimir, Prince of Kiev, capital great,
> Was enraged by old Cossack Ilya Muromets,
> He locked him up in cellar dank.
> Ice-cold and deep, in that prison caged,
> For long three years Ilya's life was waged.

Such were the first lines of the bylina "Ilya Muromets and Kalin-tsar" as presented by Trophim Grigorievich Riabinin, the most famous Russian epic chanter.

According to the chronicles, a cellar (pit) was one of the two forms of prison known in old Russia. The other one was an above-ground dungeon — a wooden jail. The first mention of the wooden jail in the "Primary Chronicle" dates back to the year of 1036 when the son of Vladimir, Yaroslav, "placed" his brother Sudislav in custody in Pskov. While the cellar as a form of a jail was first mentioned in 1068, when the Kievans rose up against prince Iziaslav Yaroslavich who "shut up their host" (the townsmen arrested by the prince's authorities) in the cellar. The fact that prisons existed under the rule of Vladimir can at least be guessed when reading the stories of his punitive measures against the brigands. However, documented evidence of the fact have been preserved only in the manuscript of Tietmar von Merseburg, a German chronicler, who recounted that in the early 11th century (between 1012 and 1015) the prince of Kiev jailed his nephew Svyatopolk, his wife, and bishop Reinbern, her guest from Poland, into some sort of a "solitary confinement" in Turov, Pinsk or Kiev. Thus, folklore was not misleading.

If we believe the bylinas, Vladimir often quarrelled with his defenders and guards, which caused grumbling and protests from their side; this resulted one day in a unified "scuffle". He schemed against them either on his own, or advised by his "evil counselors" (an attribute used in chronicles to identify persons with doubtful moral reputations). Folklore, which never holds back when characterizing its personages, calls them "crooked-bellied boyars", "prowling instigators" and "big-bellied inciters". Some variants in the bylinas, describing Alyosha Popovich's suit for the wife of Dobrynia, relate that it was the prince himself, not that simple-minded and rather unfortunate (according to some tale-tellers) sarcastic bogatyr, who concocted this improper plan and made considerable efforts to implement it. It was the prince who "drafted the letter" to Ophimia Aleksandrovna about Dobrynia's death, and it was he who would "visit" Nastasia Mikulichna until she was "compelled", who authorized his "court servants" and "gate keepers" to "hang those who utter Dobrynia's name!" As a result, Dobrynia, on his return, quoth such sulfurous words that I will not risk repeating here.

Dobrynia's was not the only such case. The bylina named "Danila Denisievich" ("Danila Lovchanin") describes another, and even more scandalous, of the prince's deeds. He decided to kill the bogatyr named Danila, and thus to lay hands on his wife, Vasilisa Nikulichna (one of the most widespread epic female names, that was also the name of the wife of Stavr Godinovich, and in some variants — that of Dobrynia). The plot seems to be based on truth, for Vladimir who, as the chronicler puts it, was defeated by "lust for women", "was never sated with lech-

ery, and brought over to himself [other] husbands' wives and maidens".
In that case, the prince was instigated by a certain Mishatochka Putiatin (alias Shatien'ka, Shat, Putiata Putiatovich), possibly a son of
Vladimir's captain, who in tandem with Dobrynia forced the Novgorodians to be baptized (although another voivode known as Putiata
lived half a century later).

The prince was on the point of anger: "Have you ever heard of or
seen such a thing — to take the wife of a man who is still alive!", and
even ordered to "execute and hang" Mishatochka. But Mishatochka
apparently knew well the weaknesses of his lord. It should be noted,
that in some variants of the bylina he was referred to as the prince's
nephew, while in the others the fact that this impertinent advisor's
name was Mishatochka, a diminutive form of the name Mikhail, was to
testify that he was not just a representative of the "round-bellied
boyars" but a highly trusted person, possibly from the department surveying potential domestic enemies. That was why Mishatochka, far
from being confused, sneered to himself and asked permission to "utter
yet another word". ("Smart was that Mishatochka Putiatin, he flipped
over at once to the other side" — shrewdly comments the bylina).

He suggested sending Danila "to the open field, to those Levanidov grasslands", "to that roaring fountain head" — to hunt down a
white-necked bird, as well as to kill "a fierce lion and bring him to the
prince to sup" (the lord, he said, was missing lion's meat at his dinner
table). In other words, Putiatin's son's idea was to clap Danila in the
devil's place in hopes that the lion himself would eat Danila for his dinner.

> Oh, liked these words the prince, he did,
> Loved Vladimir-prince the words, indeed.

Ilya Muromets, who happened to be a witness of this criminal
conspiracy, tried in vain to intervene, saying that the prince would only
harass his strong falcon to no purpose — he would anyway fail to catch
the white swan. In honor of his merits, the bogatyr was placed again
behind the bars. Meanwhile, Vladimir did not delay sending off Mishatochka with the "hastily prepared letters" to Chernigov where Danila
lived, instructing him to start out for the service. Seeing him off, Vasilisa Nikulichna gave him a large quiverful of tempered steel arrows, not

a small one, and pronounced her far-sighted warnings to her overly-naive "beloved friend":

> An extra arrow will stand you in very good stead
> But it will not fly to find the prince or boyar's head,
> Against your brethren bogatyrs you'll raise your hand.

And this was just how it happened. The lion failed to fulfill his mission. But Mishatochka, as it turned out, had an emergency variant (which he must have whispered into the prince's ear, because the balladeers heard nothing). Briefly, on his way back from hunting, the prince's huntsman turned his "spy-glass" in the direction of Kiev and discovered that

> That was no snow, burning bright,
> Nor dark mud, reflecting night,
> The Russian host was there, black and white,
> Against him, Danila Denisievich, the knight.

Only at that moment Danila understood that he had "become most unwelcome to the prince", and after "bitter tears" took up his "fighting sword"; however, he did not take up the above-mentioned bow and arrows. Now, Nikita appears, blood brother of the huntsman, in company with Dobrynia. And again Danila Denisievich sheds tears ("It's a thing unheard, unseen — a brother goes against his kin"), sticks his spear, butt down, into the ground, and throws himself onto the spearhead.

Though they had come to take Danila's life, the bogatyrs began to cry in grief. When all the tears were shed, they returned to Vladimir and reported "bold Denisych's" suicide. On hearing such news, the prince was not sad. He jumped into his golden carriage and started out, with escort, to Chernigov for the bride. Vasilisa Nikulichna took along her knife of damask steel, and on the way back, when the nuptial cortege reached the "Levanidov meadows" (please note where the reserves with lions were situated in those bygone days), she asked the prince's permission to bid farewell to her "dear friend". The guard, consisting of the above two bogatyrs, did not prevent the woman from stabbing herself and falling down alongside Danila. That was how a new hunting drama ended.

There is yet another corpse in some versions of the bylina — an angry Vladimir "awarded Mishatka with the boiling tar-pot bath".

Now Prince Vladimir allowed Ilya Muromets out of the cellar, and "kissed his head, the upper crown" for telling the truth. Ilya was lucky again — his term in jail was short, for those days.

However, Ilya, naturally, was not the only one who was imprisoned. Dounai and Sukhmanty, Duke and even Dobrynia himself — they also experienced the life of the prisoner. One version of the bylina relates that the latter was clapped in jail, by the prince, for bragging about his young wife; another bylina claims that the bogatyr was imprisoned on a charge of "bogatyr slander": a sworn brother, comrade in the frontier and counter-intelligence activities, sold him out. The last version rings quite true, because the history of such institutions — in any country — abounds with such paradoxes. Besides, we have already seen what an indecent role some bogatyrs often played.

Ilya should not have too dark memories about his stay in the cellar — his term, as already mentioned, was not very long, and his confinement was not unbearable. Nevertheless, an Old Russian cellar, especially in its epic variant, is no joke. In the bylina about Dounai, the cellar is described as being some 65 meters deep and some 16 meters wide, with walls standing two meters above ground.

The entrance to those catacombs was barred by "solid gray rocks" and "hard iron plates". The heavy doors were equipped with damask-steel padlocks supervised by the "key-stewards and castellans". The "golden keys" of the padlocks were kept by the prince himself.

In the bylina, Ilya was saved by the only daughter of Vladimir (actually Vladimir had, reportedly, from two to nine — or more — daughters, one of whom was named Predslava). Coming to understand that to put a bogatyr who could "fight single-handed for Christianity and the Fatherland" in a cellar was "no trifling matter", she took active measures to save at least his health. The maiden ordered to have "forged keys" made, and appointed some "secret men"(!) who took down to Ilya's dungeon "feather-beds and downy pillows", "warm blankets", "good viands" and a change of "brand-new" clothes. Thus, when Kalin-tsar approached Kiev with his countless host, and Vladimir rushed with his golden keys to the "bars of iron" (by the way, Ilya was to be released as early as three months and three days before), he saw that the "old Cossack. . . sits in the cellar and does not grow older". However, such things were, naturally, very rare.

By contrast, Dounai Ivanovich was imprisoned for as long as fifteen years in conditions far from those of a health resort. Some of my readers may think that such a term is symbolic, exaggerated by folklore, but the reality of life was sometimes even harder than the tales. Thus, prince Sudislav of Pskov, one of Vladimir's sons, was locked in the cellar by Yaroslav the Wise in 1036, as it was stated above, and spent 24 years behind bars!

Ilya's misfortunes did not end at imprisonment alone. He also happened to stay in "places of faraway exile", which was considered to be a good disciplinary measure, even in those days. (Addressing to the Prince of Kiev a risky request to release Dounai from jail, Dobrynia begs him in advance not to confine him "in faraway exiles"). This time, the calumnies against Ilya invented by the "slanted belly boyars" sounded very grave:

> Against Ilya of Murom they cast such doubt,
> That he speaks such braggart word:
> "I shall drive, he says, Vladimir-prince out,
> I myself shall sit in Kiev, in his abode,
> I myself shall be the prince of all about" . . .

Vladimir heatedly interrogated the bogatyr; they "sparred at each other", and the prince sent Muromets away from "fine Kiev-grad." However, Ilya had the privilege of choosing the place of exile himself, and he naturally preferred to be confined for three years in his native village of Karacharovo, at his "father's and mother's" home. He returned to Kiev when "his zealous heart was in torment" and he understood that Rus' was again in trouble. With the skill of a seasoned agent, the bogatyr left his white steed in a "wide yard" and exchanged clothes with the first pilgrim he met (the traveler was delirious with delight at seeing Ilya Muromets). Ilya learnt from Vladimir himself about the violence that the new conqueror (the pagan Idolische) had committed in town; he was generous in forgiving the humble and wretched prince who threw himself zealously at his feet, begging pardon, and then performed the deed of a true bogatyr . . .

The bylina named "Ilya Muromets and Kalin-tsar" recounts that Vladimir's tough "pedagogical system" and his defiance of the interests of those who were defending the nation once resulted in a situation where he was strongly opposed by the whole powerful alliance of bogatyrs (in another instance, angry at not being invited to a princely feast, Ilya knocked all the domes off all the town churches, and then called for all the taverns' poor folk to join him at his own banquet table).

Released from the cellar, the commander of the Russian frontiersmen found his friends in the open field and called upon them to stand for the divine churches, for "the common peasants" and for the glorious capital of Kiev. However, his ardent call was received very coldly. Samson Samoilovich replied:

> Oh my Godson, Ilya, darling one,
> Old Cossack who hails from distant Murom!
> Saddle we shall not our steeds so fine,
> Mount we shall not our riders in line,
> Ride we shall not to the open grassland,
> Stand we shall not for Faith and Fatherland,
> Defend we shall not that capital Kiev-grad,
> Fight we shall not for mother churches of God,
> Nor shall we guard Vladimir-prince grand,
> His Princess Oprakseia in addition to that.
> He has many princes and boyars proud,
> He wines them and dines them and favors abound,
> But no honor from Vladimir-prince have we ourselves found.

Three times Ilya attempted to appeal to the conscience and honor of the bogatyrs, to arouse their patriotic feelings, and thrice Samson Samoilovich word for word repeated his negative answer. And only after the dramatic adventures of Muromets in the camp of Tatars, when he had sent a charmed arrow to Samson, did the bogatyrs at last engage to fight.

10. Epos and History. Who of the Heroes Served or Could Have Served Vladimir Svyatoslavich?

Does this mean that the history "written" by the folk should be accepted without criticism? From the very beginning of Russian folklore studies, there have been controversial approaches to the problem of the historical origins of the epic heroes. Did they "really" exist? To be more precise, could they be traced back to some real historic proto-types? Or maybe all those personages were woven out of thin air and were the result of artistic flights of imagination?

In other words, was the peasant who listened to the bylina about Ilya Muromets really wrong in muttering doubtfully: "I guess, it's all lies . . ."? Among present-day researchers, B. N. Poutilin seems to express the above opinion most clearly. The scholar believes that "it is a proven fact that the historic authenticity of some of the heroes of the bylinas is doubtful. Alyosha Popovich did not come into folklore from real history. On the contrary, the fictional personage acquired the features of a true historic person under the pen and ink of a chronicler. Echoes of the epic Sadko and Vasily Buslaev found their way into the annals. Some other parallels between the names of the characters found in the chronicles and bylinas should be regarded as mere coincidences — not more".

Ilya Muromets has a precise "ancestry", but the whole of his biography is a fiction based not upon the chronicles, but on the age-old historic experience of people and a distant poetic tradition. Folk imagination may sometimes "catch" in its nets a real historic person, but it can also flourish without such material . . .

I understand the genesis of epic heroes quite differently. My presumption is based on the principle that people never dreamed something up consciously. People simply interpreted the pre-historic and historic past in their own language. Of course, most people did not read the chronicles (although even this should not be taken as an absolute truth). But real epic heroes and their deeds — the subject matter of the chronicles — served as a spark that ignited the folk fantasy and let the "thoughts flow through the tree of dreams." They created a semblance of the chronicles that changed over time due to altering realities.

The approach of B. N. Poutilov, who views the bylinas as non-historic sources and the chronicles as historic documents, is wrong. Chronicles are just one of the sources of history. If a hero of the epics finds his way into the chronicle, there is no reason to doubt his real historic background. The folk memory served as a natural reservoir accessed by the old Russian scribes.

However, proving that bylinas directly influenced the chroniclers is no easy matter. Is it not significant that no mention of Ilya Muromets, a major hero of Russian folk poetry, can be found even in the oldest chronicles? One starts to assume that the chroniclers might have come into contact with the bylina folklore through intermediate books, such as the 16th century tale about Alexandr Popovich, that survived till our day. It should be also borne in mind that the annalistic tradition has come down to us in a form that is far from the original. Many elements of the chronicles have been lost, together with the unique historic information which those preserved, known, annals lack.

I would like to share the approach of Academician D. S. Likhachyov as stated long ago. "The artistic creator in a bylina", he wrote, "like the Russian medieval literature, proceeded from a single historical fact, a specific historical person, and a specific historic event. Initially, an epic work narrated only what had happened; it could be a historic tale, a historic song glorifying a hero, a lament for a hero, and so on. Those early historic works had already elements of some artistic generalization, as well as attempts to comprehend the history . . . Then, in the course of time the events and the historical persons gradually underwent a great transformation . . . A literary work converted into another genre possessing a different degree and quality of artistic imagination. A bylina came into being. However, bylinas were still perceived as the 'truth'. The folk were very careful to preserve the names of persons and places, as well as the historic outline of any story".

My approach, as readers might notice, has dealt mainly with the skills and psychological characteristics of the epic heroes, not with the authenticity of the stories in which they played their roles. However, those features reflect the issues that confronted the bogatyrs at the real outposts, and their activities, among other duties, in the sphere of intelligence and counter-intelligence. Academician B. A. Rybakov's research and his attempt to demonstrate correlations between the epic plots and the historical reality (e.g. in relation to Ilya Muromets) might be of interest to the reader.

11. *Russian Secret Services under the Rule of Prince Vladimir. A summary.*

General remarks

Unfortunately, we know very little about the secret services of Kievan Rus' in the 10th and early 11th centuries. How did they form historically, what were their organizational structures? Indeed, the very existence of these institutions is known only through the actions of some of their leaders, officers and agents.

In the early years or decades of Vladimir's rule, those secret services were apparently led by Dobrinya — a person not only of remarkable individuality, but rather a prominent personality. The whole "intelligence support" of Vladimir's struggle with Yaropolk, and apparently that of the Korsun campaign, are to be credited to him. Whatever merits might be attributed to Dobrinya's predecessors, we have fair grounds for presuming that it was he who made the greatest contribution and even laid the corner stone of the edifice of Russian national security (under construction for a very long period of time), and provided it with relatively stable blue-prints.

As head of that institution, he firmly held the reins of government. Those who were "under him" included the persons known to us as voivode Bloud, the Varangian Zhdebern, "the man from Korsun", Anastasius, the "old man" of Belgorod, and the envoy-visitors sent to foreign countries to look around, envoy-couriers, youths assigned just one single missions. To my mind, we also should not forget the bogatyrs of the bylinas, Ilya Muromets, Alyosha (Alexandr) Popovich and the others already mentioned. Anyway, I am inclined to believe that Ilya and Alyosha are historic personages of the Vladimir era, or, to be more precise, to have their first historic prototypes in that epoch. We shall discuss Ilya Muromets later . . . The above-listed persons were mainly people of high or privileged social status, serving at the administration of the Prince. In addition to this list, there were people of various social groups and lands who dreamed about the career of a state official.

One historian wrote that the actions of any form of secret war at the time of Kievan Rus' were supervised by secret confidants and favorites of the Prince. "Secret confidants appeared at the moment when it became necessary to retain and win power, the throne of prince. Initially, the functions of these confidants were carried out by the Grid' — a small druzhina escort of the prince, consisting of his guards (hand-picked warriors), whom he entrusted with the most delicate assignments related to the elimination of rivals and foes". However, the Grid's did not include persons who could at least to some extent determine the policy and actions of the prince in such an important and delicate sphere.

A very fragmentary list of those who were so engaged enables us at most to define the main activities of the agencies in question, and some of their methods. The main emphasis was naturally laid upon military and political reconnaissance, the former being based on recruited agents and voluntary turncoats. To recruit agents, special "envoys" were sent, who, as in all times, lured their victims mainly with generous payments for their future services. In the turmoil of the internecine wars, the secret services did not disdain political assassination (Rogvolod with his sons; Yaropolk). Hit men had been "authorized" as far back as the time of Prince Oleg.

In order to deceive the enemy, disinformation was used. The general means of communication was to send couriers or "envoys" who orally transmitted the messages, instructions and proposals of their chiefs. Seemingly primitive, this method of secret information delivery has survived throughout the ages, and is still used nowadays as quite an effective and reliable means.

In those bygone days, dispatches written on parchment or birchbark were not customary, given the fact that the written language was not yet widely used. Written messages were resorted to in cases when contacts through an "envoy" turned out to be impossible (like the siege of Korsun). The number of men engaged in the services in question was apparently not very great. There would have been only two or three rungs separating the captains from the rank and file agents, in this hierarchy. The liaison went along the shortest line, without any unnecessary relays. It is hard to tell whether the intelligence (and counterintelligence) of Prince Vladimir was always directly controlled by the "center" in Kiev (initially in Novgorod), or there were "affiliates" in other big cities and border towns. But when we think back on the story about the Belgorod kissel, remembering the rugged princely existence of Svyatoslavich Jr., when Kiev would not have had time to render assistance to cities and towns under nomad attack, and when Prince Vladimir himself happened to escape under a bridge in order to avoid the disgrace of captivity, I assume that the establishment of affiliate structures is more likely.

The Secret Services of Rus' in a Historic Context

The Byzantine Empire was the center of ancient (Western) civilization, the greatest state of the medieval world, and was the cultural and, partially, political model emulated by Rus' after the adoption of Christianity; the intelligence services were similarly organized on the same basis. At that time, under Emperor Basil II, a treatise on the fundamentals of intelligence was written, according to which a "domestikos" (a war-lord of a certain rank) and the borderland "strategoi" (governor-generals, military administrators of districts, heads of garrisons) were obliged to "have such spies" through whom they would "know all the designs" of nearby countries and especially those that interested Constantinople most of all: Pechenegia and Rus'. Thus, Rus' did have a teacher to learn from, though, of course, the Empire did not share its secrets willingly.

Naturally, it should be taken into consideration that there was a great difference in the level of cultural development between the ancient Russian state, the Byzantine Empire and certain countries of Europe, Asia and Northern Africa. As a matter of fact, secret services date back to time immemorial, and seem to have appeared synchronously with the emergence of human civilization.

Passages about specific intelligence and counter-intelligence operations can be found as early as the cuneiform messages in clay from the library of Assyrian king Ashurbanipal, on Egyptian papyruses, in the Homeric legend of the conquest of Troy, and the classical historians stories about Greek, Carthaginian, Parthian, Roman and other agents, residents, couriers, and their "hunters". "Already in ancient times", writes E. Chernyak, "many presently routine methods of intelligence were well known: the sending of civilian spies, the use of messenger-pigeons and other specially trained birds . . . to deliver reports". The first attempts to comprehend these activities on a theoretical basis also date back to ancient times. For example, the Chinese treatise on the art of war, written in the 5th century BC by Sun-Tse, classifies spies as a "treasure for the state". Emphasizing the great importance of "advance knowledge" for the success of "enlightened sovereigns and wise captains," Sun-Tse insisted that the knowledge "cannot be acquired" "by conclusions on analogy, nor by means of any calculations. Knowledge about the state of the enemy can be received only from the people". That is why, continued the oriental thinker, "there are five uses for spies: there are local spies, there are internal spies, there are reverse spies, there are death spies, there are life spies". "Local" spies — are those we call turncoats; then come the moles and double agents: "internal" spies are recruited agents who conspicuously serve one state, while secretly serving another one; "reverse" spies — re-recruited agents seized by counter-intelligence. "Life spies" — agents assigned with the mission to obtain and dispatch certain information, staying alive. As for the "death spies", there was no such privilege, as they were kind of disposable agents.

Thus, the differences between the "secret services" of various countries, it seems to me, relate first of all to the qualitative aspect — the professional skill of the "staff", the efficiency of vertical and horizontal relations, the scope of the agents' network, i.e. everything resulting from the experience of each country and its national traditions.

A Brief Note on Counter-Intelligence

The above discussion actually touches only upon intelligence, which by its functions may be compared with a sword in action; whereas the shield, i.e. the counter-intelligence, has always been in the shadow. Apparently, little of the information provided by the historic sources is in congruence with the real development of this institution and its status in the whole system of secret services. I may move professionals to laughter, but I dare say that it is more difficult to find than to hide, to catch than to elude; to successfully catch spies, the appropriate services were expected to greatly outmatch the opposing enemy's intelligence.

There are exceptions, however, from this rule. Byzantium, for example, which like the ancient Roman Empire relied heavily on intelligence-gathering skills, especially under Emperor Justinian, paid too little attention to its own external intelligence. Rus' apparently emphasized the importance of spying.

It is not incidental that the chronicles and other preserved documents mention nothing or very little about the activities of domestic sleuths, and only the folkloric memory provides material on the subject. At the same time, it is quite clear, reading from the Byzantine chronicles on the diplomatic maneuvers with Rome, that the Eastern Romans' emissary-spies (not unlike the Pecheneg, Polish, Hungarian, German, Scandinavian and others) showed up in Rus' on a number of occasions. In the course of conversion to Christianity, the expanding empire of Vladimir was invaded by a real horde of Christian missionaries (who were by no means only Byzantine). A torrent of Greek (and Bulgarian?) church representatives of every rank flooded the country. The Holy See of Rome also showed up constantly, and in its own way, expressed sincere interest in enlightening the souls of the people living in the largest Slavic state.

One historian has justly noted that in those days it was "sometimes hard to tell a monk from an ambassador, a monastery from a consulate, a church from a warehouse, a pilgrim's word from an official dispatch, and a pilgrim from a resident". Let us take the above-mentioned Anastasius the Tithe as an example. Who can tell, now, for certain, that he served his second homeland honestly? Was it only the plundered estate that he carried 30 years later to Poland?

In short, if the secret services were generally in the early stages of development in Rus', so were counter-espionage activities, during the days of Dobrinya and his colleagues as well as their successors'.

A Saga about Great Chiefs. Sigurd.

Who were they, the comrades-in-arms and successors of that voivode and bogatyr, uncle and tutor of Prince Vladimir? This question can be answered only in the form of conjecture.

Using a range of evidence, it is not very hard to figure out who was Dobrinya; however, there are no reliable sources relating to other favorites of the Kievan prince. Bloud is not likely to be a serious candidate — his position as an adjutant to the juvenile Prince Yaroslav speaks for itself. This was an honorable but "peripheral" post.

The Icelandic saga about the Norwegian konung Olaf Tryggvason, related by monk Od, claims that Olaf's maternal uncle Sigurd had great influence with the court of Prince Vladimir. He was allegedly in "such honor" that he "examined and decided the affairs of the konung [Vladimir] and his court", as well as "collected tribute from all dependent countries, and decided where and how much is to be paid". In the course of Vladimir's princedom, as in the times of his father and grandfather, the Varangians possessed great influence and occupied high state posts. However, the ruler of the Russian land on some occasions was already beginning to feel oppressed by their unreserved greed. And once, having sent the bulk of the Scandinavian druzhina to Byzantium (as mentioned above), the prince confidentially recommended that the emperor promptly dispose of them. (This is one of the first known acts of Russian secret diplomacy).

But the prince still allowed some Scandinavians to stay by him; he "chose among them the kind, the clever and the brave men, and gave them honors". Among those who were chosen and granted such high positions might have been Sigurd, son of Erik. Hence, the information provided by monk Od is apparently not unfounded.

If Sigurd was entrusted with such a wide range of judicial and administrative powers, then it is very likely that he was also involved in the activities of the secret services. In fact, Varangians are generally all depicted in the sagas as brave good men, almost always enjoying the favor and the affection of the Russian princes, making bright careers and gaining glorious reputations. Such was Olaf Tryggvason himself. Yet neither he nor the Icelander Bjorn (from the "Saga of Bjorn"), who allegedly won over Vladimir's brother and received his magic sword as a sign of favor, nor their brethren warriors, were characterized in the way Sigurd was; they are left in the memory of the skalds as generic druzhina leaders and excellent warriors.

Naturally, being experienced warriors, they knew many tricks for use in planning the battles or when reconnoitering the enemy. Olaf, for instance, when he came to England and was asked who he was and from where he hailed, answered that he came with his comrades from Gardarika (the country of cities — so the Scandinavians named Rus'), that he was a merchant, and that his name was Ali the Rich (!). But this does not prove that he passed through Dobrinya's "school" (or maybe it would have been Sigurd's. . .).

An Aside on Capturing a Good Man

If we are to believe the sagas, then Vladimir did not have any problems in terms of the intelligence support of state security, and in unearthing the secret schemes of his enemies, irrespective of whoever was at the head of those services. For, "Gardarika at that time had many prophets who knew much." However, those recruited from among the magi and the clairvoyants for service in the prince's "counter-intelligence," were not very successful.

On one occasion he was informed of the arrival in Rus' of "a famous man, although yet young". He was advised that this man's happiness would be so great, and "the halo over his head would be so bright, that this light would spread over the whole of Gardarika, and over the whole eastern part of the world". However, where he was from, this man, the prophets failed to tell.

Nevertheless, this information interested Princess Allogia, Vladimir's wife (who is already known to the readers), the "wisest of women" (some researchers identify her with the famous Rogneda). All this "struck her as very important", and she decided to make a kind of personal inquest. Allogia asked Vladimir to call all the inhabitants of Novgorod (for the events took place in that city) and nearby *volosts* to the *veche* to meet (in other words, they convoked an *althing*). When the Novgorodians gathered together, the princess ordered them to stand in a circle. "I want", she said, "to see everyone's face, and his appearance, especially his eyes; and I hope that I will know who owns this happiness, . . . it will be impossible to conceal who is he by nature". In the course of two days, Allogia wandered about the *althing*, scanning the eyes of her subjects, made happy (or maybe frightened) by such attention, but no one's eyes told her anything. On the third day, an angry Vladimir ordered that everybody outside be rounded up and brought to the *veche* assembly, so that no one could avoid it. And then the princess came upon a twelve-year-old boy, dressed in an old hat with a shabby overcoat hanging on his shoulders. "She looked into his eyes and at once understood that it was he who possessed such great happiness. She led him to the konung, and everybody understood that they faced the man that they had been looking for". Here is how at least one "famous man" from abroad was caught in the net.

He was, though, a good man, in spite of having committed a murder. (Would it be possible to catch a bad man by this means, also?) His name was Olaf Tryggvason (the saga named "Earthen Circle" suggests other circumstances under which "the glorious woman and famous princess" met Olaf).

The "Saga" of Malusha

According to the story of Od, Prince Vladimir, in his turn, listened attentively to the revelations of a prophetess who lived in his palace. She was already very old and feeble, and on every feast of Jole (a heathen feast which corresponds to Christmas) she ordered that she be carried to the chamber where Prince Vladimir sat at banquet with his druzhina and retinue. She was seated in the chair in front of the prince's "high seat". All present froze in anticipation, because she "foresaw much, and everything she said came to pass"; and also, because she was the mother of the sovereign. In fact, this was Malusha, alias Malfrida, and sister of Dobrinya. She was still alive and assisted Vladimir, with her not annoying care, at least in the early or even mid

990's AD, when the Church of the Tithe was under construction. According to the chronicles, she donated the church with her village of Budotino or Budutino, where she had once been exiled by Olga, and where Vladimir was born.

Respectfully (or maybe nervously?), the son would ask: "What do you see? Is there any threat or trouble that might endanger my land? Is there any inkling of a breach of peace or approaching danger? Are others plotting to seize my estate?"

As we can see, Vladimir placed very great faith in his mother's supernatural abilities. He relied on them to solve the global issues of statehood, to reveal and prevent any insidious schemes on the part of external (and maybe domestic) enemies. That is, he tried to use Malusha the prophet as the fairytale golden cockerel. In so doing, he was not in the least embarrassed by the presence of Dobrinya and his colleagues who might interpret such questions as openly expressed mistrust towards them or dissatisfaction with their service; unless, of course, Dobrinya had prompted his dear sister in advance on what she had to say.

Although it is not known how valuable were Malusha's insights in relation to state security, she responded once that: "I do not see anything, my son, in which I can foresee danger to you or your land, nor anything that would disturb your happiness, but I do see a great and pleasant sight. The Konung's son is born today in Norway, and he shall become a famous man and celebrated leader, and he shall not do harm to your land but shall give you much . . . And now carry me away, because I shall not speak more, enough has been told".

It appears that almost all the adults of Vladimir's family had a great craving for actions relating to intelligence and investigation. His uncle Dobrinya was professionally involved, his wife Allogia (Rogneda?) — was an amateur, his mother Malusha-Malfrida — was a clairvoyant. There were also some brief mentions in the bylinas that Dobrinya's mother, too, used to write letters to Prince Vladimir concerning affairs beyond the sphere of a woman's usual interests (in those tradition-bound days).

Then it would be natural to presume that the supreme ruler of the Kievan Empire did not himself stand aside from this exciting and beneficial passion, and that, of course, is not surprising — as such was the ancient tradition. Sun-Tse wrote: "In charge of all five categories of spies must necessarily be the sovereign himself". For example, Mithridates VI Eupator, tsar of Pontus, was a brilliant leader of secret services. Vladimir might not have donned a wig or fake beard as Hannibal once did, nor would he camouflage himself as an actor, like King Alfred of England.

The bylina about Stavr Godinovich gives us an image of the Russian prince dealing with "counter-espionage" but in a somewhat satirical manner. The plot of the bylina is this: Boyar Stavr Godinovich once, while sharing the festive table with Prince Vladimir, boasted either of his untold wealth (his estate was allegedly as vast as the city of Kiev), or of his young wife (bylinas tend to have many variants which sometimes vary greatly). When he was boasting about his young wife, he sometimes went too far in declaring, for instance, that she would deceive any prince-boyar, and as to Prince Vladimir, she would indeed drive him mad. Allegedly Stavr was not boasting for all to hear, but sharing his thoughts with a tipsy neighbor next to him at the table; still, the "loyal servants" turned out to be very keen and immediately reported everything to their boss. (Notice the eyes and the ears of prince's men at the palace — quite a detail!).

The princes-boyars at once began whispering to the angry Svyatoslavich to put Stavr into the cellar. "Let Stavr's young wife . . . deceive us, and drive Vladimir the Sun mad!" The collective counsel of the "princes-boyars" also describes the features of Prince Vladimir's ruling style: the prince of Kiev took decisions on various state issues only after discussing them with his senior druzhina escort (especially in the last years of his rule when Dobrinya was already off the stage). "Volodimir loved his druzhina", reads one chronicle, "and with them thought through the order of the land."

Prince Vladimir accepted the advice, and allegedly also sent envoy Prokofy or Dobrinya Nikitich with his comrades-at-arms to distrain and seal the estate of Stavr. But apparently Stavr, too, had a trusty man at the banquet, and that unfortunate boyar's wife Vasilisa (alias Vasilista, Catherina) Mikulishna (alias Vasilievna, Perekrasovna), had already taken measures. She managed to send the officials back empty-handed: she herself dressed up as a bogatyr, mounted her good horse, took her glaive and camped at the outskirts of Kiev with her druzhina, a force that had appeared from nowhere. Then the newly fledged bogatyr appeared before Vladimir.

Vladimir: "What horde are you from, what land are you from?"

Vasily Mikulich: "I am from the Lyakhovitsky land. Son of the Lyakhovitsky king".

The son of tsar-king (in other variants — the "stern envoy" from the Golden Horde, Golden, Politovian, Venetian land) announced that he had come to marry the princely daughter (niece), Evpraksia (Zabava, Lyubava Putiatichna), (or to collect the tribute due for thirty years). Vladimir agreed, but his daughter (or niece, a princess herself) noticed that something was wrong: judging from his build, his gait and his manners, the groom was rather like a woman — walking with a mincing gait, bringing the knees together when taking a seat etc. Vladimir did not believe this (his trusty counselors seem to have disappeared), but not wishing to make a fool of himself, decided to set up a test for the guest.

He invited him to bathe together in the sauna. Vasily Mikulich did not decline the offer. But while the prince was "throwing off" his clothes in a leisurely way and "preparing", the bogatyr was already "steamed". And when Vladimir, towel in hand (we may suppose), opened the door of the steam-room (readers may embellish the picture as they see fit; there are many variants), the groom was already fully dressed. "No time to waste lolling in the *banya*" — responded Vasily Mikulich, while the Red Sun earned his name by blushing.

Some fable-tellers have claimed that, on advice from his daughter, craftier than any man (which would explain why the trusty servitors appeared to be not needed), Vladimir had sent scouts in advance as stokers and sweat-room attendants. But they too failed to discern anything intriguing or questionable. The envoy behaved in a "warrior-like manner" — "threw off" his clothes with one hand, and "washed" with the other. In short, the Kievan "counter-espionage" team's first attempt to disrobe the impostor, executed at the highest level (indeed, in order to implement it, the prince had to dress himself, if we may say so, in the clothes of Adam prior to his being cast out of Eden), and apparently destined for success, resulted in a shameful fiasco.

The next plan, likewise quite subtle, already had less chance of succeeding. They decided to expose Vasily Mikulich by differentiating the imprints or indentations left on a feather-bed after a man and a woman had slept on it. If a man (especially a bogatyr) used the bed, then the feathers would be dented by the shoulders. And if a woman — the deepest indentation would be somewhat lower.

But the "stern envoy" turned out to be on his guard again. He lay with his legs at the head of bed! The next morning Vladimir personally inspected the "material evidence." Another version of the bylina relates that the prince even watched, through the keyhole, the guest sleeping with his legs on the pillow. And still he failed to tell the lower part of the body from the upper one. After such embarrassing failures, rudimentary tests like archery contests and wrestling contests looked like gestures of despair. All the more so as, according to Trophim Grigorievich Ryabinin, who related the bylina, all those events took place at the time when Ilya Muromets had not yet reached Kiev, and Dobrinya Nikitich could not stand in wrestling against even the younger daughter of Mikula Selyaninovich, Nastasia.

It is no wonder that Vasily Mikulich managed to "outshoot" and outfight everybody. Flying into a rage, the guest was near to beating up all the feeble *muzhiks* of Kiev, but Vladimir pleaded with him to desist, lest he impair the demographic statistics.

In other versions of the bylina, the prince arranges a chess match. He tells Vasily Mikulich:

> And now I give you a harder test:
> To challenge my players,
> at pawns, at chess.

The result is, of course, pathetic. Then Vladimir sits to play chess himself and receives a mate in three moves (a feat none of today's champions can replicate). Nothing to be done — Vladimir announces the bridal feast. In vain Zabava calls for him to listen to reason:

> Oh, my darling uncle, dear!
> Marry me not to this woman here!
> Do not make me a laughing stock,
> A fool for all Kiev to mock.

The feast was in full swing, and the groom began to mope. To liven him up, they decided to bring out Stavr from the "deep cellar", for he was very good at playing the *gusli*. "Vasilyushka" perked up at once, started "going to and fro" and "dancing", and then went "for a walk" with Stavr to the open field, to the "white tent". Once in the field, he set about testing the intellectual capacity of the disgraced boyar, by proposing to solve some very sharp-witted riddles (which contributed to making the bylina so popular). The riddles gave their teller away in a most transparent manner. However, Stavr either had sunken into a torpor while cooped up in the cellar, or was not a good guesser by nature. Or maybe Vasilisa played her role too well (which makes us understand the difficulties she caused to Vladimir and his investigative team — boyars-counselors, stokers, sweat-room attendants, etc.).

In brief, "the stern envoy" took perhaps even greater pains in throwing off her disguise than in assuming it. Then Stavr finally opened the prince's eyes, with the proper pride. "The Prince — the Sun — was ashamed". And such was the final disgraceful result of the intelligence operation (that the prince had controlled personally) to reveal the identity of the "stern envoy", son of a tsar-king.

Vasilisa Mikulishna — that was the kind of person the secret services of Kiev actually needed. What native talent, suitable to a high-ranking secret agent, was hidden in her! But that does not help explain how it can be that, in fact, Vasilisa was born one hundred years later than the events described in the bylina. (As a matter of fact, the chronicles mention the historic prototype of Stavr Godinovich, Novgorod *sotski* Stavr Gordyatinich, as a contemporary of Prince Vladimir Monomachus, who actually shut him up in 1118 together with some other boyars of Novgorod.) And thus, the chief merit of the bylina about Stavr or, to be more precise, about Vasilisa Mikulishna, may be its satirically colored image of Prince Vladimir Svyatoslavich.

As it is related by epic, i.e. folk memory, Prince Vladimir the Red Sun did not live too sweet a life, as some readers might have expected. Here is how he becomes horror-stricken by the whistling of Solovey the Brigand, brought to Kiev by Ilya.

> And Vladimir in the capital of Kiev,
> with staggering knees stands he,
> sheltering in marten coat stands he,
> And his sable hat already on the ground.

Or:

And at three the prince was lying lifeless.

Here is how he complains of the excesses committed by Idolishe in Kiev:

Oh, vile Idolishe lives off me,
Lives at my palaces of stone,
And all we provide, he eats and eats,
that Tatar will eat us out of house and home.

He sheds bitter, helpless tears after hearing news of the Tatar threats:

Vladimir-Prince fell into fear,
Reading the yarlyks, burst into tears.
Or:

Bitter, salty tears he cries,
With silken kerchief dabs his eyes. . .
In tears, he cannot say a word . . .

And finally, he finds out that the only bogatyr remaining in Kiev who is able to protect him — the inveterate drunkard Vasily Ignatiev, who sleeps in the tavern — is "drunk with green wine". The prince runs there:

And seized he his coat of marten-sable,
And pulled on his boots over feet still bare,
And to the tavern made his way
As fast as he was able.

Vladimir personally serves Vas'ka cup after cup of honey, to cool his coppers. If only "the proud heart of Vas'ya is washed", "the wild head of Vas'ya is cheered up". In another passage, the prince hastily rattles a bunch of keys by the doors of the cellar, where Ilya Muromets sits, long forgotten by him. Vladimir drops to his knees in front of him, prostrating himself three times, "bowing lower and lower". But Ilya does not even look at him ("What an old one, does not raise his eyes").

Of course, we face here not so much the portrait of the historic personality but, I think, that of the folk memory — which might have caught onto something real. Vladimir's image, related in chronicles and in "books" in general, is also not quite entirely heroic, or maybe not heroic at all. This is a far cry from Svyatoslav, who is like the classical

Achilles or Hector. By his temperament, Vladimir was very agile and impulsive. He was flexible in adapting himself to changing situations, reacted easily to different circumstances; and was ready to commit both "moral" and "immoral" actions (especially prior to the adoption of Christianity).

The apparent affinity to the weaker sex is organically inherent in the nature of such a person. It seems that Vladimir did not make any significant mark on the battlefield. I have already mentioned that once he escaped from the Pechenegs and took refuge under a bridge. This fact, although certainly not in itself a proof of cowardice, still does not contradict the bylina's image of the prince sheltering in a marten coat against the whistle of Solovei the Brigand.

However, as a politician, Vladimir was an outstanding person. Like Peter the Great and Catherine the Great, so many years later, he possessed two assets that are very valuable for a sovereign: a profound and wide-ranging mind, combined with the ability to gather talented people around himself. Still, the character of Vladimir is depicted by folklore in somewhat grotesque manner.

Chapter V

SVYATOPOLK, SON OF YAROPOLK, AND VLADIMIR'S HEIRS

1. Son or Stepson?

Since the times of Yaroslav the Wise and until the present day, there has been hardly a single man in Russia who does not know the name of Svyatopolk the Accursed. However, notoriety comes in all flavors, and not all of them are complimentary. But such considerations rarely stopped people from preferring fame of any kind to the gloom of oblivion.

Svyatopolk went down in history with the nickname of the Accursed for killing his three brothers — Boris, Gleb and Svyatoslav. Nevertheless, many historians, especially Ukrainian and Byelorussian, are inclined to belittle or even totally deny Svyatopolk's guilt, which our Russian grandparents did not doubt at all. For instance, they assert that it is a "myth" that "the guilt of Svyatopolk was of the same order as that of the grandsons of Yaroslav — Svyatopolk Iziaslavich and Vladimir Monomachus."

In his recently published book, N. F. Kotlyar states, "In the Primary Chronicle and the first Novgorod chronicle of the earliest events, one should not look for historically authentic descriptions of the struggle for power in Russia between Vladimir's offspring. Instead, the annals offer the church legend that blames the murder of Boris, Gleb and Svyatoslav Vladimirovich (Volodimerich) on Svyatopolk 'the Accursed';

meanwhile *The Chronicle* by Tietmar (bishop of Mersebourg, about 1018 AD) unambiguously testifies that Svyatopolk did *not* kill his cousins. Despite the legend of his awful crimes, Svyatopolk has been mentioned in one reference work and another. Is it possible that the majority of experts in old Russian history have not read Tietmar?"

It is surprising to see such a respected researcher straightforwardly contrasting one kind of historical interpretation to another. True, the annals are generally considered more trustworthy than the hagiographic sources, especially in their reconstruction of the actual outline of events. But such preference does not provide the slightest basis for treating "church legends" as incomplete historical documents. Only concrete analysis can determine how much any of them conforms to the truth.

As far as I can judge, nobody has succeeded in discrediting the anonymous Legend *of Boris and Gleb* or Nestor's *Reading* about them. Possibly, the first is based on the annals' material itself, and the second was created by the chronicler.

It does not at all follow, from the story in the *Chronicle* by Tietmar of Mersebourg, that Svyatopolk did not commit the crimes with which he is charged. The bishop simply does not say anything about it, probably due to ignorance. Further grounds for speculation are offered by *The Eimund Yarn*, which is comprised in the *Saga of Olav the Holy*, which narrates Yaroslav's murder of one of his brothers. But the inconsistency of the presentation does not allow for the reconstruction of any clear picture of the events that could be an alternative to the version of the "church legends". Let's go through all of this, step by step.

In June of 978 (or 980), Vladimir Svyatoslavich, who reaped the fruits of the betrayal committed by Bloud and of the murder of his own brother Yaropolk, was enthroned as King in Kiev. The winner not only came into possession of the throne of Kiev , but the widow of his unfortunate brother: a beautiful Greek woman whom Svyatoslav Igorevich had brought home from one of his campaigns and married to his elder son.

Soon Svyatopolk was born. Whose son was he? In historical reference books and indexes Svyatopolk has one of two patronymics: either Yaropolchich, or Vladimirovich (Volodimerich). However, it seems that the chroniclers and early biographers had no such problem. The *Legend of Boris and Gleb* — the literary monument of the late 11th century — narrates Svyatopolk's heritage with extreme clarity: "His mother had been a nun, and was born Greek. And she became the wife of Yaropolk, brother of Vladimir; she was defrocked for the beauty of her face. And he conceived by her Svyatopolk the Accursed. Vladimir, with the pagans, murdered Yaropolk and married his wife. . . She gave birth to this Accursed Svyatopolk who had two fathers, who were brothers. Vladimir did not love him — as if he were not his son". The story is almost the same, only a little more confused, in both The Primary Chronicle and Nestor's *Reading about Boris and Gleb*; other medieval compositions do not convey anything new.

Those who doubt the veracity of the story point to the fact that neither *The Legend* nor the annals was composed immediately after the events, and, most importantly, they are quite biased: for them, Svyatopolk is certainly the Accursed. But the charge would be valid only if Svyatopolk were not the cousin but the natural brother of the sons of Vladimir, killed by him; in that case he would be deprived of any moral excuse for the crimes committed. It is clear, however, that Vladimir himself was not blameless in the fratricide that followed his death. So, if the ancient writers could possibly be accused of anything, then, most likely, it would be their truthfulness. The accepted picture of the tribal symbol of Svyatopolk, by the way, also confirms this.

Vladimir must have known that Svyatopolk was not his son (he was probably born by the end of the year 978 or in early 979; or, similarly, in 980 or 981). He did not suspect, he was not plagued by doubts; he *knew*. This, apparently, fostered his attitude to his stepson: quiet and even-tempered, but not very friendly. Certainly, it was annoying that among his children there should be one who was "not by him". Maybe the very sight of the boy made him depressed, and recalled the murder of Yaropolk; especially if Svyatopolk resembled his father in appearance or habit. But generally speaking, Vladimir must have felt morally calm.

All this continued for some time. Svyatopolk was growing up. It became necessary to think of his future. Vladimir undoubtedly was worried by the death of his elder sons Vysheslav and Iziaslav. Now, Svyatopolk and Yaroslav became the most adult offspring in his large nest. It was clear that to make Svyatopolk his successor, the heir of supreme power, would mean the ruin of everything for which he had been struggling. I think that the Kievan prince, by transferring Yaroslav from

Rostov to Novgorod, hinted at his choice of successor — after all, Novgorod was the capital of his great-grandfather, the founder of the dynasty; it was the largest center of all the northwest region and the city from which he started his path to Kiev himself.

However, there are strong arguments for another assumption — that Vladimir's favorite son Boris was expected to succeed him. Svyatopolk should be kept out of sight, but not too far — it must be easy to keep an eye on him. And, when Vladimir sent Svyatopolk to Turov, or to Pinsk (we do not know exactly when it happened), Vladimir certainly did not forget to appoint agents to watch him.

Events progressed in this way, until all of a sudden the "German-Polish-Pecheneg card" came into play.

At the beginning of the year 1007, Bishop Bruno (Bonifacius) of Kwerfurt visited Kiev while he was traveling from Hungary to the Pecheneg steppe. At that time, he was one of numerous western missionaries infatuated with the idea of disseminating the gospel among the pagans. He did not succeed in Hungary (as King Stefan greeted the activity of the German emperor's political emissary with alarm). Now, the bishop intended to take revenge in the camps of the "wildest" nomads and barbarians. Vladimir received the visitor with great hospitality, entertained him for a whole month, and all this time in every possible way sought to discourage him from the dangerous and useless undertaking (". . . opposed my intention and bustled about me, as if I were one of those who voluntarily rush to die" — wrote Bruno to King Henry II).

Despite all the external deference, the behavior of the Kievan prince very much resembled the behavior of Stefan. Vladimir obviously did not want to allow Bruno to approach the Pechenegs. He fully realized that, after the Roman priests, would come German or Polish diplomats and councilors (as Bruno was connected with the ruler of Poland, Boleslav the Brave). It was better to deal with the steppe rulers face to face than to have them become vassals of close or distant neighbors who were strong enough even without this new support. Apparently, it was considerations such as these that made the prince's smile so good-natured, and his hospitality so obliging.

However the bishop, apparently, let it be understood that the complexity of the task did not deter him, and that he offered himself as an intermediary between "the Russian sovereign" — "famous for his power and wealth", radiant with virtues — and the nomadic barbarians, and would seek to persuade the latter to come to peace with Kiev.

This changed the situation. Vladimir was deeply touched. Besides, as the prince told his guest, he had a dream that frightened him very much — that in three days the young bishop would lose his head. For some reason it followed from this that the German preacher should leave Russia as soon as possible. The prince would hate to have this sad event happen on his land, which would implicate him indirectly. Therefore, he did not detain Bruno for another day but almost pushed him out, and he even decided to personally accompany him to the border — so that nobody would offend the great man on his way to the steppe. Besides, this would help keep the bishop from "straying" unnecessarily or giving rein to excessive curiosity. Who knows what secret instructions his powerful patrons must have given him?

When they approached the rampart, everyone dismounted and walked out through the gate. Vladimir, accompanied by his senior army staff (druzhina and host) went up a hill and, seeing that Bruno and his retinue were heading off, sent a boyar after them with such words: "I have accompanied you up to the place where my land ends and the unfriendly one begins. I ask you, for God's sake, not to lose your young life, to my dishonor. I know that tomorrow before three o'clock you will suffer a cruel death for no reason and no use at all". From this farewell speech (which seems to have been quite obscure, as recorded by Bruno, with one thesis contradicting another), it is only clear that the prince was concerned about the further destiny of the bishop. But what was the reason for such worry — was it Christian anxiety for a brother or more complex political considerations?

However, everything ended happily (for Vladimir). Bruno's missionary activity with the Pechenegs failed, just as it had with the Hungarians. He baptized only 30 people. But in five or six months' time the bishop returned to Russia, and he pleased the Kievan prince with the success of his peace initiative. The Pechenegs had nothing against good neighborly relations with Kiev, and to confirm the sincerity of Vladimir's intentions they suggested that he should send them a hostage (most likely, the talk was about an exchange of hostages). Bruno suggested Vladimir send them his son. Which one? Many researchers suppose that it was Svyatopolk.

Who else could be sent? The mission was important, and it meant traveling far away from the principality. Besides, the Pechenegs had once been friends with Yaropolk. His man — Variazhko — had launched many raids from there. That would mean that Svyatopolk would feel much easier with them than the other sons would, and one would hardly wish to put his own legitimate sons at risk. This might have been Vladimir's line of thinking, more or less, when he was making the decision. And, I do not exclude the possibility that the Kievan prince's decision could have been influenced by information that he must have been receiving from the agents assigned to his stepson. For, if Svyatopolk was sitting at that time in Turov, certainly he was not wasting his time. It is very probable that he was actively, although cautiously, establishing relations with the adjacent Poland. Or, with Czechia or with the hostile and reserved Polotsk. Vladimir would not want to allow that to happen under any circumstance. One may suppose that, sending an ambassador or a courier after the stepson, he would have given instructions to deliver Svyatopolk to Kiev by all means, and if necessary, by resorting to assistance from the Kiev "diaspora". But it seems to me that everything happened in a totally different way, the way that Vladimir and his councilors were afraid it would.

2. The Shadow of Yaropolk

Whether the Kievan prince had told the young Svyatopolk about his true father or not, we will never know. However, it must have been impossible to keep such a "state secret" from the interested person. And Svyatopolk would sooner or later come to hear about it.

Besides, one should remember that the desire for revenge, for a congener, was not perceived as shameful in early medieval society. Its moral lawfulness was certified in the very first article of the most ancient written monument of Old Russian law that is known to us — Yaroslav the Wise' *The Russian Truth* : a brother avenges his brother, a son avenges his father, a father avenges his son; this law applies also to nephews. Only when there is no close kin capable of such an act is the issue decided by a large penalty.

Vladimir, at least formally, had taken revenge on Yaropolk for the loss of his close relation — his brother Oleg. And actually, in murdering his brother Yaropolk, he was only implementing the moral precept of the common law and restoring justice, since Yaropolk had killed their brother, Oleg. However, Svyatopolk could object that, in the first place, Oleg Svyatoslavich himself had committed a murder (of Lute Sveneldich). Therefore Sveneld, his victim's father, had the right to demand revenge from Yaropolk. Secondly, Yaropolk never killed his brother. Oleg actually died incidentally at the end of the combat near Vruchiy (Ovruch). When the body was found, Yaropolk was crying over Oleg's body and reproaching Sveneld for what had happened. I do not know whether it is possible to find anyone entirely innocent or entirely guilty in this knot of crimes. But it seems clear to me that Svyatopolk's subsequent actions resulted from these events and were not the actions of a pathological maniac. The huge shadow of Yaropolk, the shadow cast onto posterity, covers the Russian land. This punishment "sanctioned by God" and redemption through the blood of innocent people were only to be expected.

Having gathered Turov (or Pinsk) under his reign, Svyatopolk apparently organized vigorous covert activities. His nearest neighbor to the west was Boleslav the Brave, ruler of Poland. It was to him, I think, that Svyatopolk's secret ambassadors rushed in the first place. What could Yaropolk's son want this time? What was he counting on?

Historians already long ago came up with the idea that Svyatopolk was aiming to separate his principality from the eastern Slavic federation and make it independent. Or semi-independent, at least, under the temporary protectorate of Poland. Svyatopolk certainly understood that he would have to pay tribute to his ally. Boleslav, for his part, as further developments show, had nothing against establishing closer relations with Turov and achieving closer political infiltration to Russia. Poland had already established — maybe with the help of bishop Bruno (Bonifacius) — preliminary relations with the Pechenegs, a quite enviable perspective in the East. Therefore, Svyatopolk's diplomatic forays should have met with Boleslav's most favorable response.

However, the Polish prince was very busy, even without Russia. The war with the German king came at high costs in every respect, and Svyatopolk may have understood that he could not count on Boleslav's military help. It is not known whether he tried to establish friendly relations with anybody else — for example, with the Czechs or with Polotsk. But if he tried, it appears that he did not meet with success.

And then (or maybe much earlier) the eyes of the Turov prince himself turned towards the southeast, to the Pechenegs. His father's past connections with them could not have been a secret. I am convinced of one thing: Svyatopolk tried to establish ties with the Pechenegs, and he achieved that.

Vladimir and his advisors made a big mistake in calling Svyatopolk to Kiev and sending him to the Pechenegs. (Apparently, Vladimir's secret services were not at their strongest at this juncture. Malousha, Vladimir's mother and his prophet, had died. Dobrynia had left the scene, too.)

Looking after the departing stepson and his finely garbed retinue and waving them good-bye, Vladimir did not suspect that he was blessing the first of the great series of tragedies, which nearly eliminated his dynasty. Svyatopolk most likely had won the first round of confrontation between the two secret services.

3. Fortune Smiles on Svyatopolk

Only one man — Tietmar, Bishop of Mersebourg — narrated the important events that followed. He wrote the chronicle of events in Europe during his era, events that were of interest to the politicians of the Holy Roman Empire of the German nation. And Kievan Russia swung into the orbit of his attention.

As Tietmar says, dramatic changes in Svyatopolk's life came with his marriage to the youngest of Boleslav I's numerous daughters. This dynastic marriage apparently was seen as necessary by all the three parties who agreed upon it: the bridegroom himself, his uncle and the future father-in-law. Although, of course, each one had different and to some extent contradictory interests. Vladimir and Boleslav saw this step as an effort to consolidate the peace between them, while fully realizing its fragility. That is why, one should think, they secretly must have been sharpening their swords. Both of them had to be interested, for example, in the fate of the "Cherven' towns" — important trade centers that had been captured by Vladimir.

In Svyatopolk Poland potentially obtained an ally, and through him — the "legal" justification to interfere in the internal affairs of the huge Slavic state to the east. And Svyatopolk, having established connections with the Pechenegs, and having gained the friendship of Boleslav, could hope to shed the heavy guardianship of his uncle and become an independent governor in Turov. And when his uncle eventually died, it would be possible, with God's and the Poles' help, to claim his rights to Kiev. His Polish father-in-law would support his claim. It was under approximately these circumstances and with these political ambitions and expectations in mind, I think, that events unfolded.

As far as one can understand Tietmar, the leading role in the marital negotiations was played by Vladimir. Things developed as follows. The bride, Boleslavna, with her entourage and confessor — Reinbern, Bishop of Kolobzheg — arrived in Russia. Then (but it is not clear, how much later) Vladimir, as Tietmar informs us, "having heard that his own son, in secret with Boleslav, was preparing a revolt against him, jailed him with his wife and Reinbern in separate cells". Such a thunderbolt out of the seemingly blue sky!

Clearly, Kiev's reconnaissance was on alert. And judging from the fact that not only Svyatopolk himself, but his wife and a representative of the Roman church who accompanied her, were arrested, Vladimir and his secret service obviously suspected an international plot. The Kievan prince would have hardly taken such a step without good reason, knowing the foreign policy complications it could (and did!) bring.

What Boleslav and Svyatopolk could wish, generally, we have understood. But one can't help noticing the rapt attention that Tietmar exhibited towards the figure of the bishop Reinbern. He barely mentioned Svyatopolk and Boleslavna, but he dedicated an extensive (albeit rather vague) panegyric to one of the archbishops of the Polish Church. Reinbern, apparently, was a compatriot of the bishop of Mersebourg. They were also political and spiritual cognates. (Although the separation of the Churches had not yet taken place, the opposition between Rome and Constantinople was already far enough advanced so that the two principal Christian centers were spiritually hostile to each other.)

About Reinbern, Tietmar writes that in prison "the venerable father was secretly working over what he could not do openly (as we may understand, he subjected himself to wearisome fasting and prepared himself for his reunion with God). When, thanks to continuous humble prayers emanating from a sincere and grieving heart, his sacrifice reconciled him with the Supreme Being, and he was freed from the tight prison of his body, with joy he passed to the freedom of eternal glory". Simply put, Reinbern died in prison. "In heavenly bliss, the bishop with a smile meets the threats of the impious man and, being sure of his righteousness, impassively looks on the vindictive anger of the voluptuary — for, by the testimony of our teacher St. Paul, God condemns adulterers". The "impious man" and "adulterer" is, certainly, Vladimir. He probably interrogated "the venerable father" himself but, according to the opinion passed on by Tietmar, he did not get anything out of Reinbern, got mad, and kept threatening him even after his death.

How to explain such an attitude toward Reinbern on the part of the Kievan prince? He probably considered him to be the central figure in the plot, while Svyatopolk was only a pawn in the hands of this artful and treacherous neighbor. Probably, this followed from the evidence that Svyatopolk and his wife gave; the determination and the fanaticism with which Reinbern resisted him only reinforced this version.

Tietmar writes that the bishop of Kolobzheg was an educated person, and he was ordained on his merits, that is, he was a zealous missionary. Tietmar also says that Reinbern "has ruined the pagan temples and, having thrown off the four rocks, has cultivated new sprouts on the fruitless tree in the name of the almighty God, that he has planted the holy Gospel in very coarse people". Where Reinbern performed this missionary feat — whether in Kolobzheg's diocese or in the lands around Turov and Pinsk, is not clear. If we do not carp at the word "sea", as mentioned by Tietmar, the last version is not excluded. Especially when taken together with the suggestion that: "exhausting his body by continuous fasting and vigil", "Reinbern has turned his heart to contemplation of the divine sight" (that is, probably, he was admiring the fruits of his labor); Tietmar immediately focuses on Vladimir. Did Reinbern really attempted to rebaptize the country that had been already christened? Vladimir might have had every right to apply sanctions to him.

This version is supported by Reinbern's conduct during his investigation, his ecstatic self-conviction of securing martyrdom, and the substantial power obtained by Boleslav from the Emperor Otto III in the year 1000.

In the words of the *Chronicle of Gall the Anonymous*, the head of the Holy Roman Empire, Pope Silvester, sanctioned such missionary action. It says: "By his power and by the power of his successors . . . provided him [Reinbern] with authority in church affairs in the Polish kingdom and in other barbaric countries, which were conquered or were to be conquered; the pope Silvester, by the privilege of the Roman

Church, confirmed the essence of this agreement".

"Conquered or were to be conquered" — who knows how these words would be interpreted by Boleslav and Reinbern!

Understandably, Vladimir would also have an opinion based on what else he knew about the plans of Rome and its allies. It was not in vain that he held very long and cordial conversations with the no less venerable Father Bruno. It may be assumed that after Father Bruno's departure and his second visit to Kiev, during the same year of 1007, the prince, with his superior retinue, held important conferences where the information received by the head of the state and his immediate assistants was discussed.

Vladimir was apparently beginning to suspect that his stepson had become a toy in the hands of the secular and the spiritual rulers of Europe. This thought is also raised by one curious fact in Svyatopolk's biography: his Christian name, as seen on his coins — Peter — was borrowed from the patron saint of the Roman Church. Certainly, he could have received this name when he was baptized as a child. Or, is it possible that Svyatopolk had undergone a second christening?

One way or another, Vladimir and his security people correctly suspected the main thrust of the intrigue. The trail led to the West. And the charge against the three prisoners of Kiev — if formulated in modern terms — would sound approximately like this: organization or participation in criminal conspiracy with foreign and domestic forces hostile to Kievan Russia with the purpose of violating its state sovereignty and territorial integrity by means of propagation of an alien ideology, and preparation of an armed uprising against the legal power.

As historians have suggested, Boleslav's youngest daughter reached marriageable age by the year 1012. This is the year most frequently cited as the time of her wedding celebration. In 1013, the Russian-Polish war broke out. Boleslav managed to conclude a short-lived piece with the empire, and "then", as Tietmar informs us, "with our help, he made haste toward Russia and devastated a considerable part of the country". Old Polish historians supposed that Boleslav either attempted to relieve those who were imprisoned, or revenged them. And indeed, Tietmar, narrating about Reinbern's death and Vladimir's powerless rage, concluded: "Boleslav, learning all this, took as much revenge as he could". Even so, the Polish prince launched his warfare only after having secured himself in the West and having found allies — including, by the way, the Pechenegs (courted by Bruno and probably brought into the alliance by Svyatopolk himself)!

In the Russian sources, however, the war of 1013 and the events connected with the arrest of Svyatopolk have left barely a trace. Coming to power in Kiev in 1015, Svyatopolk himself probably took measures to eliminate any reference from the prince's annals that could defile him in the eyes of his descendants. By no mere coincidence, the lacuna in the Kiev chronicle starts in the year 998, when Svyatopolk was 20 (or 18) years old — quite an appropriate age for one's first open conflict with his stepfather.

We know all this thanks to Tietmar. Certainly, in the Russian chronicles the events must have been described in far greater detail. In a word, Svyatopolk had his reasons to withhold one and a half decades of history from the memory of the following generations, whereas Yaroslav, who replaced him as Grand Prince, most likely did not have such reasons. (Indeed, concerning the war, not every trace was eradicated, as proven by a hint found in the Ipatiev chronicle under the year 1229. In his recitation of Prince Daniila Romanovich Galitskiy's participation in the intestine war in Poland and in the victorious end of the campaign, the chronicler proudly observes that "no other [Russian] prince would have ventured so deep into the Ladskou land — except Volodimer the Great, for he had christened the land". As we can see, not every reference to the Russian-Polish war of 1012-1013 had been completely expunged from the memory of Russian writers. It probably survived in one of the local chronicle traditions — and in Rus', of course, the story was interpreted very differently than on the other side of the border.

Apparently, Svyatopolk planned to rewrite the past, in due course, in a light more favorable to him; but he had no time. As a result, he has deprived future historians of the possibility of verifying the rather fuzzy narration by Tietmar. From his remark that Boleslav, having learnt what had taken place, "went on taking revenge, as far as he could", one cannot conclude that we are looking at a "single-act" military action. When the Bishop of Mersebourg started his story about Boleslav's campaign against the capital of the Russian state, after Vladimir's death in 1018, he would say, beforehand: "The strongly fortified city of Kiev suffered from frequent attacks by the Pechenegs, prompted by Boleslav."

From frequent attacks! Is that what it means — "revenged, as far as he could"? Then the chain of events lines up differently: in the beginning there was a war, for example, because of the Cherven' towns. The peace agreement was sealed by the dynastic marriage; probably already in 1014. At any rate, V. N. Tatishchev has suggested that in that same year the "ambassadors of Boleslav Lyadski came to Vladimir; with them there were Czech and Ugric ambassadors, to ask about peace and love; and they asked his daughters. He promised Boleslav to marry his elder daughter to the Czech, another — whom he loved very much — to the Ugric, and promised to gather them, come spring, in Vladimir-Volynsk". If this was sometime around April or May of the same year, 1014, and if the "forum" was indeed held, then they could have agreed about Svyatopolk and Boleslavna then. The ambassadors came with "peace and love," i.e., ending the state of war between Russia and Poland was a necessary first step (and so, therefore, the Kiev negotiations marked the very first probing initiatives of the parties which had been hostile until then). Almost immediately after this, only a few months later, the dramatic events took place as narrated by Tietmar of Merse-bourg.

Such a sequence seems to me more probable.

How much time the disgraced prince spent in jail, we do not know. The Lives of Boris and Gleb and an article on the year 6523 (1015) in the Kiev annals inform us, at any rate, that by the end of Vladimir's life (he died on July 15, 1015), Svyatopolk was in Kiev, but not in jail. And Tietmar writes that Vladimir "died under the burden of his days, leaving the inheritance completely to his two sons; the third one had been in prison, from which he then escaped and, leaving his wife there, ran to his father-in-law".

So, Svyatopolk was released from custody. But when and under what circumstances? Was it under Vladimir, or already during the internecine wars, as we understand from Tietmar's story? And, what is concealed behind those events? Some compromise, forgiveness, or simply a successful escape, as the bishop of Mersebourg writes?

Preference should be given unconditionally to the Russian sources. Otherwise, according to Tietmar it would appear as though Svyatopolk did not participate in any political events in Russia from the moment of his arrest (late in 1014 or early in 1015) until his return with Polish, Saxon and Pecheneg troops in 1018. ("The city of Kiev received Boleslav and his liegeman Svyatopolk, who had been absent for a long time . . ." we read in *The Chronicle*. "Abandoned by its prince, on August 4 it accepted Boleslav and Svyatopolk who was in exile for a long time . . .") — and that is completely wrong.

Probably Tietmar was poorly informed about what took place on the Russian land, and he considered the appearance of Svyatopolk in Poland to be an escape from the prison after he lost the battle (by the end of 1015) near Lubech.

But the Turov prince was set free when Vladimir was still alive, and, in all probability, by Vladimir himself! Why? Some authors think that Svyatopolk's release was one of the results of the Russian-Polish war of 1013, a consequence of a political deal between Boleslav and Vladimir. After that, Svyatopolk's position at the Kiev court presumably changed drastically, and he became either the first assistant to, or the guardian of Russia's ailing sovereign.

I do not see the slightest basis for such conclusions. We do not know any facts about Svyatopolk's rising fortunes. Leaving him in Kiev or in the nearby Vyshgorod in fact allows for different interpretations. For example — reluctance to let the cognate, who has discredited himself, out of one's sight.

Let's review. The old prince handed over his armed forces to his son Boris. He sent them against the Pechenegs. If Svyatopolk had been their hostage for some time, he knew their customs better and would have had better chances to come to a peace settlement. But evidently Vladimir did not trust his stepson. And maybe, he was still holding him in prison.

I rather believe that Vladimir might have let Svyatopolk out only during his final illness, to relieve his soul. Such a motive for releasing a prisoner seems very probable to me.

4. "Poutsha's Lads"

A new plot was being cooked up in Vyshgorod, during the pleasant summer days of 1015, in feverish haste as dictated by developing events. Apart from Svyatopolk, its participants were the boyars of Vyshgorod, headed by Poutsha. Poutsha's close buddies — "Poutsha's Lads ("chad")" — are even known by name (from the story about their attempt on the life of Prince Boris): they were Talets, Yelovich, and Lyashko. The nickname Talets probably hints at an etymology from "tal" —

"hostage", and Russia was frequently swapping hostages with the Pechenegs. He seems not to have been an obscure figure in Svyatopolk's camp. And, in the story about the murder of Prince Gleb, there appears a certain "Accursed Goryaser" (it's hard to say who that might be: is it a specific name or the nominal identification of some devil incarnate?); under his command were "sent from Svyatopolk his malicious servants, merciless blood-suckers, cruel fratricides, furious beasts who took the soul away".

So, in Vyshgorod, apparently, Svyatopolk's secret service and punitive agents started to get organized — these are indispensable arms for any force vying for power. Probably it was with the help of Poutsha and his men that Svyatopolk vigilantly monitored affairs in the capital and the prince's village of Berestov, where Vladimir was lying ill. So that at the necessary moment, they were ready to appear at the center of state affairs, not simply waiting but actively preparing for the hour.

Where was Svyatopolk on July 15 — the day of Vladimir's death? The *Lives of Boris and Gleb* and the annals give different answers to this question. According to the annals, Svyatopolk was in Berestov. Does it make a big difference? Yes, it does. In accordance with the *Lives*, it appears that Svyatopolk "concealed" Vladimir's death, so he was master of the situation; he was in charge and, apparently, by then he was already fully forgiven by Vladimir. And here we are not far from the supposition that "Svyatopolk was Vladimir's regent", etc.. Certainly, this is difficult to believe. However, it is possible to recognize as quite pertinent and even indispensable the fact that the dying prince would summon the disgraced nephew for a Christian farewell.

But why were there none of Vladimir's own sons in Kiev at this time, as it seems? (With the exception, perhaps, of Gleb?)

Let's assume that, at the time, Vladimir was at war with Yaropolk. Boris was out on the Pecheneg campaign. But Mstislav and the others? Svyatoslav, Gleb, Sudislav? Why not send some good men to bring them back home? Doesn't it seem that the great prince Vladimir did not yet feel the need for such a family reunion? Or that he hoped to overcome his illness? Is this the reason that he did not give any instructions as to the inheritance of the throne? None of the characters of the tragedy that followed made any statement about an oral will; none appealed to any written testament from Vladimir. The Western chronicler Tietmar of Mersebourg, as we remember, relates something about the two sons of Vladimir as the heirs, but there is no mention of this in the Russian sources. Or, was Vladimir's illness sudden and fatal?

It seems that Nestor knew best of all how it happened. He wrote (in *The Reading about Boris and Gleb*) that Svyatopolk, having heard what happened in Berestov, mounted his horse and "soon came to the city of Kiev". This would mean that Svyatopolk was waiting for the information at his "headquarters" in Vyshgorod and came to learn about the prince's death in spite of the attempts of Vladimir's boyars, who did not want Svyatopolk to be the first to learn about this important fact. Svyatopolk, however, had his information channels and was not slow in making his appearance in Kiev.

Viewed through such a lens, the situation can be easily understood. Having the good fortune to find himself the only one of all the claimants to the throne who was in the right place at the right time, the Vyshgorod exile must have seen immediately what he had to do — and in what sequence — to achieve his goal. Having ascertained — apparently through his well-wishers and his paid agents — that the old prince had left no clear orders about the throne, he understood that this condemned him to vying with most, if not all, of Vladimir's natural sons.

The most menacing and dangerous rivals were three: Yaroslav, Mstislav and Boris. Yaroslav was far away. Sending hired assassins to eliminate the Novgorod prince was practically unachievable. That meant that the dispute with him would have to be decided by military strength, which Svyatopolk still lacked. Mstislav was far away, too — in Tmutorakan'. Between him and Svyatopolk lay the Pecheneg steppes, a reliable barrier. Svyatopolk would take care to make it even more reliable.

Now, for Boris. Under his command were the prince's host and the home guard. With the support of such a powerful force and, along with that, the support of Kiev's citizens, he could seize power at any moment. This was the greatest hazard. And so Svyatopolk rushed at full speed to Vyshgorod, to Poutsha and his lads: "Tell me truly, whether you are faithful to me?" Hearing the desired response, the son of Yaropolk (according to "The Legend, Passion and Praise of Saints Boris and Gleb") nevertheless forbears to give at once the deadly order commanding the destruction "of all the heirs", so that he himself can "take all the power". For some time he is still emotionally ripening.

But another version is also possible: Svyatopolk had mapped out his action plan even before "D-Day." How long before? Nestor, in *The Reading about Boris and Gleb*, writes that Vladimir called his son Boris to Kiev, "having learnt" of the treacherous intentions of Svyatopolk. It is possible that Svyatopolk was already charged with plotting against Boris (and the other Volodimerichi — offspring of Vladimir) during his arrest in 1013 or 1014.

I have to admit that the Pechenegs' attack on Russia in 1015 (or the wildfire rumors about it) may have been provoked by Svyatopolk as part of his plans in preparation for the coup d'état. There is nothing improbable in the notion that someone among his agents managed to reach the steppe koshes (camps), extend courteous greetings from the son-in-law of the ruler of Poland and, calling to mind the old friendship, persuade them to mount at least a small military demonstration near the Kiev borders.

What could Svyatopolk count on, in that case? Probably, that he would be entrusted to lead the troops against the Pechenegs. And, as head of the integrated Russian-Pecheneg army, he would be able to dictate his conditions to both the ailing Vladimir, and the more so, to the inexperienced Boris. If Boris were to head the army (and this was exactly what happened), then Svyatopolk could take this occasion to recover his influence with the prince and establish relations with Kiev's populace.

One way or another, Svyatopolk's "golden cockerels" did not lose sight of Boris — judging by the fact that Yaropolk's son not only knew very well how the campaign was going, but was also aware of the exact location of the young prince. Either Svyatopolk had people in the army that set out, or he received the requisite information in a timely way from the Kiev "military office". And this once again confirms that Boris, in Svyatopolk's eyes, was the nearest and the greatest obstacle to his accession to the throne.

The murder of Boris was prepared and carried out hastily, which demonstrates the lack of the necessary skills among those who organized and those who executed the plan.

First, if we take the Russian sources' words for it, Svyatopolk's intention to resort to political assassination could not be kept secret from his opponents in Kiev (who, certainly, constantly kept an eye on the frugal competitor for the throne). And among them, apparently, were professionals from the former security service who did not wish to link their fate to Yaropolk's unpredictable descendant. Boris, according to *The Legend, Passion and Praise,* by an anonymous author, knew about Svyatopolk's plans long before an actual attempt was made to implement them. On the way back from the campaign against the Pechenegs, Boris received a messenger who had information about the events that had taken place in Kiev. (He "told him about the death of his father, how his father Basil (?) died . . . , and how Svyatopolk concealed the death of the father . . ."). So he was already reflecting upon his own fate: ". . . He did not know whom to trust . . . His brother? But he is so interested in mundane vanity and thinks to murder me. And if he spills my blood and endeavors to kill me, I will be a martyr to my Lord. . ." This must have been Boris's "inner thought" as he "was going to his brother".

Boris was uncertain of his moral strength; he doubted whether he would be tough enough to resist the temptations that were awaiting him in Kiev. There were so many people who wished to see only him on his father's throne! — "If I go to the house of my father, many people will harden my heart and will coax me to turn my brother out; just as my father did before the holy christening, for the sake of glory and of his princedom in this world . . ." Fear of committing a great unforgivable sin forced the young prince to reflect in indecision and to recall again Svyatopolk's intentions: "I know they are gladdened by the intended evil, and urge my brother to kill me." So, Boris understood clearly what lay in store for him after his father's death — long before he received open warnings.

And such open warning came right on the eve of the murderous act. (The first messenger had not communicated anything about the new Kievan prince's plans against him.) This, apparently, is confirmed by Nestor's story about Vladimir's removing Boris from the principality to Kiev, to spare him from the brewing attempt on his life. At least, we do not have any other data that might point to the sources of knowledge available to the favorite of the old prince (and to many Kiev dwellers). However, the nature of that knowledge makes one feel uncomfortable.

Boris refers to some "people, who are glad about the evil prepared", who stir up and "force" the elder brother against him, as though partially justifying Svyatopolk and reconciling himself with him. In the literary cycle about Boris and Gleb, it is impossible to find any other similar expression; perhaps that is because it is not consistent with the context of an expressly accusatory anti-Svyatopolk sermon. Meanwhile, the writer of *The Legend* incidentally leaked a rather significant fact — the formation around Svyatopolk of a party which was highly influential by its structure and by the quantity of the participants. Its existence around the active rival for the Kiev throne can hardly be doubted. With the help of none but Poutsha's lads, Svyatopolk would have achieved nothing. For those were not "birds that fly so high".

It is an unknown bibliophile who provided, on behalf of Boris, the indication that somebody else and not this honest company is meant; that "people who were glad about the evil" had the right to "force" the former appanage prince — whereas Svyatopolk himself forced "Poutsha's lads". Therefore, "the Vyshgorod boyartsy" comprised only the circle of Svyatopolk's closest agents, and they were supported by a significant part of the Kiev and, maybe, of the Turov aristocracy — those who wished to see a rapprochement with Poland, and with the West and with the Roman Church in general. In particular, apart from the above-mentioned Wolf's Tale, we presumptively can name Anastasius the Tithe, bearing in mind his future feats.

We should not exclude the possibility that Polish agents in Kiev and in other Russian cities might have increased the number of Svyatopolk's supporters to some extent. This is the sort of comment that suggests itself to Boris's speculations! However, this is not directly connected to the subject at hand.

According to *The Legend*, Boris got the warning, but only once. An anonymous author writes ("There was a message for him about his murder") in the context of the tale about the events of the evening and night of Saturday, July 23, 1015. Boris was left alone, without any soldiers, with only several boys and the priest, and, calling to mind the images of ancient martyrs who perished at the hand of their congeners, in tears and grief he prepared himself for the inevitable.

According to Nestor, this all happened somewhat differently. Despite his own story about the measures Vladimir had taken beforehand against Svyatopolk's encroachments, he assures us that neither Boris nor Gleb "ever knew" about the villainous intentions of their elder brother. Returning from the campaign and having learnt from the Kiev messenger about the events already known to the readers, he prayed for his father and "rejoiced" over the nascent princedom of Svyatopolk, hoping that he would replace his late father. And when, after this, a messenger from Svyatopolk came to him in a great hurry with honey-sweet speeches (in *The Legend*, they sounded like this: "I wish to be on friendly terms with you and will treat you as everything else that has been given by the father"). His "flattery" was apparently taken in good faith. At all events, Nestor points out: "The blessed (Boris), who came to the brother, did not guess that Svyatopolk was conceiving something against him". However, the first disturbing signal soon came (how soon, *The Reading* does not say, but we should keep in mind that the period that elapsed from Vladimir's death — July 15 — until Boris's death — July, 24 — is nine days). But it came only to the ears, and not the mind, of the prince. "And these people came to the Blessed, saying that his brother wanted to kill him. The Blessed did not believe them, answering: 'How can this be true, do you not know that, being the younger brother, I do not oppose my brother who is older?'" But in two days' time the messengers appeared again, and informed the prince of "all that had happened, and how his brother, Saint Gleb, had run away". Only then did the prince understand and make his decision: not to oppose his brother, and not to run away from him, but to stay in his place or go to Kiev, hoping that Svyatopolk would change his mind.

When Boris told his 8,000 soldiers of his decision, they answered that Vladimir had passed him over to them and them to him. With him or without him, they would go to Kiev, expel the usurper and enthrone their master. But Boris refused such help point-blank, coaxing the select Kievan troops — Vladimir's senior host and other warriors — to peacefully go "back to their homes". And "I," said he, "will prostrate myself before my brother: and he will have mercy on me, when he sees me; he will not order me killed". "And, having kissed everybody", he let them go. According to *The Legend*, it was even simpler than that. Having found out that Boris was not going to fight, the soldiers went away. Both sources seem to agree that this took place on Friday.

Nestor says that, having parted with his troops, the prince continued to stay in his own place, because he had sent one of his lads to his brother with the entreaty. But Svyatopolk "seized the lad and detained him" as he had sent already the assassins to Boris and, maybe, was afraid that the returning messenger would interfere with the course of events. "The Blessed", continues Nestor, "seeing that his lad was not coming back to him, got up and went to his brother. And there was a man coming towards him, who told him that his brother had sent people to kill him. And that they were already coming soon". It was the third warning by one of the young prince's friends in Kiev, whose name is unknown to us.

I admittedly can name only one of Boris's high-ranking well-wishers — his sister Predslava. Proceeding from the assumption that it was she who later narrated everything that had taken place, from Kiev to the faraway banks of the Volkhov River (Novgorod) — to Yaroslav, — and that it was she to whom Boris's only surviving servant (Moisey Ugrin) ran — the brother of his favorite George, according to the Pechory monk Policarp (13th century). But the prince had no means of defending himself. Having prayed to God to "deliver" him from the fury of those who were moving against him, Boris ordered that his tent be erected; he went into it and resumed his prayers. This happened on Saturday.

Svyatopolk had an eye on his cousin, not too overtly, but very closely and firmly. He undoubtedly knew those who wished Boris well in Kiev, too. And if he could not prevent their secret communications with his greatest rival, then he took measures to neutralize the possible consequences. Svyatopolk's personal ambassador followed in the footsteps of Predslava's messengers (or those of some other Kiev grandee.) According to Nestor's *Reading*, this ambassador was sent not so much with the intention of ensnaring the prince-pretender in a cobweb of false promises or to disorient him (Nestor only in passing mentions his master's speech, or a letter handed over by the ambassador), but with the purpose of ascertaining his intentions. "Ruthless was he, and he sent a man with flattery to the Blessed, although he heard him speaking; but he did not have mercy on his brother." And he either left for Vyshgorod, or called his "adviser in all things evil and the head of all lies" to the capital. And he "opened" says *The Tale*, "his foul mouth, and uttered the evil words to Poutsha's lads: 'Since you have promised to give your lives for me, be my friends, and seize my brother Boris; choose a convenient time and kill him.'" "'And swear to do so'".

According to Nestor, Svyatopolk "selected violent men, sent them against the blessed Boris, and instructed them: 'Attack him at night, destroy him, and if anybody opposes you, destroy those together with him'".

Svyatopolk's agents were distinguished by diligence and patience.

They apparently kept close watch over what was going on in Boris's camp, waited for their hour, and when he was left without his soldiers they dared to attack the prince and his "lads".

Poutsha, Talets, Yelovich, Lyashko and their assistants did it.

At least on the miniatures of the illuminated manuscript of *The Saga* ("Sylvester Collection", 14th century), and on the hagiographic icons, the whole host is depicted, in armor, and appears to be strong enough to fight all of Boris's troops. At night, Svyatopolk's people surrounded Boris's and his boys' tents on the Alta River. And, obviously being fully confident of success, they behaved carelessly, making a lot of noise and not bothering with any disguises. According to *The Saga*, Boris "having heard some sinister whisper around the tent, trembled. And then he suddenly saw them running to the tent, saw the glistening weapons and swords being drawn". Nestor, in *The Reading*, expresses himself more sharply: "And here they came, growling like wild animals, eager to swallow the righteous man. The Blessed heard them approaching. But the impious ones, when they came up, did not dare to attack the righteous man: God did not allow them to, before the Morning Prayer". Only after that, "as the prince lay down on his bed and called the murderers himself ("Come in, brothers, fulfill the will of the one who sent you"), "like wild animals they attacked him and thrust their spears into him."

In *The Tale* there is no such mystical interpretation of the tragedy. It simply narrates that after "the swords were drawn" "without mercy, the fair and gracious body of Boris, the saint and blessed martyr of God, was pierced with spears by the accursed Poutsha, Talets, Yelovich, Lyashko". The Primary Chronicle, which generally gives a plot similar to that in *The Saga*, almost like *The Reading*, states that the killers, headed by Poutsha, attacked Boris "like wild animals near the tent," after the prince, who had finished his prayer, "was lying in his bed".

The boys were a contrasting background to this noisy and horrifying sight. Quite a number of them had remained near the prince. "People kept silent," as in Pushkin's "Boris Godunov", though with all their souls they sympathized with the prince. And "his priest and the boy who served him," at the last minute before the attack, "saw their master looking old and very sad, and they cried very much," that he — "having so many warriors under his command" — "would not oppose his brother." ("And having said this, was deeply moved").

Certainly this picture, collected from separate pieces, can hardly claim absolute veracity. Its hagiographic "composition" is too obvious, the glowing tones of the icon are too clear; the pedantic spirit of its creators is felt too strongly. Actually, the "violent men" sent by Svyatopolk, like most executors of dirty tasks, were not necessary and were even counter-productive. Boris's boys could not behave in accordance with the role prescribed for them by hagiography, i.e., to resist. Especially given that there were quite a few of them. And this circumstance, possibly, confirms the fact that there was a special reason for depicting Poutsha's lads as a powerful retinue.

It is quite logical to think that Svyatopolk was prepared for an armed conflict with Boris's personal servants or was concerned that some of the warriors would not leave his side. Otherwise, four men armed with knives instead of spears actually would have been sufficient to dispose of the prince. If a savage combat had been expected, the chances of the success would be the greater, the stealthier and more sudden the attack.

And there is one more point. When heavily armed troops are on the move, it is hard to maintain quiet and secrecy until the decisive moment. Possibly, Poutsha's troops did not succeed in this either, despite (not thanks to) his efforts. We should not rule out a brief clash between the visitors and Boris's servants. "They have beaten unmercifully many of Boris's boys", we read in the annals and in *The Tale*. And the annalist describes this in the context of the story of the attack against the prince himself and the death of his favorite lad, George Ugrin, who died simultaneously with him. (Ugrin covered his master with his body and was also pierced by spears, and then he was decapitated: the greedy Vyshgorod men liked his necklace — a golden coin hanging from his neck.) In such a case one might suspect that Poutsha's retinue attacked simultaneously all the tents on the Alta field. That would be either because they had already revealed their presence, and were trying to suppress any organized resistance as quickly as possible, or because they encountered some resistance (Poutsha, according to Nestor, had an order from Svyatopolk: "If anybody resists you, kill them together with Boris"). Or, simply, they did not wish to leave any witnesses (and only one of them made it back to Kiev).

5. Two Varangians

Thinking that the prince was dead, Poutsha and his accomplices left the tent. However, the injured Boris rushed out after them. Both *The Saga* and *The Reading* agree that, in shock and unable to comprehend what was happening, he prayed to God once again, then "one of the murderers ran up to him, and stabbed him in his heart; and so the Blessed Boris passed his soul into the hands of God." This is how Nestor relates it.

In *The Saga* we also find words of prayer: "They have prepared me like a ram for the feast. My Lord, you see, I do not oppose, nor speak against, but, having at hand all of my father's warriors, and being loved by my father, I think no ill against my brother. However he, as far as he can, has gone against me . . ." In *The Reading*, after his prayer, Boris, also dies, although the details are fewer.

In *The Reading*, that is the end. But the annals and *The Tale* continue their narration, because Boris was still alive. "Having killed Boris, the accursed ones", we read in The Primary Chronicle, wrapped him in a tent and put him on pales (a stretcher), and he was still breathing. Having learnt that he was still breathing, the accursed Svyatopolk sent two Varangians to kill him. When they came, they saw that he was still alive, and one of them drew his sword and pierced his heart . . ." In *The Tale*: "They wrapped the blessed Boris in the tent, put him on pales and carried him away. And when they were in the forest, Boris lifted up his head. And Svyatopolk, having learnt this, sent two Varangians and they pierced his heart with a sword. And that is how he died . . ."

The above story can be interpreted in the following way. The existing historical documents agree that the murderous assault against Boris was implemented twice. In *The Reading*, both occasions took place at the same location and with just a few minutes' interval, yet according to the annals and *The Tale*, which are close to each other, the events take place in different locations and about one day (or even longer) apart. (The second version narrated in *The Tale* admits a triple assault.)

Each of the versions sounds credible in its own way. The first one — by virtue of its simplicity and logic, the second one — because it retains details that are not so relevant in and of themselves. Being convinced that the logic of historical facts and events, their causative-consecutive connection, does not coincide with human logic, I give preference to the latter.

I believe, from these stories, that the following took place. Having killed (as they thought) Boris, Poutsha and his comrades carried the corpse, wrapped up in a tent (apparently, this had been agreed with Svyatopolk beforehand) to their place in Vyshgorod for secret burial (which actually took place at St. Basil's Church, named for the heavenly patron of Prince Vladimir). At some point they had to cross the Dnieper River.

(We read in the Tver collection: "And having brought him to the Dnieper, they put him into the boat and came with it to Kiev; but the Kievans did not accept him, but pushed him away. And having carried his body secretly, put in near the St. Basil's Church in Vyshgorod, and buried him in the ground". Some historians make far-reaching conclusions based on this story — about the Kievans' hatred of Boris (presumably for bringing the Pechenegs into Russia). In reality, there are no grounds for this. If we give preference to the Tver' collection version, then we must remember that in Kiev at that time both Boris and Svyatopolk must have had supporters. Maybe it was the latter who, as seems likely, were waiting for the boat on the pier. They could also have been former supporters of Boris, who were disappointed in him after his voluntary abdication of power that left them in the hands of Svyatopolk.

Going through a pine forest, the prince, covered with wounds, regained consciousness (A. A. Shakhmatov felt that this would have taken place most likely in the pine forest "near Dorogozhich, where the swamps started, in which Igor Olegovich got stuck after the battle of August 13, 6654 (1146)", because there, in the St. Cyril monastery, a church was later built in the memory of "the sacred martyr".) In any case, the guards and their mournful cargo, apparently, were already on the right bank of the Dnieper, instead of the left bank, which was clear of the forests.

One can imagine the impression made on all the attendants by the victim's revival from the dead! Their reactions are described in *The Eimund Yarn* — a collection of memories of the Varangians who once served the Russian princes.

For example, I. N. Danilevsky in his course of lectures *Ancient Rus-*

sia in the Eyes of Contemporaries and Their Descendants (9th — 12th Centuries) pointed out that "The body of [...] Boris was taken to Kiev. But on the way, it suddenly turned out that the prince was still breathing. Then Svyatopolk, who got wind of it — God knows how, sent two Varangians from Kiev..." And then: "Why did Svyatopolk have to send murderers to Boris twice? Who told Svyatopolk that the 'killed' prince was still alive? And why did the murderers, carrying his body, not notice?" It seems to Danilevsky that he has revealed significant weaknesses in the domestic sources when it comes to this particular episode, showed their incompleteness and, most importantly, their unreliability. The only serious question is, why was it necessary to inform the Kievan prince, if it was clear what had to be done? A. A. Shakhmatov was also interested in this question. "Why did the murderers, having noticed that Boris was still breathing, not kill him themselves, but send a messenger to Svyatopolk? and why did he, not desiring to disclose his participation in the murder, not entrust the task of murdering Boris to the same Vyshgorod men devoted to him (Poutsha and his retinue) — why did he send for two more Varangians for this purpose?" Danilevsky, like other historians, convinced of the necessity to rehabilitate Svyatopolk and lay the fault for the committed crimes on Yaroslav, considers that the explanation is contained in *The Eimund Yarn*, which narrates how the Varangians, under orders from the prince, killed the sleeping Burislav in the tent, at night, one day's ride from Kiev, and cut off his head and brought it to Novgorod as "material evidence"; and how, implementing Yaroslav's order, they then returned to the place of the murder to perform an adequate burial of their victim. "We also find the answer", says Danilevsky, "to the question of why the prince-murderer needed to send Varangians to the already-murdered Boris: to take the head back to the corpse and to bury him".

The Eimund Yarn (a constituent part of *The Saga about Saint Olav* in *The Book from the Flat Island*) —of rather later origin, from the end of the 13th century (J. de Fris, T. N. Jackson) is considered an independent source and more authentic than some of the popular research literature. The respected historian of the past century M. P. Pogodin was probably closer to the truth when he wrote, *The Eimund Yarn* serves as clear evidence: the details at large are incorrect, but the general features (relations, negotiations, conditions, occupations, military affairs, etc.) are of the greatest importance for Russian history; they supplement, explain and revive our information about this period . . ." The parallels between *The Eimund Yarn* and the Russian literary monuments describing the death of Buritslav (Buritsleif) and Boris are not so many and convincing (in *The Tale*, the murder and burial of Yaroslav's brother are carried out by the same people, and in the annals — by different ones; it is difficult to imagine how one event could be interpreted so variously). The collective name Buritslav could integrate Boleslav, Svyatopolk and Boris. But why not accept that *The Tale*, describing the murder of Svyatopolk by Yaroslav's Varangians, borrowed some details from the Russian legend about the death of Boris? (Perhaps somebody from Eimund's retinue served Svyatopolk and participated himself in the removal of his contender).

Shakhmatov saw "the location of this episode, with the Varangians delivering the death blow to Boris, as a borrowing by the annalistic narration from some local tale that pointed to a place recognized by devout adorers of saintly martyrs as the scene of Boris's death." (The historian, in particular, suggested St. Cyril monastery in Dorogozhich). Certainly, the existence of such an oral legend is quite conceivable and even very probable. Apparently, many such were created as a result of the public perception of the dramatic events at the beginning of that millennium. Unfortunately, legends do not come with labels testifying that they are true or false.

Why did Poutsha and his lads send the messenger to Kiev, instead of finishing the job with Boris quietly, and immediately? There may be several answers. First, we should not exclude emotional shock, and confusion. After all, they were believers, whether Christian or pagan. The sign of heavenly protection over Boris (expressed by the failure of their efforts to kill him) would frighten the loyal servants of the new Kievan prince. Then, it is not necessarily true that everybody around Poutsha enjoyed the assignment given to them by Svyatopolk. They might have hoped that the prince would show mercy to his brother. And lastly, it is not certain that the cart with Boris's body was accompanied all the way down to Vyshgorod by the entire retinue and their commander, the only one who could undertake such a decision.

Let's remember, then, how Prince Yaropolk Svyatoslavich was also murdered, in June of the year 978 (980). — "And there came Yaropolk to Vladimir, and walked in past the gate together with two Varangians hiding swords in their bosoms". The formal aspects of the murderous assault provide a basis to suspect that the murder was not only of political but also of a ritual nature. Their objective was revenge for a crime (the murder of Oleg, for which Vladimir blamed Yaropolk).

It is also indicative that swords have been used as ritual tools. The sword, as we know, was the most expensive, and already for this reason, most valuable weapon in the Middle Ages, an era so abundant in wars. In the cultures of the Indo-European peoples, quite naturally it has become one of the emblems of the highest temporal power and in religious worship "the sacred weapon", the bearer of complex "religious symbolism" (F. Cardini); it is also used in pagan magic for its sacral functions connected with the same symbolism.

From the annals we know that the warriors — pagans such as Oleg, Igor or Svyatoslav, when concluding peace treaties with the Byzantines, swore on weapons, and above all on swords, which were drawn and laid on the ground. "And let the undipped [pagan] Russians put down their shields and naked swords, armor and other weapons and swear to everything . . ." we read in Igor's treaty. And further, "If the Russian side decides to destroy such love [. . .], if they have not been christened, let them not have help from God, from Perun, let them be unable to protect themselves with shields, and let them be slashed by their own swords and die from arrows and other weapons of their own". And it is pointed out that the punishment for breaking the oath applies to princes as well. "If I, or the prince, or anybody else desert our side [. . .] let him be killed with his own weapon . . . If anybody from the prince and from the Russian people [. . .] breaks anything written herein, he will deserve to be killed with his weapon." The sword's function as a sacralized weapon, of mystical or real punishment for serious crimes in early medieval Russia, is seen rather clearly.

Certainly, in principle, any weapon could play a similar role. But in "the ethical classification of weapons", which F. Cardini enumerates among the German tribes, and characteristic of medieval culture as a whole, the sword is given first place unconditionally for "its social and aesthetic significance". That is why it is not surprising that in the annalistic story of the thrice-repeated revenge of Princess Olga against the Drevlians for killing Igor, swords come into effect at the final stage (after burying alive and committing to flames). This is an act of last resort, which completes and sanctifies the entire enterprise. And the artist of the Radzivill annals precisely reflected the essence of what was happening (i.e. the confessing Drevlians), having depicted Olga's servants armed only with swords — not one spear, even for the sake of visual diversity.

Meanwhile, when Kievan and Drevlian troops met on the battleground the next year, and young Svyatoslav "hit with his spear", which hardly flew "between the horse's ears", Sveneld and his tutor Asmund exclaimed: "The prince has already started, let's join in, friends, after the prince!" — A spear starts, the sword finishes . . .

Could it be that this horrible logic dominated Svyatopolk during his action against Boris? Maybe the prince had planned this? — Poutsha and his lads inflicted serious wounds on Boris, but didn't kill him; they only transported him, half-dead, closer to Svyatopolk (just as they allowed Yaropolk to reach Kiev, not arranging an ambush to catch him on his way from Roden').

In other words, there is a strong plausibility in the notion that everything that happened to Boris in that long day of July 24 (and maybe so long that it ran over into July 25th) was not the consequence of a random, unexpected chain of circumstances, but the unfolding of a premeditated plan, the details of which had been elaborated beforehand. Poutsha might have known very well what he was doing. The attack against Boris was achieved by Poutsha together with his close confidants Talets, Yelovich and Lyashko, who were also well-informed as to the intention. The rest "dealt with" the boys, all of whom died. Except for one: Moisey Ugrin.

By the way, in the text of *The Tale* there is one moment that is difficult to comprehend. When the injured Boris, "struck dumb," rushes out of the tent, he asks for time to pray; then he says: "Brothers, as you have started, finish your mission . . ." In the annals there is no such episode. In *The Reading*, one of murderers "ran up" and stabbed the prince. In *The Tale*, after Boris speaks, we don't hear the footsteps of hurried murderers running up to him, nor the jingle of weapons being readied, only the wailing and the sighs of the prince's servants, concluded by the phrase: "And here he passed away, delivering his soul into the hands of the God." So what happened? Did the murderers "finish" their "task", or did Boris "pass away" on his own? The last version seems more probable; indeed, very probable, as Poutsha prohibited his subordinates from touching the prince (they must surely have been shouting, pointing at Boris: "Don't just stand there, staring! Kill him!"). But Poutsha had to make sure that he was alive.

It follows from this that the messenger rode to Kiev, not so much because Boris had recovered, but to reassure Svyatopolk who was impatiently waiting for him.

Of course, many objections can be raised against such a hypothesis. First, it contradicts the direct narrative of the sources, which testify that Svyatopolk sent "Poutsha's lads" to perform the murder. Second, the meaning of this whole story of a feint is not very clear. After all, Vladimir finished off his brother without any ceremony. Svyatopolk could urge Boris to come to Kiev or, at any rate, send the Varangians with swords to Alta. And lastly, we should not forget that Vladimir, when he performed the ritual revenge, was an ardent pagan, but Svyatopolk had become Christian way back in his childhood. Could he deliberately plan to repeat a pagan ritual?

As for the last question, many historians of the medieval world (among them J. Le Goff, J. Dubi, and F. Cardini) have tried to imagine the nature of the spiritual life of that epoch in different regions of the Western world. "We have before us an extremely fluctuating and fragmentary religious world," writes F. Cardini. "Syncretism was live and well, in harmony with the struggle among different beliefs. There was practically an unlimited number of combinations of coexistence." When it was necessary, for example, to seal some legal act, the Scandinavians resorted to ancient forms and to the services of ancient gods. German paganism, as a matter of fact, did not show any considerable resistance to the new belief but they resisted its forms. The Germans reluctantly parted with their ancient legends, at least partly because they were largely connected with the pattern of their society. But the Germans willingly received new cultures and rituals, too. They interpreted them only in the magic way, adding them to the former beliefs, to which they were loyal. At the beginning of the 10th century, the archbishop of Rheims wrote to the Pope that the Vikings in his diocese "were christened two times. Despite this, they still preferred the pagan way of life, kill Christians and priests, and make sacrifices to their idols". The Norman duke Rollon, when dying, "cherished the hope of getting to paradise, but he did not forget Valhalla either", and therefore "presented one hundred golden livres to the Christian priests and simultaneously made a sacrifice to the ancient gods of a hundred of prisoners of war". He may be considered one of the emblematic figures of that time.

In Russia, Svyatopolk, in many respects, was identical to Rollon, incorporating the heritage of various cultures — Greek, Polish, Varangian, Eastern Slavic — assimilating and committing to different religious and cultural forms. Of course, it is difficult to tell what may have been Svyatopolk's planned ritual of vengeance, the ritual vengeance to which his father had fallen prey. He may have thought of luring Boris to Kiev, but such a plan carried great risks.

Vladimir's own first attempt on Yaropolk's life was during the siege of Kiev. As readers already know, the Novgorod prince ordered his newly recruited "friend," voivode Bloud, to kill his brother or to help Vladimir's people do it ("If I'd have my brother killed, then I'd rather have you do it instead of my father . . . Because it was not me who started the assault on my brother, but he"). Bloud, for his part, "met privately with Yaropolk, and frequently sent messengers to Vladimir, ordering him to assault the city of Kiev, thinking to kill Yaropolk; but because of the loyal townspeople he could not kill him. (Only then the voivode-traitor worked out another script for the criminal drama, thinking (correctly) that the easiest method would be to attack the prince on the battlefield, when his enemies were close by. In the noise and the confusion of the battle, most of the defenders would quickly lose sight of Yaropolk. And then it would be possible to blame this on somebody else.)

In this case, taking into consideration the thinking of the Russian chroniclers, our attention should be drawn not by what they wanted to convince us of, but by what transpires in the narration as a slip of tongue on the part of its creators. The circumstance that only spears were used in the first attack on Boris, at Alta, and that then two Varangians with swords finished him off in a pine forest ("bor") near Kiev, relates closely to the layer of unintentional information, and that's because none of the annalists suspected Svyatopolk of an intentionally pagan revenge. Otherwise, aside from fratricide, he would have been openly charged with "paganism" (an even graver sin).

According to this line of thinking, the available information stubbornly testifies that at Alta, Poutsha and his team used only spears against Boris, although they were armed with swords as well (as was mentioned already, when they cut off George Ugrin's head to take the gold grivna coin off his neck). Also, the two Varangians sent to the pine

forest near Kiev coincide both in number and nationality with the murderers of Yaropolk (although the murder itself was probably accom-
plished not by two swords, but by one). All this makes me think that, if
the indicated bits of information from the annals and *The Legend* corre-
spond to reality, they confirm the charge preferred by the Russian
"church legend" against Svyatopolk as the initiator and the perpetrator
of the murder of Prince Boris Vladimirovich. The crime, committed for
the sake of usurpation of power, and at the same time inspired by the
idea and the feeling of a blood feud, had corresponding ritual forms.

In my view, the only point open to argument is when and how
this deeply ritual component of the bloody drama manifested itself. Did
it color the general intention of the perpetrator from the very start, or
was it an unexpected improvisation, a sudden flash that lit up Svyatopolk's consciousness when he was informed about the "resurrection"
in the pine forest? I have tried to prove the likelihood of the first possibility. The version given by the Tver collection, in my view, confirms
this. It is very likely, or at least, it is quite probable, that Svyatopolk
ordered to have the wounded Boris brought to Kiev with the purpose of
making his execution resemble as nearly as possible the murder of his
father: not only in the method, but also in the place.

And this whole story began in the "early dawn of July 24, 1015, on
Sunday . . ."

6. Crimson Dawns

However, the death of Boris did not quell the fire in Svyatopolk's
soul, it did not appease him, it did not make him shudder at his own
conduct. On the contrary, crimson dawns started to blaze in his heart
with ever greater force, and it is rather more difficult to understand
that. Indeed, it seems that at the price of crime he had achieved all that
he wanted. He had secured the throne against the sole (at the time) real
rival, and paid "the debt of justice" towards his father, in the way that
he understood this debt. Having remedied the evil done by Vladimir
and restored trampled justice within the princely family, he, it seemed,
should have become softer at heart and become henceforth an advocate
of peace and brotherly love.

Furthermore, if he were to go after anyone else's head at this
point, it should be Yaroslav's or at least Mstislav's, but not Svya-

toslav's-Gleb's. Scholars aspiring to prove Svyatopolk's innocence also
cite the insufficient motivation for his behavior as related in the frame-
work of "church legend". Why would he do it? However, the same
question could be asked in regard to Yaroslav. For what purpose
would he have killed?

With the apparently meager information at our disposal, one may
look for an answer in the sphere of psychology, or even pathologic psychology, as in fact the ancient Russian scribes did. From their point of
view, from his youth Svyatopolk had been obsessed by the idea of becoming absolute ruler of the Russian land by eliminating all his rivals.
He was "taken by Satan", who invested in him "Cain's purport" of
dreams of fratricide. Although the author maintains that this was pre-
destined, given his sinful birth to a defrocked nun by "two fathers-
brothers".

However, while Nestor in his *Reading* depicts a prince-murderer
who is a superfluously single-minded maniac, the anonymous creator of
The Legend, to the contrary, keenly perceives the tremblings and oscilla-
tions of a human soul, shocked by the madness of his acts and the sense
of an inescapable evil curse.

As a historian, Nestor might be very "perceptive", but in this case I
say he was mistaken. As an artist who described life through his own
experience, he most likely was not able to imagine a man who, since his
birth, could not tell goodness from evil. And in this he was right. This is
how he saw Svyatopolk after the death of Boris: "No", says the scribe,
"the prince did not repent at all". On the contrary, "all of a sudden, Satan came into his heart and began to incite him to commit acts even
worse than this one, to commit many more murders".

In other words, one could somehow understand a single crime, a
single human slip; but when that becomes just the first link of a chain,
then the only possibility is that Satan is involved. Very likely; but the
key detail is that for the author of *The Legend* this is not so much a verdict as an occasion to mumble excuses, "I am inquiring of my own soul:
'What shall I do? If I stop with the crime I have committed, then I must
expect one of two outcomes: when my brothers discover this they will
repay me a hundredfold. Or, they will drive me out and I shall be deprived of my father's throne, and pity for my land will devour me, and
the abuses of abusers will conquer me, and my reign will be taken over
by another, and no living soul will be found in my courts. For I have

destroyed the one who is beloved by God, and added a new sore to the disease, added lawlessness to lawlessness . . .'" It is doubtful that such semi-informational meditations were in Svyatopolk's nature at this time. But anxious thoughts over the consequences of Boris's massacre are more than probable. He pondered what he must do next; and might really have found no answer but to go on as he had begun. Any reconciliation with the princely sons of Vladimir, after they found out what had happened, seemed to him unattainable.

Of the pair of princes-martyrs, revered throughout the 11th century, the leading figure was Gleb, whom the scribes called the Saint, while Boris was usually honored only with the epithet of "Blessed". Gleb's innocence, enhanced by his tender age, was too apparent. And the anonymous writer considers the murder of Prince Boris a crime *with motive*, whereas the destruction of Gleb was *unmotivated* and indicative of the degeneration of a human soul.

While analyzing *The Legend*, V. N. Toporov (in his book *Holiness and Saints in Russian Spiritual Culture*) came to a somewhat different conclusion as to the inner motivation of both the separate actions and the overall behavior of Svyatopolk. He focused on the subject of the prince's sinful origin, believing that it had formed the essence of his personality and predetermined the fatal sequence of his actions. Svyatopolk, says V. N. Toporov, "like Oedipus, turns out to be a personage who acts in double paradigm: he appears at the same time in the roles of son and nephew of Prince Vladimir, his father and uncle; the duplicity of parentage and hence the actual status becomes an integral feature that characterizes his moral make-up".

Svyatopolk is certainly a villain, but the villainy itself finds its way (is implemented) through his fatal division ("duplicity") between thought and word, word and deed. Hence the special role of hypocrisy, lies, double-dealing, and double-talk in Svyatopolk's behavior, which is in great contrast to the first fratricide, Cain. Svyatopolk himself, perhaps, was not to blame for this "duplicity", but it came to be that such a fault predetermined Svyatopolk's sin and crime. While accepting Toporov's observations, I would nevertheless emphasize the psychological portrait of Svyatopolk as presented in *The Legend*.

A sense of pathological underpinnings seems to me very important in coming to an understanding of subsequent events. Of course, I do not mean to say that Svyatopolk's attempt on Gleb's life does not have any rational explanations. Scholars usually overlook the fact that Gleb was the only natural brother of the deceased Boris, which could not but knit them together within the wide kin of the Volodimirich. And one should probably believe Nestor when he says the brothers were inseparable: "Boris praying all hours, and Saint Gleb listening to him, sitting close by the Blessed Boris, day and night listening to him".

But even if it were not so, blood ties remained too important for Svyatopolk to ignore. However, *Reading* and *The Legend*, while being more or less similar in the description of the murder of Boris, differ fundamentally on the story of Gleb. The author of *The Legend* claims that by the time of Vladimir's death, Gleb had been the prince of Murom. And when Svyatopolk decided to commit a new murder he sent a messenger ("ambassador") to him with the false words: "Come as soon as possible. Father calls you and he is very sick". An "evil advisor of the Devil", he was obviously in a hurry to take advantage of the fact that the young prince of Murom was not keeping up with current events, presuming with good reason that that would not go on forever. In that case, the innocence of Gleb is absolute. "With a small force" he moved in haste to Kiev, and somewhere in the field by the Volga his horse stumbled over a ditch (a bad sign), hurting the horseman's leg; and Gleb has to continue his way in a boat ("small ship"). Here, at the Smyadyn' River, he is reached by some messengers from Novgorod. Yaroslav, who has just received news from Predslava, warns Gleb: "Do not go there, brother! Your father has died, and your brother was killed by Svyatopolk". But the prince continues on his way. At the mouth of the Smyadyn' he is met by the "wicked servants" of Svyatopolk "with the soul of cruel beasts". They are led already not by Poutsha (let us remember our considerations above about him and his "folks"), but by Goryaser. The boat with the assassins, having turned round, reaches the vessel of Gleb. The prince thinks that they have come to "kiss" him on behalf of his brother, and welcomes them with joy. But the moment the boats come abreast, Goryaser's men, unsheathing their swords, jump into their victim's "small ship". Gleb's oarsmen are stunned, he himself tries to beg those "very cruel brother-haters" not to slay him, because he is yet "infantile" both in age and "ill will" (i.e. hatred against anyone has not yet ripened in his soul). But "accursed Goryaser orders them to slaughter him immediately". This instruction is executed by Gleb's cook, Torchin, who "butchered" the prince "like a lamb, pure and kind-hearted". This happens on September 5, a Monday.

Some researchers find many holes in this story. First of all, why would Gleb choose a roundabout route from Murom to Kiev via Smolensk? — asks Danilevsky. — As the authors of Russian sources note, he was in a great hurry to find his father alive, wasn't he? And for that matter, how did Yaroslav, being in Novgorod, not only manage to get news from Kiev but also to warn Gleb of the impending danger? The route from Kiev to Novgorod and from there to Smolensk adds up to over 2000 miles, which would take no less than a month and a half to traverse, even if the messengers never stopped for a single day. And how did Yaroslav's envoys know by which road Gleb was traveling to Kiev? And whereto did they disappear when the people sent by Svyatopolk arrived there at practically the same time?

In fact, things are not so complicated and mysterious. One may suppose, for example, that Gleb, having received news of his father's illness, sent a messenger to Yaroslav, being in no doubt that Yaroslav too would hurry to Kiev, and therefore offering to meet him in Smolensk. In such a very probable case, two puzzles are solved at once; and Nestor offers an answer as to why didn't they wait for Goryaser and his armed forces.

Nestor asserts that Svyatopolk's aversion to Gleb was allegedly as old as his repugnance towards Boris. "Accursed Svyatopolk was furious not only with Blessed Boris, but also with Blessed Gleb, and both the Blessed were not aware of that . . ." If this is not a pure literary device, then such an "aside" makes one wonder.

Ponder again Svyatopolk's plot. Did he think that the simple murder of both brothers (as blood brothers) would be a worthy revenge for his father's death? Really, the circumstances of Gleb's murder — his "slaughtering" with a knife "like a lamb, pure and kind-hearted" — are more than expressive. Nestor depicts these events with naturalistic clarity: "and the above-said cook, having knelt down, seized the head of this Blessed and cut his throat." It was in just such a way, since biblical times, that pagans had made their sacrifices. That was how Abraham prepared to slaughter Isaac.

According to *The Legend*, Goryaser's punitive team caught up with Gleb's boat and bristled with swords "shining like water" (note that: with swords, not with lances). Then they "jumped" into the boat, although if they'd used their lances they could have struck their victims while staying aboard their own boat. A miniature in Sylvester's collection shows the warriors, armed with spears, absolutely passive, while two of them, in ceremonial dress, are swinging a sword and a saber.) Then why did not they take the lances with them to Gleb's boat, unless they did not intend to use them for some reason? And what could that reason be?

Indeed, no other weapons were used but the services of the poor prince's cook. "As for Gleb's cook, Torchin by name, he took the knife and, seizing the Blessed, slaughtered him . . ." Then what, again a ritual murder?

However, I think that this in no way resolves the above-mentioned doubts as to whether Svyatopolk was mentally ill, because he soon committed the third murder. Svyatoslav, Prince of the Drevlians, became the new victim. What did he do to arouse the wrath of Svyatopolk, indefatigable in his vengeful rage? Why did he have to abandon everything he possessed and rush to his kin in Hungary in an effort to escape Svyatopolk's tentacles? Unfortunately, nothing is known about this. Of course, there must have been some motive.

It is possible that Svyatoslav might have been present, with Gleb and the other young brothers, when Vladimir issued some final orders, before he died, contained provisions that were unacceptable to Svyatopolk.

No wonder that his escape failed, that Svyatoslav was run down by the Kievan "goryasers", who possibly set up an ambush; and this prince too was killed. This shows the atmosphere of terror created by Svyatopolk against his apparent and potential rivals and ill-wishers. They not only lived under the fear of punishment, but their tracks were already being followed by the bloodhounds of the new secret service and by the butchers of the punitive forces. Hypertrophied lust for revenge, irrepressible lust for power in the name of the restoration of the "legitimate" dynasty, and satisfaction of the personal ambition of power, hidden fear of retribution — all this pushed Svyatopolk to the moral abyss. Having bathed his hands thrice in blood, he burned all bridges behind, and did not expect any reconciliation with the remaining brothers. Now his strength alone had to be his main argument. And he had it.

Using gifts and promises, to which he had resorted in the first days of his rule, Svyatopolk gradually won over the vast majority of the Kievans. "Svyatopolk sits in Kiev after his father, gathers the Kievans and starts to distribute to them estates" — reads the first Novgorod chronicle — "They accept them, but their hearts are not with him, because his brothers are with Boris". That is, the Kievans hesitated at first, fearing that if Boris should come with his regiments (according to Nestor, his army had about 8,000 men), then these "estates" could turn out badly for them. And family ties weighed heavily on their "hearts". But they nevertheless "accepted" the gifts. This decisive success was a gift that fell into Svyatopolk's hands when Boris turned down the offer to fight.

Now, having done away with actual or imaginary enemies, he deprived his principal rival Yaroslav, of potential allies, and secured himself against war on several fronts.

Now Svyatopolk could concentrate entirely on preparations for the war with Yaroslav.

7. How Yaroslav the Wise Came Close to Becoming Yaroslav the Daft

Svyatopolk probably took all possible precautions so that his sensitive brother to the north should find out as late as possible what had happened and what was going to happen at the dynastic level in the Russian land. It is easy to guess that patrols and outposts, sent by him, tightly covered all the routes to the "midnight countries", and controlled entry and exit from the capital as well as from other cities having ties with the Volkhov region. Nevertheless, if the description in the *Chronicle* and *The Legend* is true, one day in the middle of August a tired-out courier on horseback delivered word from his sister Predslava to Yaroslav, Prince of Novgorod: "Your father has died, and Svyatopolk sits in Kiev; he has killed Boris and sent killers to Gleb, and you must keep a sharp watch out".

The tone of the message leads us to believe that Predslava was afraid. She did not call on her brother to go to Kiev with an army. She just warned him about the danger now threatening him. It seemed to her that someone among Svyatopolk's "goryasers" must be at that very moment spurring toward Novgorod, with a knife inside his shirt, and/or "a deadly potion" in his ring.

Yet, Predslava's envoy failed by just a few hours, because just the day before, Yaroslav received troubling news from the banks of the Dnieper. The nature of the troubles? The Varangians, employed by the prince. Bored after a long period of inactivity, the mercenaries had begun to roister about in an increasingly bold manner: "And the Varangians began to do violence over married women", says the Novgorod chronicler. The townsmen did not like it, "and having gathered together at night, they trounced the Varangians at Poromon's yard". These sudden "guerilla" actions were led by "cuckold husbands" and "glorious warriors" from among the Novgorod "thousand".

Yaroslav took that dashing and merciless raid as a personal offense, and with some reason. The mercenaries cost him a pretty penny, but with them he was as safe as if behind a stone wall. And now he had lost this wall. In a fit of rage, Yaroslav could think of nothing better than to serve the obstreperous townsmen with the same sauce. He went to his village, Rakomo, and having put on the mask of resignation, sent a herald to tell the townsmen his reaction: "It is already impossible for me to baptize them" (Meaning, what can I do now?). "And he sent for the cuckolded husbands who had flogged the Varangians, and lured them in, and flogged them a thousand times," reads the Primary Chronicle or the Tale of Bygone Years ("Povest vremmenykh let").

And just after this, as if by heavenly punishment, "in the same night" Yaroslav received word as to the affairs in Kiev. He must have realized the foolishness of his action since, the next day, addressing "the rest of the Novgorodians" (i.e. those who survived) at the *veche* (people's assembly), he said (according to the Novgorod chronicle): "Oh, my beloved and honorable druzhina. Yesterday in my madness I flogged some of you, and now I cannot repay their precious lives with gold". (In the Primary Chronicle: "Oh, beloved druzhina! Yesterday I beat you up, and now I need you.")

It seemed, at that point, that fate would have left us with Yaroslav the Daft, if Svyatopolk found out what had happened and came with his army to the walls of Novgorod, the city still bleeding as a result of that sudden execution; he could have taken Yaroslav "with his bare hands". But Svyatopolk did not find out about it. Yaroslav was favored by Fortune. Although he had to live through many more anxious hours, he pulled himself together, recovered from his fear, and made a quick reassessment of his deployment of forces.

But maybe he did not have to deal with the situation alone; Bloud, who is given a significant role in the chronicles, remained a tutor and a voivode, and hence one of Yaroslav's closest advisors. As to the Novgorodians, they appeared to be forgiving and diplomatic.

In short, after Yaroslav "dried his tears" and, having turned to "business", finally explained the reason for his grief (the first Novgorod chronicle says, "Brothers, my father Vladimir has died, and Svyatopolk rules in Kiev. I want to go against him; help me"; Primary Chronicle: "My father has died, and Svyatopolk is in Kiev, killing his brothers"). And the Novgorodians responded curtly: "And we, our prince, will go with you". (Primary Chronicle: "Though, our prince, our brothers were flogged, we shall fight on your side").

Yaroslav managed to collect under his banners 3,000 Novgorodians, and added to them another 1,000 of the surviving (or newly recruited?) Varangians (according to the Primary Chronicle, "other warriors," except the Varangians, counted for 40,000). Finally, the northern forces camped on the banks of the Dnieper, not far from Lubech.

We shall not sidestep the battle that took place there, because judging by the first Novgorod chronicle, the reconnaissance services of at least one of the opposing sides, namely Yaroslav's, proved to be very active. Events developed in the following way. Having received word from one of his outposts on the movements of the enemy, Svyatopolk "collected countless number of warriors, headed to Liubech, opposite to the enemy, and camped there on the field. Yaroslav came and stood on the bank of the Dnieper". Svyatopolk managed to secure the Pechenegs' assistance. He located his camp between the two lakes. The Pecheneg cavalry occupied the opposite shore of one of the lakes. Neither of the enemies risked making the first move. Three months passed while everyone waited.

Cold weather set in. Once, Wolf's Tail, the voivode serving Svyatopolk, evidently shivering with cold, went down to the river and, "galloping along the bank", began to harass the Novgorodians. "You came with this lame man, what are you — carpenters? We shall put you to hew our mansions!" It is certainly very possible, though, that Wolf's Tail bawled out such abuses not because of the cold, but in accordance with the instructions of the Kievan prince's war council, in order to lure the enemy onto their side of the river, by any means possible. (In order to provoke an opportunity to push the opposing troops right into the freezing Dnieper.)

According to the version in the Primary Chronicle, they succeeded in stirring up Yaroslav's men. But either Svyatopolk did not expect such an immediate response from Yaroslav, or the Wolf Tail's eloquent pitch was out of line with Svyatopolk's secret strategy; either way, when the enraged Novgorodians appeared before Svyatopolk's camp at dawn the next day, they took the Kievan prince by surprise.

Fighting the cold, Svyatopolk had "drunk together with his guards all the night through", and did not care to form up a common line of defense with the Pechenegs. That was why, when the battle began, "the Pechenegs could not help from beyond the lake, and Svyatopolk was pushed to the lake, and stepped onto the ice; the ice broke and Svyatopolk's warriors were drowned in the waters, and Yaroslav began to win. Seeing this, Svyatopolk started to run . . ." However, the Novgorod chronicle renders the circumstances under which the battle began in an essentially different way.

Still lame but wiser now, Yaroslav swallowed the insult from Wolf's Tail. Having chosen the appropriate time, he sent a scout to Svyatopolk's camp to establish a liaison with his secret collaborator. "And the Dnieper began to freeze", says the chronicler. "And Yaroslav had a loyal friend in Svyatopolk's camp; and Yaroslav sent his youth to him at night. And his youth told him: 'What do you advise him to do? there is little mead brewed, but there are plenty of troops!' And he answered this man: 'Tell Yaroslav: there is little mead, but many troops: attack at night'. And Yaroslav understood that as an order to fight at night". As far as one can understand, the "youth" asked, roughly, the following: "OK, what's-your-name, what would you recommend we do, if your force is great and our force is small?" And the secret friend replied: "If you have small forces, attack at night". This was a coded conversation between scouts, the first known to us in Russia and a distant prototype of present-day verbal codes and passwords.

Yaroslav followed the advice, and that same evening (not at dawn) he crossed the river, ordering his warriors to cover their heads with towels so that they would not cut each other in the darkness ("use towels on your heads, as our sign"), and already before the "light" they defeated Svyatopolk. Svyatopolk fled — according to one source, to the Pechenegs, according to another, to the Poles. Most likely, he ran first to the Pechenegs (or to their protection, as they did not participate in the battle), and from there, to shelter under the wing of his father-in-law.

Ilyin believed that the version presented in the Primary Chronicle was more truthful, while Shakhmatov tended more to favor the first Novgorod chronicle. I (reluctantly) join Shakhmatov, and thus credit the valuable advice of the scout for the outcome of the battle. Of course, one might call him a traitor, as did Ilyin, for example. Such a variant cannot be neglected, but it is by no means binding. One should not forget that there were many people in Svyatopolk's camp at that time who had been forced to hastily adjust themselves to the new political situation, and they might have suffered from the burden of making a wrong choice. Though one should also admire Yaroslav's reconnaissance work, since he was able to find a useful man in the enemy's camp and to establish a reliable liaison with him, which is always far from easy when a war is underway.

8. Svyatopolk's Return. An Interpretation of the "Eimund Yarn"

Yaroslav soon learned where the fugitive had gone. He arrested Boleslavna and began active preparations for a battle with her father. Boleslav at the time was deeply involved in the war with the German Empire. As Vladimir had done, Yaroslav engaged in talks with Henry II and concluded a treaty with him. According to the new treaty, he was to attack the Poles from the east simultaneously with the Germans' attack from the west. He kept the promise and, according to Tietmar, in 1017 he went with his army to Berestie (Brest) and laid siege to another Polish city — albeit without much to show for it. According to Nazarenko, Yaroslav managed to capture the city, but "it was no success". Ilyin thought these comments were about the city of Berestie, taken over by Boleslav, that Yaroslav tried to liberate; but Yaroslav soon had to go back to his capital which was under attack by the Pechenegs, instigated by the Polish prince. ("Boleslav in his turn moved Pechenegs onto Kiev.") Nazarenko also points to Berestie, for he thought that Svyatopolk was there at the time.

However, one can hardly imagine that the siege laid by the Russian prince, in his own Russian stronghold, had anything to do with the treaty concluded between Henry and Yaroslav. How could Svyatopolk escape when the city had been taken over? Then Tietmar, in a different text, clearly indicates that "Yaroslav captured a town that had belonged to his brother in 1018". That is why I am inclined to think that the chronicler meant a Polish stronghold on the Polish bank of the Bug River. Why, then, would Yaroslav discontinue a war march that prom-ised good booty? The manuscripts do not happen to mention any trou-ble in Kiev except for some churches that were burned down in the Russian capital. Such news could be interpreted in various ways. A. A. Shakhmatov, for instance, refers to atrocities committed by the Varan-gians that Yaroslav had brought in; Tietmar refers to an accident at St. Sophia cathedral. Only the "Eimund Yarn" asserts that the Russian stronghold, where the Kievan prince and his Varangian assistant and benefactor were besieged, was attacked not by the Pechenegs but by the Biarmans (Finnish and Ugric tribes from the north or north-east). "Burislav" or Bouritslav, whom some scientists take for Boris, is sup-posed to have brought them there; but I tend to go along with those who think it was Svyatopolk.

It is quite probable that the nomads had help from other parts. Boleslav could not possibly appear at Kiev. But Svyatopolk . . . One still has serious doubts as to the saga's credibility and its chronology is rather confusing. Some historians think that the events revealed in it date from the beginning of the conflict, that is, from the battle at Liubech late in 1016 (?), crediting Eimund and his host of 600 men with making a substantial contribution to the Novgorod prince's victory over his opponent. (Eimund had persuaded Yaroslav to repel his brother, criticized him for hesitation, and drafted a bold — even risky — battle plan, in which he got around behind the enemy and "struck from the rear".) But it may also indicate that Eimund arrived in Novgorod from Norway only in 1018 or 1019. If we leave out some minor details (which we more or less must do, since the town defended by Yaroslav and Eimund was not named) then one may assume that the attack on Kiev was led by Bouritslav-Svyatopolk. The saga discloses some details on the preparations for battle on both sides, namely about the actions of the intelligence service. It appears that the shortsighted Yaroslav, who thought that his brother had perished during the previ-ous battle, did not take any serious steps to consolidate his advantage; it appears that he was resting on his laurels, and would have come in for a real shock if it had not been for Eimund.

It is rather odd that talk of Svyatopolk-Bouritslav and Yaroslav's intentions comes up only during the conflict brewing between the Kievan prince and the mercenaries. What if it happened some three weeks earlier? There was too little time left to undertake any serious countermeasures. But let us not find too many faults. If Eimund had been engaged in intelligence gathering, most probably he interrogated merchants and other travelers who had come to Kiev on one errand or another, and got wind of Svyatopolk's trail in Pechenegia. Eimund must have dealt with the matter anonymously and did not share, for some reasons, his information with his Russian counterparts, who for their part did not seem to be very effective in their actions. That may reflect the order (or disorder) in the country and the fact that the Varangians mostly disregarded the interests of the state and its rulers. According to the saga, Eimund easily proved his point, for he had to be paid for the information. So the wise leader of the mercenaries easily converted the intelligence that he had into money that he did not have. The intimidated Yaroslav hastily extended the treaty with the Varangians. He was at a loss and asked Eimund what should be done — gather an army for battle, or flee the camp? If troops were to be gathered, then where? Here in the capital or at the frontier, in the steppe? The brave Eimund, who was appeased by the clink of gold and the soft weight of exotic furs, must have felt his morale lifting; he took on the burden of the preparation himself. The brave Varangian exhibited the full extent of his military talents: he built a camouflaged moat filled with water, reinforced two gates where they might either fight the enemy or use them for retreat, planted trees on the walls for protection from arrows and sent richly clad women with gold ornaments to walk along the walls, to show the Pechenegs that they were not expected — and to whet their appetite.

Bouritslav, for his part, was afraid that it would be difficult to storm the city where the "konungs" (Yaroslav and Eimund) were, and he took every precaution to keep his arrival secret in order to take them by surprise. He must have approached via roundabout ways and detoured around the outposts and border guards. His reconnaissance teams must have captured all those who could warn Kiev about the impending invasion. So when he arrived at the city and saw fancy women walking the walls and gold rings glinting in the sun (some invention of the manuscript compilers), the prince thought that his efforts had not been in vain. (Bouritslav, and his troops, came out of the forest to the city, and surveying the lovely scene, he thought he was clever enough to have gotten there unnoticed.) He did not even suspect that his crossing of the border had been duly noted by Kievan reconnaissance (Yaroslav and Eimund had learned all about konung Bouritslav, who came from Gardarika to their city). So that, according to the saga, was the background of the Kiev battle; and Svyatopolk very much prized the military art of the Normans (Varangians). Don't ask how Eimund learned of Svyatopolk's opinion, for flattery travels fast. During the battle the Varangians displayed miraculous heroism and saved the badly wounded Yaroslav, whose leg was injured, and fended off the onslaught. "All the Biarmans who survived fled and Bouritslav retreated with his retinue. Many of them were slain. Eimund with his men pursued them until the woods and killed their standard-bearer. There was a rumor that the konung was also killed and they could boast a great victory!"

That is how the yarn described it.

9. Svyatopolk's Return in the Chronicles. The Battle at Volhyn'.

The Battle at Volhyn'

According to the annals and Tietmar's chronicle, Svyatopolk came back to Russia only in the summer of 1018 (this conflicts with A.V. Nazarenko's thesis about capturing Berestie with the help of Boleslav in late 1017 or early 1018). He returned not alone but with an army; a foreign army. One cannot make out for certain whether it was Svyatopolk's troops or some enemy army that crossed the border, seizing, in its wake, a stray prince. Well, there is no need to beat around the bush — foreign regiments had come to the eastern Slavic lands even before Svyatopolk. But they were hired troops of Varangians or Pechenegs who took orders from the prince or a voivode and did not claim any independent political role in events. This was the first time in Russian national history (as we know it) that a foreign army entered the lands of the Kievan state under the command of its own lord. And he was a person who would not yield to anyone at the political table. For he was Poland's ruler, Boleslav the Brave.

Besides his own troops, he brought regiments of Saxon and Hungarian mercenaries, and some Pechenegs as well. So Svyatopolk had the dubious honor of becoming the first Russian ruler who used foreign intervention in order to restore his power. Unfortunately this "honor" belongs to him forever. Well, according to his notion of honor, he was right in fighting for what was his by birthright. But he was at liberty not to exercise that right when it entailed such a high price (his father Yaropolk had disdained a similar opportunity, when Variazhko offered him to ask the Pechenegs for support; but that was quite another matter).

I want to emphasize that a political personality always has a choice. But Svyatopolk, like most potential claimants to a throne, in any era, had an incurable lust for power. For his paramount view of power was as a source of privilege and not as a position imposing social obligations. Certainly, the notion of self-respect was understood differently in the 10th-11th centuries than nowadays and Svyatopolk did not consider himself a traitor. That epithet was confined to his nephew, the Kievan prince Iziaslav Yaroslavich, who some 50 years later also brought Polish troops to Russia, headed by Boleslav the Bold. But here is what happened next.

Yaroslav's intelligence officers seem to have shown their superiority this time; and so did the border guards. When Boleslav and Svyatopolk approached the Bug River, they saw Yaroslav's regiments deployed along the opposite bank near the town of Volhyn'. This time, good fortune was not on the side of the lame Yaroslav. He did not prevail, but had to flee to Novgorod. Boleslav and Svyatopolk reached Kiev unimpeded, having overcome only brief, although fierce, opposition from some citizens true to Vladimir's son. He then entered the city.

That was the chronicler's version. Tietmar has it somewhat differently. "On June 22, Boleslav came to a river, and ordered his men to make camp there and to get ready to negotiate the river. The Russian prince was sitting on the opposite bank, waiting for the outcome of the proposed battle. When the battle commenced, the Russians all of a sudden fell back from the river. Boleslav ordered his allies to get ready, and made a hasty crossing of the river. The enemy scattered into small detachments and tried in vain to defend the motherland. After they yielded to the first thrust they could not resist further and gave way. A great number of fugitives were killed and only a few of the winners". The bishop must have written that on hearsay from the Saxons who came back from the march. That would be why the description is more plausible and factual. Voivode Bloud was not so much to blame for the enemy picking at Yaroslav's troops.

The main reason why the Russians were defeated is that they struck not with a fist but with an open palm. It is not clear why their battle formation was shattered at the very beginning and why they were scattered all over the place. In any case, that was, above all, the voivode's fault. Yaroslav, brave soldier that he may have been, did not show his superiority in this case. So he had to take off for Novgorod in a disgraceful retreat (and old Bloud lost his head, grey hair and all, at the Bug). "Boleslav went off in hot pursuit after the scattered troops". After a triumphant march through the Volhyn' and Kievan land, the Polish, German, Hungarian and Pecheneg troops soon came to the Russian capital, which stood in opposition — but not for long. Tietmar wrote: "Kiev was defended by its townsfolk but soon yielded to foreign forces. Abandoned by its prince, on the 14th of August, it accepted Boleslav and Svyatopolk who had been in exile for a long time. The land was subjugated because of the prince's popularity and because of fear of the Germans" (as if it were not Boleslav's army that made up the bulk of the aggressors but the 300-Saxon troop).

Svyatopolk's popularity among the townsfolk should not be exaggerated, for both in Kiev and in other cities there were many adherents of the surviving sons of Vladimir. But it also should not be disregarded. For Svyatopolk was eager to retain the sympathy of the population. He was afraid to lose it. And that explains to a great extent both the sense and the logic of the prince's actions that followed soon after his triumphant arrival in Kiev.

Plunder. Son-in-Law Against Father-in-Law

Boleslav and Svyatopolk entered Kiev on the Assumption Day, probably the most sacred day for the Tithe Church, at least, that is how they emphasized the event. Then systematic looting and plundering of the city began. "Boleslav took, in Kiev, untold treasures", wrote Tietmar, "most of which he distributed among his allies and comrades in arms, and some part of it was sent to his homeland." This was the first time that the wealth of the Kievan prince's house, the state treasury of a great country, was devastated. Wolves were in the sheepfold and they hid neither their appetite nor their disdain for their Russian ally.

Though there was not enough momentum for an open revolt, in the end the situation turned sour for Boleslav. His troops began defecting. Soon after Svyatopolk's triumph, and after the local population swore their allegiance to him, Boleslav let his mercenaries go. It was hard to feed such an army and they were depleting Kiev's supplies. He had to re-deploy his Polish troops all across the country. "Boleslav ordered his troops to be stationed at different towns and villages — notes the scribe — and it was done so". Then the accursed Svyatopolk, who had helped to implement the order, added: "Whenever you meet Liakhs — slaughter them". "And so it was done." After that, the scribe accused the prince of folly.

Just moments ago, Boleslav and his son-in-law had displayed such touching unity as the Kiev metropolitan, according to Tietmar, hailed them in the Church of St. Sophia (which had been reconstructed after a fire). That showed that the Kievans' friendship with the uninvited guests was dubious, at best. This is such a drastic change of the picture, and so inexplicable, that some historians tend to think that it did not take place at this time; rather, they place the events described here in 1069 during the rule of Iziaslav Yaroslavich. (The Liakhs were stationed in certain cities and were slaughtered then, too.) That opinion is shared by A. A. Shakhmatov and N. N. Ilyin.

The similarity lies in the fact of invaders being slaughtered, which is explained by the repetition of similar historic situations, although the personalities of the princes are different and their roles in the events vary. Iziaslav did not play any particular role in the events of 1069. He simply provided the Polish troops with "living premises" in some towns (at least, that is what the chronicle says). Svyatopolk took the initiative.

How then should one understand Svyatopolk? What made him act so oddly? I do not think there was anything extraordinary in his action. On the contrary, it complies nicely with the general logic of Svyatopolk's behavior. It was a decisive action characteristic of his "style". That is, it involved bloodshed and was secret, on the sly. It is clear that he used such means to get rid of the Poles. One cannot possibly overlook such coincidences. One can only note the similarity of "the handwriting".

One may wonder at such a phenomenon but it is easy to identify the faulty party: it was both the circumstances and the personality of perpetrator. In his political struggle Svyatopolk used the same method — going after his prey when he had a chance: Boris, Gleb, Svyatoslav and Boleslav (or his troops). Svyatopolk acted like a predator; that was natural for him. Some historians are confused by his "unexpected last jump". But that is only a superficial impression. One cannot rebuke Svyatopolk for being illogical. On the contrary, he acted straightforwardly and decisively, as if he was carried away by a fixed idea (as we have shown earlier). He again attacked the prey that he considered most dangerous at the time, when he thought he could overcome him. In this case, it was Boleslav.

One may only ask why Svyatopolk turned against his father-in-law who had helped him to regain Kiev. The answer is simple.

Boleslav was a ruthless and authoritative person. He had high political ambitions. He was lucky in his maneuverings with the German Empire, with which relations were rather complicated. He managed to gain both from the war and the peace and extended Poland's boundaries to the south and north, at the same time watching with great interest the east where the powerful Kievan state was constantly growing and gaining strength. His ongoing efforts to establish a union with the Pechenegs and the war of 1013 with Russia leave no doubt that he intended to dominate the east European region. He was a shrewd man and he understood that he could not cope with Vladimir, either by force (as was evident from the war) or by ruse. But he had a trump card up his sleeve for the future — his son-in-law Svyatopolk. Both fathers-in-law, consenting to such a marriage, expected to use it for the good of their own countries. And time proved that luck was on the side of the Polish prince. He won. He reached Kiev, and sooner than he had expected. He felt himself a winner in the city, for his foe was already in the grave and his friend was at his side. Not merely a friend, but actually a vassal. Boleslav did not take his son-in-law seriously either as a personality (and he may have been wrong in that) or as a person with real power and force. It was all within his reach. If so, he should not miss the chance...

When he was leaving Gniezno, Boleslav must have discussed with his son-in-law the conditions of his military support. He would take him to Kiev with the help of Polish lances and would help him gain his father's throne. One should never doubt that there was an obligation on the part of the Russian prince to reward his savior with a large sum of money in repayment for the efforts incurred, for the inevitable sacrifices and as a token of great respect. But how much? Did Svyatopolk risk Kiev's treasury alone, or did he promise territorial rewards as well? Once in Kiev, Boleslav may have increased his demands, seeking a revision of the previous conditions. That may have caused a violent reaction on the part of Svyatopolk. Both Russian and foreign historians, describing Boleslav's stay in Kiev, fail to give any answer to the question but they do provide some interesting details.

The Russian Primary Chronicle gives the following description of the Polish prince's actions after Svyatopolk declared an "impeachment" on him. "Boleslav fled Kiev, having taken Yaroslav's possessions, and boyars, and his sister, and Anastasius who was in charge of the tithe — for he had seduced him. He took along with him many people, and he also took possession of the Cherven' towns. Then Svyatopolk began his rule in Kiev". Thus according to the chronicle, Svyatopolk's action was crowned with success and the talented Polish prince forbore to tempt his fate; he chose to go home. He made no secret of his departure. He did not slip out at night, quaking at the sound of footsteps, but left in triumph in the full view of all the citizens and with military horns playing in his honor. He left the land, taking all his men and a good number of the local nobility (who came back only some quarter of a century later). He took with him cartloads of goods belonging to his beloved son-in-law and ally. His chief prize was Anastasius from Korsun, who was called "The Tithe" in Kiev and who expected to be given some new and more graceful moniker in Gniezno.

Some researchers think that Anastasius made a fool of Boleslav. "The sly Anastasius", according to N. M. Karamzin, "had been Vladimir's protégé and later managed to secure the trust of the Polish king; he became Vladimir's treasurer and took the treasure with him, leaving Kiev. He had betrayed his first motherland, and then he betrayed the second one for his own greediness." O. V. Tvorogov treats this note about Anastasius somewhat clumsily: "He put Anastasius in charge of the Tithe Church treasures, for he had won his trust by deceit".

How did Anastasius deceive Boleslav, though? He took the treasures belonging to the Russian state to Poland, but Boleslav did not mean to give them back at the Russian border. Or maybe Anastasius harbored a thought of straying from the road and sparing at least the most valuable items for the sake of Russia? I think both "protagonists" were of the same caliber. Each of them looked to his own profit. Boleslav knew that in Anastasius he had gotten a zealous keeper of the treasures, for the latter knew every coin, cross and bracelet in it. He was sure that the treasure was in safe hands and nobody, including the guards, would get anything from it. Anastasius acted as he was wont to do in earlier times. He sensed that the strife in the Russian land would last a long time, that Svyatopolk was not worth dealing with, and that it was time to find as reliable a patron as Vladimir had been. And he decided he could not find any better than this stout giant from Gniezno. Maybe he was inclined to trust those who wore the halo of victory. Having used his wit (as he had done in Korsun), he may have sold some state secret again, and hit the bull's eye — again.

Anastasius is of interest as a symbol of the epoch. Renegades always appear in times of trouble. They are a proof that foundations are about to crumble and that the time for change has come. For the renegades, this means choosing a new boss.

The chronicler does not specify what goods Anastasius took to his third "home". Some of it may have been from the Tithe Church where Anastasius had been the treasurer. Tietmar noted that the Russian Orthodox Church authorities did not much mind having Boleslav and his army stay in Kiev. The chronicler did not say anything about them either, and only pointed out Anastasius. Tietmar tells us something about the loot, based on what he heard from one of the mercenary Saxon knights who came back with them. The Polish prince was shown an unbelievable treasure, most of which was given to his allies and adherents. The rest of it was sent to his homeland. But, I repeat, it was not only the treasure amassed by several generations of the Riurik princes; much of this booty was collected from the Kievans themselves. If it was "incalculable", then one can imagine the Russian capital was completely plundered. If we believe Tietmar, the treasury was left empty. That is, Boleslav bankrupted his ally in recognition of the help he had provided.

It is worth noting that part of the plunder was given to the "adherents" of the Polish prince, that is, to those Kievans who sympathized with him. Boleslav, being a discreet politician, was procuring agents with a long-term view. One of them was Anastasius, who showed the prince the treasure. I do not think that Svyatopolk did that on his own initiative; he may have even sworn that Yaroslav had taken the treasure away.

Kievan Jews, most likely, were also among Boleslav's new converts. At least the Polish chronicler of the 15th century, Yan Dlougosh in his *History of Poland,* tells us of acts of arson targeting Jewish houses in Kiev. So that seems quite plausible. The Jewish community in Kiev was settled mostly at Kopyrevo and Kozar. They were fairly numerous and quite influential. Many of them were engaged in trade and usury, dealt with Russia's neighbors, had economic ties with them and were on friendly terms with them unlike most Kievans. So they were Boleslav's natural confederates and they could easily find common language with him.

So Boleslav plundered Kiev and took away its state and (probably) church treasures. Svyatopolk was thus left destitute. Boleslav must have undertaken this action not only out of excessive cupidity but with the aim of depriving Svyatopolk of any financial means in the political and military struggle against Yaroslav. What resistance could he put up without money?

One may ask: was this not a reply to Svyatopolk's previous hostile action? But it would be very naive to suppose that Boleslav would have acted otherwise under different circumstances. The Polish chronicler of the early 12th century, Gall the Anonymous, makes it clear. "Boleslav ruled the richest city and the most powerful Russian principality for ten months. And he kept sending monies to Poland all that time." Well, if not ten months, then he may have cleared all the treasuries of their contents in ten weeks. The main thing is, he started plundering Kiev just about as soon as he'd entered the city. That was a premeditated act, without any provocation on the part of the citizens. One may only debate when such an idea had come to his head: at Gniezno, or in Kiev when he saw the riches of Vladimir for his own eyes.

Predslava's Tragedy

One more thing may have stoked Svyatopolk's wrath — Boleslav's arrogant conduct toward the prince's relatives, mostly the women. According to Tietmar, he took along with him Vladimir's last wife and nine of his daughters. He had sent to Novgorod a high church official with a proposal to swap them for his daughter, who had been taken by Yaroslav. Nevertheless, he behaved in the chambers of the Russian princesses like an unscrupulous conqueror. The most pitiful was the fate of the beautiful Predslava, the most daring and charismatic of Vladimir's daughters, who was not afraid to meddle in men's affairs. Boleslav may have proposed to her while Vladimir was alive, and been refused. According to Gall the Anonymous, Boleslav was furious about the rejection and started the war with Yaroslav with that as part of the fuel. The same information is found with Dlougosh. This version is rather doubtful but it does tell us something of Boleslav's attitude toward Vladimir's daughter.

Once in Kiev (and such a turn of fortune happens only once in a lifetime) he made up his mind to stretch his luck to the utmost. "Then he laid Predslava, Vladimir's daughter, Yaroslav's sister, onto his bed", we can read in the latest versions of the Russian chronicles. Or in the Yermolinskaya chronicle one reads, "He had raped Predslava, Yaroslav's sister". Even Tietmar did not doubt that, since he relates the unhappy fate of the nine sisters of Yaroslav in such words: "*Quarum unam, prius ab eo desideratam, antiquus fornicator Boleslaus, oblita contectali sua, injuste duxerat*".

Polish chroniclers do not conceal the fact and even admire the acts of their hero. Gall the Anonymous wrote: "Boleslav, having entered the great and rich city, struck the golden gates with his naked sword. To those who wondered why he had done so, he replied with sarcastic laughter: 'As this sword strikes now at the golden gates of the city, so the next night will be the night of dishonor for the twin sister of the coward king who refused to give her to me in marriage. She will not be taken as a lawful wife but only one time like a concubine; the offence to our people will be avenged, but for the Russians it will be dishonor and disgrace.' So he said, and confirmed his words with action". Here is "the last paladin of Slavonic unity" as Boleslav was called by L. N. Gumilev! Here is the knight "beyond reproach" who brought to Kiev the rightful lord and showed himself as a magnanimous patron and glorious champion, in N. M. Karamzin's naive opinion. At least A. Nazarenko had a different view.

Having come to Kiev as a friend, he dishonored the daughter of the Great Vladimir, the sister of his own son-in-law and his would-be bride, whom he had so desired. He did not even pretend to cover his action by a forceful marriage, "he just wanted to enjoy his vile revenge," conceded Karamzin. That was not personal revenge on the part of a man who would not tolerate rejection. According to Gall the Anonymous, that was a conscious offence inflicted on a foe, not a friend. And if the Polish prince meant Yaroslav as his foe (though incurring risk for his own daughter), he mostly offended the Kievans and probably Svyatopolk. *Antiquus fornicator!* Well, this affair was not supposed to have meant much to Svyatopolk. What feelings could he have had for a cousin who had fought so fiercely against him? It is quite probable that, still in Gniezno, the prince had stirred Boleslav's imagination about Predslava's charms. Still, while they were there, beyond the Vistula, Svyatopolk had been a *déclassé*, whereas here at the Dnieper he was a full-fledged ruler (at least in his own eyes). Any humiliation of his (now) subjects by a foreigner must be supposed to be a personal offence against him. In this case, members of the princely family were involved. And their treatment must have revealed Boleslav's true attitude toward Svyatopolk's own kin.

Svyatopolk and Rus' in Boleslav's Dreams

The question as to what role Boleslav would assign to his relative and ally in Russian affairs was of utmost importance to Svyatopolk. He must have wondered who was he in real life: the authentic Kiev prince, the ruler of a great power, or a marionette at a fair with a buffoon tugging the strings? And he was hardly content with the answer. We shall repeat the words of Gall the Anonymous: "Boleslav owned the richest and most powerful city of Russia for ten months and kept sending money from there to Poland. In the eleventh month he began preparations for going home, for he had a very large kingdom. He did not consider his son Mieshko capable of ruling Kiev, and placed there a Russian who was his relative; and he started on his way home with the remaining treasures." This "eulogy" is in fact an exposure of the "magnanimous patron" and the "last paladin". It exposes a common conqueror who has dropped the mask of protector of the Russian prince who had been offended by his father and brothers. For it was he who possessed "the richest city and the powerful kingdom of the Russians".

He kept on sending Kiev's treasures to Gniezno — as if it were military booty. He paid no heed to his son-in-law to whom, as nominal sovereign, the treasures belonged. When leaving, he put a Russian in his place! "In his place!" The words testify to a gross violation of law. "A Russian!" Even his name was not mentioned. But was it really so?

Polish medieval historians are of one mind when talking about Boleslav's campaign in Russia as a march into an enemy country, not to the land of friends. Gall the Anonymous, speaking about Boleslav II the Bold, noted that he, like Boleslav I the Brave, "entered as an enemy into the capital of the Russian kingdom." Speaking of Boleslav the Brave, he said: "bravely invaded, boldly encroached". That is why there were legends about the sword with which the fierce Liakh struck the golden gates, and about iron poles placed at the mouth of the Soula, near the Dnieper, as a token of the conquered Russia etc..

It is important to add some foreign policy background to these flagrantly aggressive actions. Let us recollect Boleslav's words before the battle on the Bug River: "If you lose the battle", he said to his knights, "you will become Russian slaves though you are of noble descent; you and your sons will be punished for the offences inflicted". What more can be said? Vincenty Kadloubek, who wrote a century later, also thought that Boleslav had placed an iron pole at the Zaale River, a tributary of the Elba (in Saxony), in order to mark the western boundaries of his power. That idea is further developed in the *Great Chronicle* (*The Great Polish Chronicle*) of the 13th – 14th centuries. It says that "the above-mentioned King Boleslav after having established the Polish state's boundaries in Kiev, which is the capital of Russia, at the Tisza and the Danube (rivers in Hungary and Carpathia), at the river Solava (Zaale), flowing through Turingia towards the North Sea, he bravely restored the borders lost by his ancestors and erected many strongholds at the outskirts of the kingdom in order to preserve his own state and repulse the enemies — mostly at the rivers of Solava and Laba (Elba)". He most certainly did not construct any fortresses west of Kiev and only appropriated the Cherven' towns that he had taken at the beginning of his campaign.

That means that Boleslav made an attempt to subjugate the territory west of Kiev and make it dependent on Poland. But can one explain in the same way his diplomatic activities on the Dnieper heights? "Encouraged by his success in capturing the city, Boleslav sent the archbishop of this city to Yaroslav, asking the latter to give up his daughter for his wife. . . . He also sent his favorite abbot Touni with great gifts to our emperor in order to secure his benevolence and support, assuring him that he would act according to his wishes. He also sent ambassadors to Byzantium and promised benefits to the emperor if the latter were his loyal friend; otherwise, he declared he would be a staunch and invincible enemy". That activity was evidence of his impatient wish to inform the most concerned persons about the impending geopolitical shifts. They could now send their ambassadors to Boleslav not only in Gniezno but also in Kiev, to what once had been Prince Vladimir's palace.

Mstislav's Silence

One may recollect that some years later the same division along the Dnieper River was proposed by Mstislav, who ruled in the faraway Tmutorakan', to his brother Yaroslav. Then Boleslav's intentions do not seem so improbable.

Boleslav may have held preliminary talks, in secret, with the Tmutorakan' prince, the last of Vladimir's sons, who may have craved power too. It was not so difficult to send his ambassadors or intelligence officers across the Pecheneg steppes. It seems rather strange that such a brave and valiant soldier as Mstislav kept himself quietly sheltered away, beyond the Cimmerian (Kerch') Straits, during the long and bloody conflict between the Volodimerichi. (It is hard to believe that he was unaware of what was going on in his fatherland).

But it is quite another matter if he was in touch with Boleslav and Svyatopolk and had an agreement with them, centering on a friendly neutral position in exchange for which he was promised the left bank of the Dnieper territory, with the throne in Chernigov. Would not such an agreement explain the following aggressive actions of Mstislav against Yaroslav? The campaign culminated with the battle at Listven of 1024 and led to a division of the Russian lands along the Dnieper River, though according to Polish chroniclers that had happened six years earlier. Mstislav, having defeated his brother, intended to take the throne in Kiev, "but the Kievans did not accept him".

Did Mstislav really detain Yaroslav? Or was it that because of Boleslav, who still ruled in Gniezno with his iron hand, Mstislav did not want to start a new and difficult struggle with him or his heirs? Though Mstislav was a valiant soldier and was also called the Brave, he may have deemed it wiser to distance himself from two strong foes and wait and see what the outcome would be. He had behaved likewise during the battle of Listven, when he set the regiment from Chernigov against Yaroslav's Varangians while he, with his host, took positions on both flanks. When he paced up and down the site of the battle, after it was over, he was quite content: "Here are dead Severians, here are Varangians, while my men are alive!"

It is significant that having voluntarily ceded the Kievan throne in favor of Yaroslav, the elder brother, he did not then take part in the war march on the Galician town of Belz, that was mentioned in the chronicle before the death of Boleslav. Only in 1031 (when Mieshko III Lambert ruled in Poland) we can read in the Primary Chronicle: "Yaroslav and Mstislav with a large army went after the Liakhs and took many of the Cherven' towns and many Polish lands". Is that not testimony of an agreement between Mstislav and Boleslav and his henchman Svyatopolk, an agreement that may have been concluded between the autumn of 1015 and the spring of 1018, and stipulating a division of the Russian land along the Dnieper River between Boleslav's protégé and Mstislav? Such an agreement might have enabled the Polish ruler to meddle in the affairs of his eastern neighbor. I think that Boleslav would not have ventured to start such a campaign without assurances on the part of the powerful and militant prince of Tmutorakan'. (In case Yaroslav had made such an agreement with his brother, Boleslav may have renounced such encroachments altogether.) I suppose that the Polish chroniclers in 1018 and the Russian chroniclers of 1024 were speaking about the same events, events that were wrapped under the shroud of secret diplomacy. There are good grounds for such speculation.

Svyatopolk's "Quiet Revolt"

When speaking about Boleslav, our chronicle tradition bears testimony to Kiev's status under the Polish prince and is unanimous in its assessment (from the early versions of the 11th century, reflected in the Primary Chronicle, until the 15th-16th century versions). For example, we read in the Lavrentiev Chronicle, "Boleslav was sitting in Kiev", and the same in the latest existing version of the Primary Chronicle: "And Boleslav sat on Vladimir's throne". This was written in 1448 in the 1ˢᵗ Sophia and the 4ᵗʰ Novgorod chronicles. Such was the shame that Svyatopolk brought upon himself — after his father-in-law arrived, on the pretext of bringing assistance, he had perched for the rest of his rule on the edge of the prince's throne. He seemed to like it.

Who was ruling in Kiev at the time? N. M. Karamzin, enchanted by the hero, wrote: "The people again took Svyatopolk for lord and Boleslav was content with his fame as a magnanimous patron and brave soldier". In reality, the Pole was satisfied neither with the plundering of the Russian capital and country, nor with the atrocities against the women in the prince's palace, nor with the illegal usurpation of his own younger relative and well-wisher's power. One gets the impression that he was possessed by the same desire as Svyatopolk: a desire for revenge.

According to Tietmar, he kept on taking revenge for as long as he could during Svyatopolk's collusion against Vladimir's heritage. His long-cherished dream of vanquishing Vladimir, of taking possession of the proud and grand Kiev, one of the greatest cities of the Christian world, had come true. He was elated, intoxicated, and could not stop subjugating and offending everything Russian; he was intent on seeing the capital of the huge eastern Slavic power subdued and humiliated; he was eager to see Vladimir's widow, his daughters, stepson and every last citizen meek and servile. Only one thought bothered him: his greatest enemy and his only worthy foe, Vladimir (who had caused him so much trouble during the war in 1013), had not lived to see it — he did not know that neither Boris, Yaroslav nor Svyatopolk had inherited the land he had built, but that Boleslav, of all people, now disposed of the fate of all who lived in this country.

The Polish ruler was evidently sure of his might and power; he took Svyatopolk for a reliable henchman and did not doubt his loyalty. Otherwise, as an experienced commander, he would not have committed such a blunder: he would not have sent away his mercenaries and would not have deployed his own army at several cities throughout Kievan Rus'. But Svyatopolk held a different view of himself and assessed the situation differently. His father's-in-law's behavior in Kiev must have opened his eyes wide.

He saw what a humiliating role Boleslav had assigned to him. He saw that he had acquired a haughty new boss who ruled Kiev and the

Russian land as though it were his own and who treated Svyatopolk as an obedient servant who should cater to his whims and run his errands. Boleslav's plundering of the national wealth, his humiliation of Predslava and Vladimir's memory as lord of the Russian land, could not help but anger Svyatopolk. And he could not stand Boreslav's arrogant and disdainful attitude toward himself. He had grown up with an offended conscience, he had felt dishonored all his life and burned for revenge and justice, he was excessively self-conscious and suffered any encroachment on his honor very acutely.

One may well imagine how he felt at being so offended and insulted as a true heir to the Kiev throne. Boleslav was unwilling to quit the capital (when he did flee, it was because he was forced to do so); and his intention to make that part of Kievan Rus' that lay along the right bank of the Dnieper dependent on Poland (according to Polish chronicles, subjugated) contradicted the original agreements and must have caused rather a negative reaction on Svyatopolk's part. Being a decisive man, he was wont to act immediately (although not always adequately), and he could not leave his father-in-law's outrageous behavior without response. In the present circumstances, he could not find any other means of self defense but to give a secret order to his trusty men: "Strike at the Liakhs!".

He was taking a great risk in issuing such an order. By radically changing the political rapport of forces, he placed his future at stake. He had had only two allies — the Pechenegs and the Poles. And it had not been easy to enroll them. Now, in the face of Yaroslav, who was gaining strength, he had to renounce the more powerful of the two. It was evidently difficult for Svyatopolk to get at Boleslav, and it entailed risking not only his political future but also his head. His revolt had to be pursued under the shroud of "friendship and mutual understanding". Some evidence of that can be seen later. Still, such a decision he made indeed.

Svyatopolk, like some of his cousins (Boris and Gleb), and unlike Yaroslav, was a passionate man. According to L. N. Gumilev, that is a "person whose passionate impulses are greater than the instinct of self-preservation". That description evidently suited Svyatopolk. He was capable of taking great risks. He saw himself as a full-fledged prince of the Russian land and he fought his destiny without scruples over the means.

I think there was another reason that impelled him to act like that — the discontent of the populace. V. N. Tatishchev, whose information — unlike Karamzin's — is quite plausible, reveals the population's complaints against the Poles. The plundering of the prince's treasury and national wealth was of concern not only to the prince. In varying degrees it infringed on the interests of all strata of the population: the boyars, merchants, craftsmen, peasants et al, for it was a major resource in maintaining state and public stability. If one assumes that the invaders of Kiev behaved in more or less the same way as the Varangians did in Novgorod, then a conflict was bound to come. Can there be any doubt? Since Svyatopolk had come to power, this is the first time that he showed that he was mindful of public support. Now, forced to choose between "Polish assistance" and "public opinion", he took the side of the latter. And that was the mainstay of his future might and power.

There is little to be said about "the slaughter". Karamzin describes it like this: "Villains do not know gratitude. Svyatopolk, fearing the long term patronage of his father-in-law and wishing to establish his independence as soon as possible, gave secret orders to the mayors to kill all the Poles — who thought they were living among friends — and he did not take any precautions [we are not sure of that! — *author's note*]. . . He may have reserved such a fate for Boleslav as well, who was sheltered in Kiev, but he learned about the collusion and left the capital . . . " We agree here with the author's assessment of the events and of Svyatopolk's intentions (we have said enough about "friends" and "gratitude" earlier).

Svyatopolk, true to his style, arranged a new collusion, the fifth, (one against Vladimir plus his three sons) and may have harbored plans for revenge against Boleslav himself, should circumstances ever allow for that. Boleslav learned too late about the plot that resulted in the "slaughter" of the Polish troops, otherwise he would have taken measures against it. We do not know the places where the action unfolded, we do not know who arranged it and who executed it. It is only clear that the Polish regiments and detachments must have been stationed not far from the capital, for instance in Vyshgorod, Belgorod, or Vasilev. Boleslav could hardly risk dispersing his forces at great distance, for fear of Yaroslav's hosts appearing near Kiev.

Karamzin's guess about the mayors who acted on Svyatopolk's orders is no more than a logical assumption, although it may be true to a certain extent. In my opinion, the leading role was assigned to officers from the prince's secret service, whom he managed to preserve during his wanderings and to find after his return. Without drawing undue attention, positioned in the proper places, they delivered their boss's orders to the proper men, who were to gather small mobile detachments capable of implementing the prince's will and arrange night-time attacks on the Poles' premises. Success depended to a large extent on the sympathy and the cooperation of the local populace.

The fact that the Polish troops were swiftly eliminated seems to confirm that sympathy and cooperation. It is more difficult to reconstruct what happened in Kiev at the time. The Lavrentiev chronicle has it that Svyatopolk gave orders to kill "Liakhs" all over the city, i.e. Kiev. But other ancient scrolls speak about "towns". That's right — for Boleslav must have had some means to prevent such a course of events in the capital (otherwise he could not get out of there safely). But a certain amount of turmoil evidently sent a tremor through Kiev nevertheless. And "towns" may certainly have included the capital itself.

Let us recollect Dlougosh's testimony about the Kievans' actions against the Jewish community in Kiev. L. N. Gumilev puts it this way: "As soon as it turned out that the Poles, and the Jews associated with them, supported Svyatopolk at his second (?) return to the throne, the Russian troops who had enthroned him attacked the Jews living in Kiev and burned down their houses." (Later on, the scholar asserts that the citizens changed their minds as to the great prince and killed the Poles stationed there.) I do not think there is any basis for referring to "Russian troops" who brought Svyatopolk to the throne and the Kievans' enmity to him immediately following his arrival in the capital in the company of Boleslav. He certainly had some friends and some foes in the city. And the prince's revolt against the Poles (covert though it was) may have only enhanced his popularity.

I can accept Gumilev's opinion of the situation in Kiev in September and October of 1018 only with such reservations: that a "quiet mutiny" took place in Kiev, and it induced Boleslav to "quit the city", as was asserted in the chronicle.

Triumphantly Running Away (with Yaroslav's Horsemen in the Background)

A. A. Shakhmatov was firmly opposed to such a view. "Does such an explanation of Boleslav's departure from Kiev conform to reality?" he asked; and he gave the unequivocal answer — "Absolutely not!"

First, we have information that Boleslav took with him Yaroslav's belongings and boyars, his two sisters and many prisoners. Could a fugitive, fearing that he would be disarmed in an enemy country, act that way? Second, Tietmar of Mersebourg, a contemporary of the 1018 events, describes Boleslav's triumphant return to Poland after the brilliantly executed military campaign. So one should count Boleslav's flight from Kiev as no more than the "patriotic elation of the chronicler."

One may, however, argue that Napoleon also left Moscow without any pressure on the part of the enemy, with a still-powerful army and a convoy of plundered loot. Still, that was not a triumphant march but a retreat, induced by implacable circumstances, and resembled very much a flight. That was what happened to Boleslav. Or, at least, that was how he read the "alignment of the stars". Why did he make such a hasty retreat to Poland, leaving his son-in-law alone? Had he suddenly recollected some urgent business left unattended at home? Boleslav managed to leave Russia with the remaining troops, with dignity, and took along with him the Kiev treasures, the widow of Grand Prince Vladimir and some of the Prince's daughters, including Predslava (who was treated like a slave), and also taking with him some noblemen from Kiev. That means he did not flee the city but managed to effect a timely retreat while the situation was still under his control, a retreat that he could present as the triumphant return of a monarch who had successfully fulfilled his mission. If Svyatopolk and the citizens allowed him to act that way, it follows that they lacked the essential military force (as Gumilev thought).

We could leave the story of Svyatopolk's "fifth conspiracy" at that, but for a curious remark by Dlougosh. Clearly confused as to the dates (in this case he meant 1018, instead of 1008, when Vladimir was still alive) the Polish chronicler relates Yaroslav's constant and abortive attempts to overcome his foreign rival who was more talented in the military art. According to Karamzin, "In 1008 Boleslav defeated Yaroslav at the Bug River, captured the capital and stationed his army in several cities. Yaroslav came to Kiev but suffered another defeat and retreated to Novgorod. The Polish king plundered Kiev because of Svyatopolk's infidelity; he wanted to go back to his fatherland but Yaroslav attacked him at the border with a host of Russians, Polovtsy (who had not yet made their debut on history's stage), Pechenegs, and Varangians, was crushed again and fled."

N. M. Karamzin treats that piece of information as a folktale, "a mixture of Nestor and old Polish fables that rather stretch the imagination", though M. Stryikovsky and some other chroniclers repeated it later. There is, of course, a lot of fantasy in Dlougosh's story but should one treat it as a "fable"? Gall the Anonymous also speaks of a battle between Yaroslav and Boleslav at the end of the Polish intervention, when Yaroslav allegedly chased the retreating enemy. One may recollect the "short remark" in the Russian Primary Chronicle that sums up the Kiev events. Boleslav "came back to his land and Svyatopolk began reigning in Kiev. Yaroslav went after Svyatopolk and the latter fled to the Pechenegs." One should point out that Yaroslav's march on Kiev is listed in the chronicle under the same year 6526 (March 1018 — February 1019). As soon as Boleslav left Kiev, about the middle of October, the Novgorod prince could have learned about this retreat from his informers in the capital; but not before mid-November or thereabouts, if he was, at the time, on the Volkhov riverbank. That means that he had about three months for preparations and the march from Novgorod to Kiev. He could hardly have managed that in a shorter time. It is quite another matter if his troops were deployed at the northern boundaries of the Kiev land, for instance in the vicinity of Liubech. These considerations, along with the information from the chronicles, make the latter version more probable — especially since it contains a story about events in Novgorod late in August or early September of 1018.

At the time, the "military leader" who had just come back from the Bug River with only four attendants made an attempt to sow panic in the heart of his own (Swedish) father-in-law overseas. But the Novgorodians, headed by their mayor (posadnik) Constantine (son of the famous Dobrynia) did not let him do that. They "broke up Yaroslav's boat" and said: "We want you to fight Boleslav and Svyatopolk". They began actively collecting resources (cattle) from boyars, men and foremen. "They brought Varangians, gave the cattle to them and Yaroslav gathered many troops."

It is important to note that the Novgorodians did not wait until Boleslav quit the high banks of the Dnieper and left the country. They made preparations for war with him, and not only with his henchman. They had to start the march as soon as they had collected an army capable of fighting. Considering the sequence of events, one may conclude that the Novgorodian and Varangian troops left the Riurik capital about at the same time as the Pole left the plundered nest of his descendants, or even earlier. And it is quite possible that Boleslav was aware of these preparations for a military and political revenge. He may have got the crucial information from his own or from Svyatopolk's scouts. It is also probable that Yaroslav had sent small reconnaissance details to the Kiev borders, where they would have met with Polish guards.

If Boleslav knew that Novgorod was preparing for a war, he could hardly have waited for them behind the walls of Kiev or even on the Russian land. That would mean being hit from both the front and the rear. And, while Svyatopolk did not miss his brother, most Kievans looked toward Dorogozhich and Kapich with hope and expectations. It was not in Boleslav's interests to give the enemy such an advantage, so that in the event of failure, he would have found himself in the heart of a hostile country like a bear in a trap many miles from his den.

Such a gloomy prospect was quite probable since his army had suffered tangible losses, and he was quite aware that Yaroslav was about to come from the north with a "sizable force" — or may have already started the march. He may have had this in mind since October, and this time he was quite right. For if we believe Dlougosh or Gall the Anonymous about the Novgorodians' clash with the Poles, at the Bug, late in autumn or that winter, then we should think that Yaroslav had mounted his charger somewhat earlier and moved faster than Boleslav could, burdened as he was with a convoy and prisoners. One may also assume that he knew from his informers about Svyatopolk's "relative's" intentions and movements, so he was in a hurry to get to Kiev and rescue the prince's family, state treasury and property. But he was late, at that. Maybe his avant-garde troops managed to prick at the rearguard of the retreating Poles.

Thus an analysis of Russian and Polish sources leads me to conclude that, in the late autumn of 1018, Yaroslav began a second march against Boleslav in order to defeat him in a field battle, or to lay siege to the capital and prevent its being plundered and the Russian power's being humiliated. This campaign together with other actions against the Poles in some cities on Kievan land (and probably in Kiev itself) did not prevent Boleslav from implementing his base intentions but all these military actions did induce him to hastily quit the territory of Russia (to fly from it, as one scribe put it). So his projects and plans for the division of the Russian state and its vassal domination remained futile, although they were reflected in some chronicles and so have reached us in posterity.

Vanity of Vanities

In the autumn of 1018 Yaroslav and Svyatopolk, though they remained foes and did not conspire together, started a united struggle against the common enemy of the eastern Slavic state. And they were eventually crowned with success. Svyatopolk was the first to triumph. But, as readers already know, that triumph did not last long. The struggle between the brothers was nearly over. Yaroslav, slowly but surely, was gaining ground. No failure could impede his thrust. And his opportunities seemed inexhaustible. Svyatopolk was also stubborn; but his resources were dwindling day by day. No matter how he tried to preserve unity with the Kiev population, whatever sacrifices he made, that unity was crumbling. The people must have remembered too well his edgy father-in-law's stay in Russia. They were also fed up with the Pechenegs, who too often came there and caused trouble. Svyatopolk was constantly sawing the very branch he was sitting on. He could not manage without foreign help. He also could not keep his grip on the foreign swords and sabers. Abusing his foreign support meant that he was left without any swords at all. In such a situation, his demise could not be far off.

To our regret, the chronicle gives too brief an account of the events in Kiev after Boleslav's retreat. Boleslav left for Poland and Svyatopolk "began his rule in Kiev". When Yaroslav came, Svyatopolk headed off to the Pechenegs. Svyatopolk had worked hard but he had to cede the Kiev throne to another claimant. That implies that he did not manage to gather an adequate army in Kiev and its vicinity to counter his brother in the field, or even to shelter safely within the city walls. He seems to have left the city soon after his father-in-law and had little chance to properly savor his power.

Nestor wrote the following in the *Reading about Boris and Gleb*: "God did not permit the Accursed to kill all his brothers and harm his land. There was a mutiny and he was chased away, not only from the city but from the country too". There it is! Mutiny is collusion among the people. First of all, the Kievans, but surely others participated too. One may assume that the revolt took place even before Yaroslav's horsemen appeared to the north of Kiev, though they may have been expected. The mutiny was evidently organized and headed by the adherents of the Novgorod prince, who managed to win over the majority of the townsfolk. In part, this would be because during the Kievans' struggle with Boleslav, Svyatopolk did not prove himself as the leader of the people's resistance. He may have taken a certain part in driving the Polish out of the Russian land, but in Kiev he must have been too invisible. Either he did not believe in the success of the enterprise and was afraid of falling prisoner to his vengeful father-in-law, or he was afraid to sever his relations with him for good.

As a result, Boleslav left Kiev, taking along with him everything and everybody he wanted. One of the reasons for the Kievans' discontent with the prince was the large number of prisoners and hostages taken by Boleslav. "He took a great many people with him" — wrote the scribe. Who were these people? They were predominantly Kievans, mostly those who had participated in the revolt against the Polish. There were also some other men that were connected to it, their relatives and families. Svyatopolk either did not want to or was not able to help them. Moreover, he allowed the enraged Boleslav to devastate the city, in the end. The Polish prince took only those boyars who had served Yaroslav; he spared those who were loyal to Svyatopolk. He did not want to spoil his relations with his son-in-law in such a strenuous and unpredictable situation. But that was not all.

Svyatopolk, who was so fond of the tactics of collusion and intrigues, became the victim of circumstances that he could not master. He left Kiev forever. He attempted a return the following year with the help of the Pecheneg cavalry. According to N. N. Ilyin, Svyatopolk managed to gather some local troops under his standards for the battle that, according to chronicles, took place in 1016, but actually took place in

1019. It is tempting to attribute it rather to late 1018, since it was a year later that Svyatopolk came with the nomads and waged another battle with Yaroslav at the Alta River. Such a version would set straight the chronology of the Eimund saga, but if one meddles with historical documents in such a way it may lead to the rewriting of actual historic events. N. N. Ilyin's version, though supported by some scholars, remains rather doubtful.

It was the last time Yaropolk's scion came to terms with the population of the Kiev land. He became alien to them and turned into an enemy. The fierce battle at the Alta River, where they grappled three times, did not bode well for Svyatopolk — even if he had prevailed. But he lost, in any case.

10. Svyatopolk's End. A Version of the "Eimund Yarn"

An Agent Must be Paid

Russian and foreign sources give different accounts of what happened afterward. The Eimund Yarn does not mention the battle at the Alta, but some time after the glorious defense of Kiev the Viking again came before Yaroslav and spoke of wage arrears (he did not seem to come to the prince on other matters). He rebuked his "employer" that he and his men had earned much more than had been paid and told him that this was not "right". For many of his men had suffered losses, "some lost legs, others — hands, some have injured other limbs or had their weapons spoiled". So he asked for redemption from the prince, without which they would leave.

Yaroslav: "I do not want you to leave, but we cannot pay such high wages for we do not expect war".

Eimund (supplying the bait): "We need money, our men do not want to toil for food only. We would rather go to other konungs and would seek honors there. There does not seem to be a war here, but are you sure that the konung is dead?"

Yaroslav: "I think that he is, for his banner is with us".

Eimund: "Do you know where lies his grave?"

Yaroslav: "No".

Eimund: "Would it not be wise not to know it".

Yaroslav: "Do you know more about it than other people?"

Eimund: "He was not so sorry to relinquish his banner in order to save his life. I think he is still at large and a danger; he was last winter in Turkland and he thinks to declare war on you. He has an army that would not retreat: they are Turks and Blokoumen (Valachs? – Auth.) and many other wild people. I was also told that he wants to quit Christianity and to divide the country among those savage peoples if he manages to take Gardariki from you. If these things come to pass as he has conceived, one may expect that he would drive all your relatives away from the country in disgrace".

Yaroslav: "How soon will he come here, with his wild army?"

Eimund: "In a fortnight".

Yaroslav: (perplexed): "Whatever shall we do? Now we cannot do without your advice".

Ragnar, a friend of Eimund who was present at the talks, said it was Yaroslav's own problem. But Eimund gracefully agreed not to leave the prince in trouble and suggested that the only thing to be decided was when to rally the host — now, or later, when the Normans would be exhausted defending the country (but only if the lord paid them their wages in full!) Yaroslav replied that rallying the host would be better done later. But Eimund retorted to the contrary, saying that he was not at all sure "how it would turn out on the part of those who had insisted on it". (We can deduce that there had been some talk in the Yaroslav suite about rallying the host, although nobody had been getting ready for war.)

Then they went on about the fate of "Bouritslav".

Eimund: "Whatever shall we do, my lord, when we get to the konung — shall we slay him or not? There will be no end to strife while you both are alive."

Yaroslav: "I will not urge people to fight konung Bouritslav; nor will I blame anyone if he is dead . . ."

As one can see, this is an old scenario. Eimund goes to Yaroslav for the wages and gets a cold reception, for the prince does not expect a war. The Viking agrees that war is not likely, but . . . Bouritslav will come to Russia in a fortnight with a host of "savage people". Then he easily gets what he is after.

Leaving aside many inconsistencies in the saga, we again find our-selves facing a romantic element: the vigorous Varangian reconnais-sance has produced something entirely new this time, namely, Bourit-slav's intention "to estrange himself from Christianity". Judging from the sense of the tale and its context (openness to making a territorial deal with the nomads) there is no talk about reviving Svyatopolk's pro-Western allegiance as one may assume (for there was no digression from Christianity in that). The message is that he was ready to accept the religion and the culture of the nomad East, to turn "infidel", as they would say somewhat later.

Such a move would have been quite consistent with Svyatopolk's adventurous character. By breaking relations with Boleslav, he could have broken his ties with the West in general. Rus' was becoming alien to him. He could have returned there only as a conqueror. But one al-ways has to pay for help, at least with promises. He might well have promised some territorial concessions, and a spiritual and religious rap-prochement. As soon as he became strong, he could forget about all that and retrieve what had been lost.

According to the saga, this talk between Yaroslav and Eimund had decided the fate of "Bouritslav" (in other words, Svyatopolk). Ilyin thought that the saga depicts Yaroslav as a "sneaky sly person capable of fratricide and ready to shift the responsibility for it onto others, a person from whom Eimund gets only half commitment to the plan". But the initiative was not the prince's and his half consent was for a single combat. The sly Vikings decided that a single battle would be too risky, and that a different approach was needed. As events proved.

Incarnations of Agents: Merchant — Mendicant — Executioner

"They went on about their own business", the saga continues. They did not rally the troops and they did not prepare their arms. Many people wondered why not, given that such a scourge was near at hand (the secret had somehow leaked out). Somewhat later, they learned that Bouritslav had come to Gardariki with a large host and many sav-age people.

Eimund feigned ignorance, and did not try to stop it. Many said that he did not dare to fight Bouritslav. We must admit that Eimund had the excellent features of a professional scout: he knew everything (as we shall find out later) and kept a straight face when everybody around him talked about an impending invasion. That inspires a certain respect for him. If the saga does not lie, there were very few spy masters of such high professional skill in Russia at the time — although the James Bond of the 11th century made a laughing stock of himself when he started his "hunt" for Bouritslav.

"Once, early in the morning", relates the saga, "Eimund summoned his relative Ragnar along with ten other men. They took horses and left the city, all the twelve of them." They took along "a spare horse and loaded it with munitions and supplies. They were clad like merchants, and people did not know what their voyage meant and what cunning lay behind it. As the reader knows, merchant camouflage was an old and safe form of cover. Other Varangians and Kievan onlookers watched them go, noted their passing, but did not recognize the voivode and the reconnaissance chief and did not know where they were going. It was essential that no one could tell, in case any of Bouritslav's spies should have spotted them. But everything went well. Eimund and his entourage "entered a forest and rode through it all day long until the night fell. Then they left the forest and approached a big oak. There was a nice field around and wide-open space. Then konung Eimund said: 'Here we shall stop. I have learned that konung Bouritslav will make a night stopover here and they will put up their tents for the night.' They went round the trees and walked along the clearing looking for the best place for the tent. Then Eimund said: 'Here konung Bouritslav will set up his camp. I was told that he always chooses a place near the woods so that he can hide there if necessary'."

The reader can assess the quality and the timeliness of the information at Eimund's disposal, even though neither he nor Yaroslav had left the capital before that. Accurate intelligence is expensive in any age. One could hardly obtain it by interrogating chance passers-by or aimless wanderers. So if one believes the saga, one should bear in mind the likelihood of a chain of interconnected paid agents capable of obtaining such information.

Now, Eimund had devised the following. He took a rope, went to the clearing and had one of his men tie one end to the branches of the tree. They bent the tree so that its branches reached the ground. Then Eimund said: "To my mind, that would be good enough". Then they tightened the rope and fastened the ends. As they were finishing, night fell and they heard the noise of an approaching host. The Varangians hid in the woods and kept watch. They saw a large army and a splendid cart, with many people following it; and a rider carrying a banner was leading the group. The host went exactly to the place that konung Eimund had supposed was best suited for the tent. They set up the tent there and the host settled near the woods. It was quite dark by that time. The host's konung (Bouritslav) had a magnificent tent. It consisted of four sections, and one pole stood above it, on top of which there was a golden orb with a weathercock. The Varangians saw from the woods what was going on and kept quiet.

The host lit their fires in the camp and the Varangians understood that they were getting supper ready. Their stomachs growled. Eimund decided to go on a bit of a scouting mission once again. "We don't have too much food", said he; "I shall go to the camp and get some." Eimund put on the clothes of a mendicant, applied a goat's beard to his chin, took two staffs in his hand and went to the konung's tent asking for food. Then he went to the next tent and collected further provisions, thanking them for their kind attitude. Then he went back to his friends and handed over a good supper; but Eimund had gathered more than a good meal.

When the camp grew quiet, Eimund left six of his men near the horses, on guard, and took the others along to the clearing, to the tents. There did not seem to be any trouble. He left two men with axes near the oak so that they would cut the ropes that were pinning it to the ground. The third one was to hold another rope, which Eimund and two other helpers would tie to the top of Bouritslav's tent. "We shall give you a sign and you, with the two other men, will cut the rope. God willing, the tree will rise and lift off the tent." Bjorn, with Eimund and Ragnar, approached the tent, made a loop in the rope and, reaching with a lance, set it over the weathercock on the top of the tent. Everything was quiet. The men in the tents slept soundly, for they were tired after the march — and they were drunk. When everything was ready, the Varangians started pulling the rope and snugged it up. Eimund came closer to the tent, for he wanted to be nearby when it leapt up. They gave the rope a jerk, the guard gave the signal, and the other two cut the rope. The tree shot back upright, taking the konung's tent and throwing it far into the woods. All the fires went out at once.

Eimund had noted the place where the konung slept; he went straight there and slew him and many others. He took Bouritslav's head and fled to the woods. Bouritslav's men tried to follow him but could not find his trail. Bouritslav's surviving followers were terrified when they saw the full scale of the disaster, but Eimund and his men took off, and arrived home early in the morning.

When Eimund met "Yaritslav konung", he related to him the truth about Bouritslav's fate.

Eimund: "Have a look at the head, my lord. Do you recognize it?"

The konung flushed red when he saw it.

Eimund: "That was done by us, the Normans, my lord. Now take care to bury your brother's body with honors".

Yaroslav: "You did this hastily and you should take the trouble to bury him. What are his people going to do now?"

Eimund: "I should think they would assemble a council and suspect one another, for they did not see us. Then they would disagree, and none of them will believe another, so I do not think that they will mourn and bury their konung".

The Varangians returned to the scene of the "bold deed". "It happened as Eimund had expected. All of Bouritslav's men had gone away in disagreement. Eimund reached the clearing and saw the konung's body. Nobody was there with it. They collected the corpse, joined the head to the body and took it home. Many people knew about the burial. All the people in the country took konung Yaritslav's side and he became king of the principality where they had both ruled before that. People took an oath of allegiance to Yaroslav (and he became the only ruler)."

Such is the story. Some researches believe it, others — no. Indeed, the saga is charming in its precision and details that either incline one to believe it and take it as actual truth or to reject it as a complete fabrication. But sagas in general and the *Eimund Yarn* in particular contain many verified historical details; to reject it does not seem right. On the other hand, in the description of Eimund's deed many dubious and ambivalent situations and assertions are found. Can one imagine that an army coming into a strange country and having set up camp at one day's distance from the enemy's capital would fail to place guards on duty, even by the tent of their leader? If the guards were stationed as usual, Eimund's chances for success would have been next to zero. The Varangians would have been captured while making a loop for the weathercock on the pole (if the suspicious mendicant hadn't already been detained before that).

Can one imagine that the "savage people," after Bouritslav's demise, scattered all over the place but did not plunder the nearby Russian towns and villages? They had come there with that very purpose in mind. Hence we have to deal with a legend where reality and imagination are intertwined and the real facts may have been corrupted beyond recognition.

Among the saga's heroes, Bjorn from Iceland allegedly beat the best Russian warrior, even on his own terrain; that makes the story less probable and casts doubts on the origin of the yarn. The use of a tree as a catapult has been known in literature since olden times. One can also establish a similarity with the saga of Harald the Stern by Khakon Ivarsson, as it depicts the assassination of Sven Asmund, turned into a robber. The historical actuality of Eimund's deeds remains quite dubious.

As we have mentioned earlier, some researches consider that the subject of this saga is not Svyatopolk but Boris. Indeed, the saga describes "a broad and pleasant meadow" one day's travel from the capital, where at different times both Svyatopolk and Boris camped. It may have been in the Alta valley. The circumstances of the assassination and the place of burial (at home) are also similar to the Russian church legend about Boris. The names of Boris and Bouritslav bear some resemblance (as A. V. Golovko observed). Of course, Boleslav also sounds similar; and Bouritslav is well-known in Scandinavian literature dealing with other circumstances and other lands. If one assumes that the Eimund Yarn concerned Boris, then all the events about "the hero from the bright valley" (Bjorn) and his mates have been inflated for the purpose of glorifying the Vikings and have nothing to do with actual facts. Boris was not the main and constant rival of Yaroslav; he did not bring the Pechenegs to the Russian lands (they were, in fact, allies of Svyatopolk and Boleslav); so, was he slain by his natural brother and not by his cousin? To my mind the person depicted in the saga is first and foremost Svyatopolk.

I would cite some domestic specialists on Scandinavian sagas. "What is the description of the struggle between Yaritslav and Bouritslav? Certainly it is based on actual facts, but they are also colored by the tradition of burnishing Eimund's image. Most of the events that are known to the author have been revised and edited in a literary manner, including the story of Svyatopolk's death. Killing with the help of an arched tree is known from ancient times; among the Russian historians, Leo Diacon and Saxon Grammatik mention it when describing Prince Igor's death. The notion of dressing up as a wanderer is evident in *The Yarn about Torleiv, Scald of Yarls* and in the *Saga about Khromound Grippson.*

The severing of one's brother's head is a motif represented in both old Scandinavian and European literature. The story recalls an episode from the *Saga about Harald the Stern* and *The Land Circle.* Yaritslav instigates Eimund and Sven instigates Hakon to slay Asmund, but neither one gives a definite order. Yaroslav, like Sven, accuses the murderer of overstepping his powers, but does not punish him for that. In both cases, the assassin shows the head of the victim to the konung and asks if he recognizes it, and the konung turns red in the face upon seeing it. It is quite probable that the episode in the *Eimund Yarn* is modeled on the pattern of the *Saga about Harald the Stern*, using the language of the time.

As one can see, the episode of Bouritslav's assassination is composed of some possible existing traditional lore with an ending borrowed from an earlier and well-known saga. No actual facts can be attributed to reality. The attempt to identify Bouritslav with Boris and not with Svyatopolk Vladimirovich does not make the picture clearer, even if both men are confused here as one and the same person. Most likely, the episode must have been composed by the author on the basis of Svyatopolk/Bouritslav's death after the last battle with Yaroslav. He did not know much about the death of Yaroslav's rival and simply used well-known motifs in order to glorify Eimund (G. V. Melnikova-Glazyrina, T. N. Jackson, E. A. Melnikova).

11. "Between the Czechs and the Liakhs." The Russian Version

Vengeance

Russian sources tell us that after the Alta River Battle, Svyatopolk fled either to "the Liakhs" or, first, to "the Pechenegs, later on to emerge again in Berestie" (Brest). One may suppose that the Pechenegs, having suffered a heavy defeat, would have refused any further help to him and that Svyatopolk was obliged to appeal to his mighty father-in-law in order to get back on his feet. On the way home, he may have visited his Turov principality, seeking shelter and some cooperation there — although Karamzin denies that he met Boleslav of Poland again. "His men brought him on a stretcher to Brest, a town in the Turov principality, and he ordered them to go further abroad. He was pursued by heaven's wrath, his mind was wandering, and he had visions of his foes chasing him; he was scared nearly to death." So he may have decided not to try Boleslav's magnanimity once again, but passed through Poland and ended his vicious life in the Bohemian wilderness, brooding over his deserved anguishes, remembered by his contemporaries and by posterity.

Failing to get any help from his father-in-law, Svyatopolk did not go back to Turov but must have turned south. He found himself someplace between Poland and Czechia, in some "desert" where he ended his life under uncertain circumstances. The mysterious death of the mutineer who roiled Russian history for so long has stirred the imagination of the Russian people ever since.

"A church legend", reflected in the Legend, Passion and Praise of SS. Boris and Gleb, interpreted the event as a sign of God's wrath and commented: "And when he fled, Satan afflicted him; his bones became soft. He could not ride a horse, so they carried him on a stretcher. They brought him to Berestie. He told them that they were being pursued, so he urged them to go with him further. They sent someone out to reconnoiter, and there was no one following them and no one coming after them. His men replied: 'Nobody is following us', and they would not go further with him. He was sick and cried out from time to time: 'Here they come!' He could not stand to stay in one place for long. He passed through the Liakhs' land and arrived at a desert between the Czechs and the Liakhs, where he turned west. His truth had proven to be false. He suffered like one cursed by the heavens. His injury was mortal and he passed away in great pain. His grave is still in that desert and it stinks foully . . ."

This is the essence of the story. During his flight from the last battle, Svyatopolk must have suffered a nervous breakdown, a shock, and found himself partially paralyzed. He was taken on a stretcher to Berestie, but he imagined he was still being chased. Yaroslav may have sent somebody after him, but was that the main reason for his flight to Poland? He may have counted on keeping a low profile in the Turov backwoods before taking some definite decision. Maybe he developed another disease, the paranoia of being pursued. He imagined pursuers everywhere, chasing him like the wind. "Here they come, here they come", he would shriek, sitting up on his sickbed and pointing in one direction or another. His servants would send guards to search in every direction for an imagined enemy.

Svyatopolk crossed Poland and reached a deserted place at the frontier of Czechia. By "desert" they meant some thinly populated place, maybe a forest or a mountain. That was his last place of abode. He was not killed in battle, or executed, but died as a result of this illness.

"Is it not an impressive description?" I. N. Danilevsky asks. "One gets the impression that it was written by an eyewitness who ran away with the cursed prince. The picture is so vivid that it is convincing as to its authenticity. The scribe's attitude vis-à-vis the dying Svyatopolk is also quite clear. The overwhelming majority of historians get this same impression from the text."

But one should interpret all the details presented in the story as clues to an opposite conclusion, advises Danilevsky. Historians' attempts to locate the place of the "desert" have turned out to be futile; the expression "between the Czechs and Liakhs" is a way of saying "God knows where". If one insists that, "as can be seen from the text, the scribe knows for sure where Svyatopolk was buried" then one is mistaken, for that "direct" knowledge is not so "straightforward" as our common sense would have it. The expression, "the grave survives to this day", is present in the Primary Chronicle in the description of every pagan prince's death, even when the author of the chronicle clearly did not know its location.

"And there is more to it," notes Danilevsky. He proves that this description of Svyatopolk's death first appeared in the late 11th century. Furthermore, the description itself is not very original, but a pastiche of biblical stories from the *Chronicle of Georgy Amartol* about Irod Agrippa and Antioch IV Epiphan. Svyatopolk in the "desert" resembles the passage about Azazi-El in the apocryphal *Book of Enoch*.

Further, as the author points out, the scribe shows a persistent propensity to rehabilitate the "cursed prince". First, he hints that he was just a "scapegoat" (as in the biblical Aaron and his "scapegoat" in the desert), then when he compares Svyatopolk's actions with the biblical Avimelekhs (according to Danilevsky), and not least when he points to an alleged similarity between Vladimir's sons and Jacob's sons.

See also *A Tale by Epiphany of the Cypress about the 12 gems on the robe of the first priest*, where, as Danilevsky notes, the order of the gems determines the presentation of Vladimir's sons. Svyatopolk was similar to Dan, the investigator recollects, as the latter was preying on his brother Joseph like "a lynx upon a goat", but God did not allow him "to perform the evil deed". "As we can see", Danilevsky concludes, "the chronicle tells the story of a crime that was never perpetrated!" The riddle requires explanation.

It is the last argument in favor of Svyatopolk's personality. In sum, the chronicler's implicit hints allow him to assert that:

1) "At close examination, the story of Svyatopolk's flight and his death is a revival of the Bible's position on 'what should be the consequences of a fratricidal crime'. The actual demise of the former Turov prince would be established".

2) Svyatopolk was a product of his time. He may have been cruel and perfidious, but not unlike most of his contemporary chieftains. Yet few of them were so denigrated in posterity as he. Even after his death, he was plagued by what we call politics. A great many political crimes were ascribed to him, although some of them were perpetrated by others, let us say by the Yaroslav the Wise."

True, Yaroslav proved himself a shortsighted ruler, an untalented soldier and a not very appealing personality. But should we condemn him for actions that the Old Russian tradition treats as having been perpetrated by Svyatopolk?

Like the authors of the *Readings* and the Legend, the historian apparently did not have accurate information about Svyatopolk's death, though he knew about his illness ("bones weakening" etc.) and the approximate location of his demise. On these premises, he picked up some similarities from the Bible.

By the way, in both chronicles there is also another reference — to the Roman emperor Flavius Claudius Julian who is better known under the name of Julian the Apostate. Nestor mentions him rather vaguely and briefly: "He [Svyatopolk] went to foreign lands and died there. The death of the sinner was awful; many of those who saw him in the darkness likened him to Julian the Transgressor". Normal people could not have seen him in hell's darkness, so one may assume that darkness of the mind was meant there. In the Legend, the similarity is presented somewhat differently: "Like the Caesar Julian, he had spilled a lot of blood from holy martyrs and had a bitter and inhuman death: his heart was pierced by a lance. He was running away and took in the end such an abominable death." One may also interpret this passage as a suggestion that "his pursuers were unknown" and there is also a hint that he did not die a natural death. That version may be accepted.

The ancient Parimiynik, confusing Lemekh with Avimelekh, tells us that the former born (Svyatopolk's parentage was also less than straightforward) of adultery, also "slaughtered his brethren" and "was killed by his own wife, who used a broken millstone for that purpose". But it would be quite improbable to look for a woman with a stone in her hand in connection with Svyatopolk's demise. The chronicler who left us the Primary Chronicle also used Parnimiynik's text but he excluded the passage about a "wife with a stone".

On the whole, both the chronicle and the other sources pertinent to the topic depict Svyatopolk's demise as being a result of the disease sent to him by God, "a morbid injury" that eventually brought him to a miserable end, either by itself or by virtue of unknown forces. The description of the illness that was provided only by the unknown author of the Legend is rather authentic, and that makes this version of the prince's death quite plausible.

I may add that there are no existing alternatives in the data that we have at the present time. There is only one exception to it, in the *Yarn about Eimund*.

But even assuming that the essence of Eimund's story is true, and attributing the episode to the struggle between Yaroslav and Svyatopolk, we do not contradict the version suggested by the Russian scribes in the chronicles (at least what is given in the original collection, in the Primary Chronicle, the Legend, the *Readings*, Parnimiynik's reading and prologue oration) where the circumstances of Svyatopolk's death are not specified.

Also, like Emperor Julian, pierced by somebody's lance, the prince may also have been the victim of villains who remained unidentified. The parallel provided by Nestor is the only one. Is it accidental? Might it carry a hint that we fail to discern? Maybe the scribes were not at liberty to tell the whole truth? Could that have been in accordance with the church line? (The Kiev Church at the time played a rather ambivalent role and its activity is treated with silence by both the chroniclers and other writers).

The main reason may have been Yaroslav's and his heirs' reluctance to cast too much light on certain of the facts in the story of his life. Let us remember Eimund's story about Yaroslav's red face when he saw the head of his enemy and his hasty orders to bury the body with due respect. There was no obligation on the part of the scribes to make up that detail. Their Christian consciences were clean. Their way of presenting it was rather subtle and covert, comprehensible only to an advised witness.

Perhaps here is the answer to the riddle of Svyatopolk's demise. Maybe it was omitted in the chronicle because it seemed too embarrassing to certain figures (for example Svyatopolk II Iziaslavich or Vladimir Monomachus). Fratricide was not exceptional, but neither was it an asset for Yaroslav. Ioann, Nestor and Sylvester, who in turn were in charge of the Kiev chronicles, may have introduced some corrections into the text (such as the comparison to Julian that was so vague and imprecise).

The events took place not on the plains of Russia but at the boundary between Poland and Czechia. One cannot assume that Yaroslav was indifferent to the destiny of his fugitive brother. All that we know about the fierce struggle of the Riurikovichi (descendants of Riurik) for the Kiev throne bears witness to that. Yaroslav must have thought that if Svyatopolk were allowed to remain free, he would inevitably cause him another headache. He was sure to attempt a comeback, either with the Czechs or the Liakhs, with the Huns or the Pechenegs, or maybe even with their brother Mstislav. He would certainly fight for his "truth" and try to avenge his offense until his last breath. One could never count on peace with him. Yaroslav could hardly have had any doubts in that regard. So he had to draw his own conclusions.

Bylina about Ilya Muromets and Sokolnik

If indeed an action to liquidate Svyatopolk took place, in fact, Yaroslav may have been involved more directly. Let us consider the bylina about Ilya Muromets and Sokolnik (the Falconer) in this light. The bylina starts with the top Russian frontier guard detecting a foreign and boastful intruder while he is surveying the borders of the Kievan state through a spyglass. The "transgressor" comes, as one understands, from the north.

> Ilya was looking northward
> And saw there a sea of blue
> And saw there a broad field —
> The glorious Kulikov field.
> In the mist he saw a beast or a bird,
> A beast was running or a falcon flew,
> Either the isle of Bouyan was seen through the fog
> Or the Saratov heights rose from the bog.
> A bogatyr rode, speaking boastful words,
> A gray wolf ran before him,
> After him ran a black cur,
> A sparrow sat on his right shoulder,
> On his left one a white falcon did stand.
> He held an arrow in his right fist
> And a tightly strung bow in his left hand.
> He was aiming his arrow at an eagle,
> The eagle was sitting in an oak tree
> Making a nest on a gray stone.
> He shot the arrow at the bird,
> He did not drop the arrow on the ground,
> He seized the arrow during flight.

If one may judge a person by his ways and actions, this one was extremely naughty and arrogant. Unimpeded, he reached the white tent of the Russian bogatyrs, took pen and paper, wrote a letter and left it at the entrance. The letter was to the effect that:

242

Now I am going to Kiev, capital city,
I am going to storm it and bring it to pity,
I will burn the churches and cathedrals down,
I will devastate the prince's taverns and town.
I will trample all the books into dirt,
I will throw the icons into the mud,
I will boil the prince in a cauldron of blood,
And will take his wife into my own bed.

When Ilya read the "document", he alerted his carefree friends and sent Dobrynia after the enemy. But Dobrynia unexpectedly failed, and Ilya was obliged to go himself. After a dramatic man-to-man fight, the old bogatyr interrogated the man and learned that he had just been fighting with his own son. They made their peace, and Ilya told him his story and invited the fellow with his mother to come to Kiev.

You will be the first bogatyr among us,
Nobody will be your rival.

But Sokolnik went home, killed his own old mother and decided to head back to Russia in order to do away with his father.

His heart was rotten,
It was rotten and black.
He said to himself:
"Now I have slain my own mother,
I will go and kill my old father, the Cossack,
Who is sound asleep,
So loudly he snores
Like the river-rapid roars".
So went Sokolnik to Kiev city,
He took nothing to eat and nothing to drink,
He paused not a moment, he slept not a wink.
His armor was damaged, dented and chinked,
His clothes were worn out, rags at the most.

And so he came to the border-guard post,
And nobody there a lookout was keeping,
Only the old one he found there, sleeping.
Sokolnik sprang down from his speedy mount,
Entered the white tent,
And took a lance out.
He stuck it right into the old one's chest.
The victim was lucky, despite being old —
By great chance the lance struck a cross,
A wonderful cross made of gold.
The lance glanced off it,
And the oldster woke up.
He leapt from the chair,
And took Sokolnik by his black hair,
He lifted him above his head
And threw him onto the brick floor,
Here Sokolnik met his demise.
The old one took him, in fact, by surprise,
And tore off his arms and legs.
He scattered the pieces over the field,
And the body tied to the horse's rump.
He gave it to the wild birds for food
And the gray wolf tore up the bones.

Who was that Sokolnik? How could Ilya Muromets' son turn out to be a foreign bogatyr who wanted to devastate Kiev and subjugate Russia to a strange power? Answering the question, many point out that "the theme is common among many peoples", that "it is an artistic conception of tragic contradictions during the transition from a matriarchate to a patriarchal society".

"Under the conditions of the formation of statehood in Old Russia, Sokolnik takes on the features of a foreign enemy threatening to destroy the people and its culture". The fact that he turns out to be the son of the principal defender of the Russian land "only enhances the nature of the conflict" (F. M. Selivanov). "A dramatic situation in which one does not recognize the son, daughter, brother, sister or father is well-known in the folklore of many countries and nations" (V. I. Ka-lougin). To this day, scholars have not managed to ascertain how this theme has made its way across centuries, civilizations and continents. But in this case, the theme is quite consistent with the historical reality. How is that?

"Russian bogatyrs have surely met on the battlefield their 'unrecognized' children, who had been taken hostage in their childhood." The attempt to detect in the bylina some documented historical events leads us to the 12th century. I suggest one should also think over the nickname of the boastful bogatyr, Sokolnik (Podsokolnik). An image of a falcon (sokol) that, in flight, drops like a stone on its prey, had become the heraldic sign of Riurik's house. It refers to the meaning of the name of the founder of the family. Does that mean that the antihero of the epic also belongs to the family? Ilya's first impression of the transgressor, when he looks through the spy-glass, is this:

> In the mist, in the fog, he sees a beast,
> Either a beast or a falcon.

Is this depiction only a reflection of the folkloric nature of the bylina? If one admits a historical parallel, then the first historical personality that comes to mind is certainly Svyatopolk (whose name also begins with the same letter as the person in question). For he was the one who came three times to Russia with foreign troops and could rightly be identified, himself, as a foreigner. In the exotic escort of Sokolnik — the wolf, the cur, the sparrow and the eagle — one may also discern the totemic symbols of Yaropolchich's allies — the Pechenegs (their different tribes) and the Poles.

In this case the whole bylina and its final episode could be translated as a story of the life and fate of Svyatopolk. Here, Svyatopolk-Sokolnik, having suffered a defeat, violates peace and friendship, comes back to the capital city of Kiev and tries to strike a blow at his enemy on the sly, and attacks him, unawares, in the tent while he is asleep.

One may also recollect the scene when Boris was killed. But here it is given in a more general way, showing Svyatopolk in a chain of crimes perpetrated against his country as revenge while seeking to seize power. Ilya, in this case, is a symbolic figure and that is why he is immaculate. He represents the whole of the Volodimerich family and is saved from the Accursed only with the help of the Orthodox cross. In the end, Ilya wins and gives the mutilated body away to the final judgment of the nature elements. The ensuing fate of Sokolnik also reminds us of Svyatopolk's fate, as it is related in the Russian annals. It is also mysterious and frightening.

I do not know how convincing are the parallels drawn here, but they may help to explain the sympathy that Yaroslav showed towards Ilya Morovlin (besides their supposed family feeling). For he was buried in the St. Sophia Cathedral (the Austrian Emperor's ambassador Erich Liassota saw the remains of the crypt there in 1596) and Yaroslav also named his firstborn son Ilya. One may imagine what a physical and nervous strain the struggle with his enterprising and stubborn brother was for him ("Yaroslav stayed in Kiev and toiled hard with his host, securing the victory" — thus the Kievan chronicler concluded his narration about the four years' strife). So, although it cannot be proven, such an assumption may appear quite logical. It is not clear what role Ilya played (or could have played) in determining Svyatopolk Yaropolchich's fate. Did he capture him or was he only the head of the detachment that was sent after him, and did he then bring to Yaroslav the news of Svyatopolk's demise? In any event, he must have been of great help to Vladimir's son during the hardest years of his life.

THE FIRST PRESERVED REPORT FROM A RUSSIAN AGENT

Everything that readers have managed to learn about the oldest period in the history of Russian intelligence work is based on documents containing the so-called historic memory. That is: they relate historic events and occasions that are distant from those documents, either in time or in space. Though they are important, they are not as convincing and emotionally compelling as are "historic artifacts", that is, extant remains of the reconstructed historic events, products of the activity of the people who took part in them. For the topic we have chosen, here are the most important documents, written by the "coqs d'or" of medieval Russia. I would like to introduce the first Russian intelligence report known to modern research.

It was discovered in Veliky Novgorod during excavations conducted by an archaeological expedition of the Academy of Sciences and Moscow State University. The report was inscribed on a sheet of birch bark that was found in 1981 in the Commercial Side (Torgovaya storona) of Novgorod. It was at the "Slavno" (Slavensky konets) end of the city, in one of the homesteads at the intersection of Noutnaya Street and Slavnaya Street — that was the main thoroughfare of the district. This was the 590th birch bark scroll found in the soil of the greatest city of northwestern Russia.

V. L. Yanin, a renowned Russian historian who was for many years in charge of the Novgorod expedition, gave the following description of the document: "The scroll is quite unusual in its form. It is a large piece of a birch bark, more than 40 cm long and more than 10 cm wide (about 15 x 4 inches). It was totally blank, except for a spot along the left margin where there is a clear inscription in two lines. On the left, there is a sign resembling a musical treble clef. The inscription is somewhat hidden inside the roll. Unrolling it, one may lose patience and decide that it is just a blank sheet. The inscription has an important message but has no address. It seems to be an agent's report that is

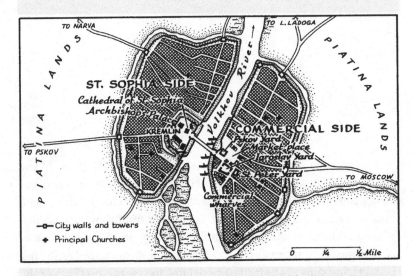

of great significance for a certain person in Novgorod". I do not think that it "seems" anything. One can hardly interpret the document otherwise. To whom could it have been of interest but to certain agents and those who used their services? For it dealt with relations among the peoples adjacent to Novgorod.

The text was written at the very bottom of the scroll and did not contain the name of the author or any identity. This means that the message and its contents were a great state secret.

So we have a report of an unknown scout from an unknown place addressed to an unknown chief. The only thing that one can say for sure is the place where the report was found. Let's designate that as site "A". Who lived there at the time, we do not know. But I do not think that its character changed, and we do know that later on, it was a boyar's yard. And such a letter would most probably be sent to a boyar. Who was in charge of the intelligence service in medieval Novgorod? Maybe the commander of a thousand (tysiatsky) or someone close to him. Sometimes such a position was hereditary, as was that of the mayor (posadnik). This comes to mind because of the following.

At the neighboring homestead "B", another rather mysterious scroll was found, dating back to the late 13th century. It, too, omits the names of the author and addressee, and the text reads to this effect: "This was brought by two men who fled on horses not belonging to them. And Thimonia is dead". What happened there? V. L. Yanin supposed that it could be "a report from the border garrison" or "a message from some tax collector who encountered opposition among the tributaries or betrayal by his assistants". Betrayal there was. But whose and why?

Considering the fact that the fugitives did not have their own horses, they may have been brought from Novgorod under guard, maybe by the very Thimonia who later turned up dead. Most probably Thimonia was a man in the service of a Slavno boyar who, at the destination, tried to protect the two messengers from the banks of the Volkhov. And the two men fled at the very time of Thimonia's death. To my mind, the Novgorod messenger did not die according to the scenario proposed by V. L. Yanin but perished under uncertain circumstances. The men he charged used the opportunity and fled (if they did not slay him themselves). Only in this light does the message become coherent and not fall to pieces. It is quite probable that the place of action was near the border; not at a fortress, from which it would be hard to escape, but at some outpost. It may have taken place at the border with some frontier tribes where conflicts happened quite often. Local authorities tried to quench such conflicts, using the help of the local population, but the equilibrium was fragile. Maybe that was the case.

The Novgorod counterintelligence officer Thimonia and his two underhanded companions attract our attention because of the above-mentioned item's connection to the head of the secret service at the center of northwestern Russia. This was a hereditary position and in the 11th–13th centuries it must have been in the hands of a Slavno boyar family. At the time when the letter was delivered, the head of the intelligence and investigative service lived at the address we have called Homestead A: Noutnaya St., Commercial Side, Novgorod. He had received the letter not at his office (at the Detinets, or Yaroslav's Court) but privately, confidentially. Having read it, he did not destroy it. That may mean that the report had to be kept safe and certain actions may have been taken because of it. That is about all we have on the chief.

As to his subordinate, there is little to be said. He left us with his secret signature, indicating that he was a learned man. At the very edge of the letter, he left an involved symbol resembling the cyrillic letters "P" and "C", similar, to a certain extent, to the pictures drawn by his contemporaries on the plaster of the St. Sophia Cathedral. The sign was not likely to have been accidental. It may have indicated the identity of the secret addressee or testified to the importance and secrecy of the document. Now, we can only guess. On the reverse side of the birch bark there is a near-circle printed by a press. Is it a sign that the letter was read, or some other testimony of divulging its content?

What was the message that the Novgorod intelligence chief read, having unrolled the entire 40 cm-long roll? There were only four words there: "Lithuania has risen on Karelia . . ." The message was very brief but extremely important. It dealt with an international incident of grave significance for Novgorod, for it was close to its borders. That may have been not the only intelligence report given on a topic of such great concern for the Novgorod author. And the author had no doubt that his message would be understand, even in such a concise form.

Further analysis is difficult for the modern historian. It is not easy to guess where the two peoples clashed, for they had no common frontier and vast expanses of Slavic land separated them. "First, the stratigraphic dating of the birch bark at the Noutnaya excavation site was not accurate", wrote V. L. Yanin. Letter #590 was attributed to the late 12th century and associated with the events of 1188, during the conflict between Novgorod and Sweden, when the Karelians in alliance with the Russians marched on the Swedish capital Sigtouna. The chronicle did not mention any Lithuanian participation in this and one might think that this would be another testimony of the events.

However, it turned out that the message could not be dated either to that time or to the time of Alexandr Nevsky. It was written much earlier, late in the 11th century, "probably in 1065-1078 — for that was the age of the cabin near which birch bark #590 was discovered". Though Lithuania was only just beginning to appear in the Russian annals at that time, it may well have begun to take actions near the Novgorod borders or even on Novgorod's own land by then.

V. L. Yanin was right when he established links between Lithuanian actions in the northwest part of Russia and the actions of the

Polotsk prince, Vseslav Briachislavich, a prince who was amply described in the *Lay of Prince Igor's Host*.

In 1066, Vseslav first attacked Novgorod and captured it. Three years later, he made another assault on it. "On the 23rd of October, 1069 Vseslav again came to Novgorod", wrote a historian from the banks of the Volkhov. "The Novgorodians put forward a regiment at the Zverin Monastery and God helped prince Gleb with his host. The battle was fierce, a great number of troops fell, and they [sic] let the prince go, grace be to God". It is worth noting that Vseslav and the Polotsk army had, as allies, Vod'-Finnish-Ugric tribes living on the southern shores of the Gulf of Finland.

It so happens that, at that time, the prince did not come from Polotsk.

On the 3rd of March, 1067, he was defeated by the three heirs of Riurik: Iziaslav, Svyatoslav and Vsevolod, at the battle near the Nemura (Nemiga) River (that was their revenge for his capturing Novgorod). Soon after that, on the 10th of July, Vseslav fell into a trap and was taken prisoner with his two sons. He was jailed in the Kiev prince's cellar. On the 15th of September, 1068, when Iziaslav Yaroslavich with his brothers suffered a defeat at the hands of the Polovtsy, there was a mutiny in Kiev. The horsemen told Iziaslav to send some reliable people to the jail to murder the dangerous prisoner from Polotsk, but he did not dare to perpetrate another crime. The townsfolk freed Vseslav from the prison and proclaimed him their prince. His enemy fled to Poland.

In the spring of 1069, Iziaslav Yaroslavich, like Svyatopolk before him, came back to Russia with the army of his ally, Boleslav the Bold. Vseslav led the Kievan troops against the Poles but, having reached Belgorod, fled to Polotsk at night. On the 2nd of May, Iziaslav took back the Kiev throne, and then he chased Vseslav from Polotsk. For a while (until 1070) the prince was an outcast and the winds of fate brought him to the Baltic seacoast.

V. L. Yanin explains the situation and suggests that the new attempt to capture Novgorod in the autumn of 1069 was made from exile. The chronicle clearly shows the losses suffered by his troops at the Gzen' River; and the place from which he started his 1069 march was the Vod' land. It was there, or en route to Novgorod, that the encounter between Vseslav's allies (the Lithuanians) with the Karelians (the neighboring Vod') took place; that was referred to in the birch bark scroll #590. It was quite natural that Vseslav could have some Lithuanian troops with him, since even before the Lithuanians formed their own state they were under the influence of the Polotsk prince. The message received in Novgorod relates to the conflict between the Lithuanians and the Karelians within Vseslav's troops heading toward Novgorod. One cannot exclude the possibility that the defeat suffered by Vseslav at the Gzen' was also due to internal strife.

One can agree with such interpretation of the unknown agent's report in light of the existing chronicles, though Yanin did not specify the location of the Karelians who took part in the conflict. Either they were a part of Vseslav's army or they just came in handy during the battle. It could have been either way. Otherwise, the Lithuanians would hardly have appeared at the Gulf of Finland. Vseslav used their help, the Vods' and Karelians', out of necessity. Probably Iziaslav's attack at Polotsk was a surprise and he did not have time to amass even his own troops (only Vod' troops are mentioned during the battle at the Gzen'). So he went looking for mercenaries wherever he could. The Lithuanians provided some, but not enough, so Vseslav went north. He may have convinced the leaders of the Vod' and the Karelian tribes to help him and then he may have gone to Novgorod with that army. Why Novgorod and not Polotsk? Most probably he considered that the throne in Novgorod would be easier to reach than his own hereditary throne, held first by Mstislav Iziaslavich and then by Svyatopolk. So he might have thought that the best route home was via Novgorod.

Novgorod had long been of great political importance for the Polotsk prince's family, eager as they were to establish their predominance in the northwest part of Russia. The Old Russian capital, under the influence of Kiev, was an impediment to the achievement of the far-reaching plans of Rogneda's scions. If he had managed to control Novgorod, it would have changed the whole balance of forces on the vast expanses of the Eastern Slavic state. One can understand Vseslav's father's stubborn attempts to subjugate Novgorod while fighting with Yaroslav.

"Briachislav came from Polotsk and took Novgorod", wrote the chronicler in 1021. "Yaroslav gathered many troops and overcame Briachislav. Yaroslav fought with Briachislav for a long time". So Vseslav just went ahead with what had been bequeathed to him. In 1069, he was doubly interested in Novgorod. Why was he so sure of his success?

Novgorod was a strong fortress with a large population capable of fighting. It would be risky to tackle it with a hodgepodge of tribes (as the battle confirmed). Probably the previous successes led him to have confidence in such a thrust. Besides, Briachislav and his son may have had people in the city who could be expected to help.

I think that some religious considerations were relevant there, too. The pagan faith had not altogether disappeared in Russia after Christianity was officially recognized. The forms of religion had changed but the mass conscience was still in the state of dual faith. The pagans' positions in the Polotsk and Novgorod lands, far from Kiev, were much stronger. They were neighbors and their faith had much in common. One may also recollect that the Polotsk prince Vseslav Bria-chislavich retained in the Russian people's memory the notion of the *volkhv*, the charmer and magician. He is shown as such both in folk and written tradition. According to many researchers, he is presented in bylinas alongside with the prophetic Oleg as Volkh Vseslavievich or Volga Svyatoslavich, who seems to be one and the same person. "The story of Volkh's birth, as it is presented in the bylina, contains a hint that the great hunter and volkhv could be fathered by a beast", wrote V. Ya. Propp. "A volkhv is born during sunrise or moonrise. At the time, thunder is roaring, land and sea tremble". The chronicle describes his birth as follows: "His mother conceived him by pagan miracle, and he had a birthmark on his head, that remained visible for all his days. Because of it he is prone to spill blood". Propp also mentions: "A volkhv may turn into a beast, he catches fish in the guise of a pike, birds — as a falcon, and forest beasts — as a gray wolf. He is a charmer and a were-wolf".

Here is an excerpt from the *Lay of Prince Igor's Host**.

> During the seventh age of Trojan Vseslav cast lots for the maiden he desired, and, cunningly leaning on the lance, he leaped to the city of Kiev and touched the golden throne of Kiev with the staff of his lance. Like a fierce beast he leaped from Belgorod at midnight, under the cover of blue mist. He managed to cast thrice a lucky lot: he opened the gate of the city of Novgorod, he tarnished the glory of Prince Iaroslav, and he leapt like a wolf to Nemiga from Dudutki. On the river Ne-

---

*The Lay of Igor's Raid, courtesy of the University of Durham, at http://www.dur.ac.uk/-dml0www/igorraid.html

miga they built haystacks of heads. They are threshed with steel flails and lives are left behind on the threshing floor. Souls abandon their bodies. The bloody shores of the river Nemiga were sown with misfortune, were strewn with the bones of Russia's sons. Prince Vseslav used to judge the people. And, as prince, he ruled over the cities. But, in the night, he prowled like a werewolf. He was able to go from Kiev to Tmutorakan before the cock could crow. And, prowling as a werewolf, he crossed the way of great god Hors. At the Church of St. Sofiia of Polotsk the bells tolled the matins for him, and he could hear them in Kiev.

What a wonderful and colorful image! A magician who could get at the throne with a lance, a wild beast who could outstrip the Sun God of Hors going from north to south in the sky. Such was Vseslav! Surely he was not a pure pagan hiding in the guise of a Christian. The chroniclers emphasize his faith in the cross, the power that freed him from the dungeon; they mention that he took with him the gold cross of the Novgorod prince Vladimir. Still, the faith of his ancestors dictated many of Vseslav's actions and his logic. That is why the author of the *Lay* ascribes to the prince such adventures as his first assault on Novgorod.

Thus it was, apparently, in 1069. That is why the mention of a volkhv that appeared in Novgorod at the time is so interesting (most historians attribute it to 1066-1069). The Primary Chronicle relates that during Gleb's reign in Novgorod, a volkhv arose there, presented himself as a god and seduced nearly all the city. He denigrated the Christian faith and said, "I will walk on the Volkhov River in plain view of everybody". There was a mutiny in the city; they wanted to slay the bishop. The bishop took a cross, donned a clerical robe and said: "Those who stand for the volkhv, go to him; those who have true faith, come to the cross". They split into two parts. Gleb and his host went to the bishop, the rest of the people stood for the volkhv. A great strife broke out between the factions. Gleb took an axe, hid it in his robes, came to the volkhv and said to him: "Are you going to stay here from morning until night?" He replied: "I will stay here forever and perform great miracles". Gleb pulled out his axe and slew him. He fell down dead and the people scattered . . .

This vivid picture from the life of medieval Novgorod has attracted the attention of historians. It was explained in different ways:

either as social discontent with a religious form, or as political trouble in the northern capital that undermined the people's faith in the powers that were (the same thing happened in the 11th century in Suzdal, Yaroslavl and Byelo-ozero). It may have been a reaction to poor harvest or other natural calamities and people blamed the authorities for that. Any of the above-mentioned factors may have been at play — but I would stress the great resistance factor of the Russian pagan traditions that tried in any event to contest the position of the Christian church.

In that case one may ask: "Was not Vseslav's assault on Novgorod the cause of the Novgorod volkhv's appearance?" In other words, could "the magician" have been one of the Polotsk men, in the usual sense? According to The Primary Chronicle, the volkhv appeared in Novgorod all of a sudden and nobody knew him. That is why they believed him (no man is a prophet in his homeland). It does not follow that he was a "pure" agent, or a priest of a pagan god (or nearly a god himself). He only pretended to be such. One may also point out that, in contrast to his counterparts in Byelo-ozero, he did not promise to tackle local social and economic issues but only stressed his ability to work miracles. He was free to choose his actions and who knows what that could have come to. He may have canvassed for Vseslav — although Vseslav had an evil reputation in Novgorod by that time. If indeed he managed to walk across the Volkhov River, as he boasted he would do, then certainly he might have extracted any payment that he wanted from the city.

If these suppositions about a volkhv appearing in Novgorod at the time were true, that would shed new light on how the unnamed scout and his chief in Slavno acted in the circumstances. The latter had to keep a close watch not only on Vseslav's troops but also on the mutiny close at hand. One cannot be sure whose side he was on; was he "the enemy" and did he withstand the intrigues of the volkhv? Though I. Ya. Froyanov asserts that nearly all the townsfolk fell to the volkhv's lures, it is evidently not so. The chronicler painted too gloomy a picture. He had to concede: "Many were lured, nearly the whole city". Some portion of the city's elite remained true to Christianity.

On the other hand, only Prince Gleb Svyatoslavich found "solid" arguments against the volkhv. He put an end to the conflict with a stroke of his axe. Was it like that in reality? We shall never know.

Maybe that was of no concern for our unknown scout, who hid in the western reaches of Novgorod's territory and sent his urgent dispatches to the city via his men. He was not alone, and we can only guess toward what end he was working. Was he simply monitoring what was going on in the enemy camp, or did he influence the events one way or another? Was it he who instigated the quarrel between the Lithuanians and the Karelians, rendering them useless to Vseslav? In any case, he worked hard, and it was not in vain that he risked his neck.

BIBLIOGRAPHY

Russian and Ukrainian citations do not translate readily into English; however, we offer the following list of resources, in the original as well as in translation/transliteration, in the interests of encouraging further research. Place of publication is generally Moscow (M) or Leningrad (L).

SOURCES

1. Byliny. Compiled by F. M. Selivanov / / Library of Russian Folklore. Moscow 1988.
2. Dobrynia Nikitich and Aleshke Popovich. Compiled by Yu. I. Smirnov and V. G. Smoliloky / / Literary Monuments. M. 1974.
3. Ilya Muromets. Compiled by A. M. Astakhova / / Literary Monuments. M. 1958.
4. Complete Collection of Russian Chronicles. Vol. I (Lavrentiev), M., 1997; II (Ipatiev), M., 1998; III (Novgorod first—earliest and latest edition), M., 2000; IX-X (Nikonov), M., 2000; XV (Rogozh chronicler; Tver collection), M., 2000; XXXVIII (Radziwill, L., 1989; XLI (The Pereyaslavl-Suzdal' chronicler (chronicler of the Russian tsars)). M., 1995.
5. Tatishchev V. N. Russian History. Vol. I / / Tatishchev V. N. Collected works. Vol. I, M. 1995).
6. Radzivillovskaya Chronicle. Vol. I. Facsimile reproduction of the manuscript. Vol. II. Kukushkina M. V. A study. Description of miniatures. St. Petersburg-M. 1994.
7. Legend of Boris and Gleb (Sil'vestrovskiy collection). Facsimile reproduction of manuscript. M. 1985.
8. Library of the literature of Ancient Rus'. Vol. I. XI-XVII centuries. St. Petersburg 1997.
9. Life of the holy martyrs Boris and Gleb. Compiled by D.J. Abramovich. Petrograd. 1916.
10. Ukrainian-Russian monuments of XI-XVIII c. on the princes Boris and Gleb. Compiled by A. Bugoslavs'kiy. Kiiv. 1928.
11. Afanasy Kal'nofoyskiy. Teratourgema. Kiev. 1638 (in Polish).

12. The "Great Chronicle" of Poland, Russia and their neighbors in the XI -XII c. M., 1987.

13. Gall the Anonymous. Chronicle and actions of princes or rulers of Poland. M. 1961.

14. Earliest foreign sources on the history of ancient Russia. Compiled by Ye. A. Mel'nikova, etc. M., 1999.

15. German Latin-language sources IX-XI c., compiled by A. V. Nazarenko. M., 1993.

16. Latin-language sources on the history of ancient Russia. Germany. IX-first half XII c. Translation under the direction of M. B. Sverdlov. M.-L., 1989.

17. Leo Diacon. History. (Appendices: Ioann Skilits. Excerpt from the chronicle). Translation M. M. Kopylenko. M., 1988.

18. Snorri Sturluson. Krug zemnoi (Heimskringla). M., 1980.

19. Iceland royal sagas about the history of ancient Russia. Vol. I-III. Compiled by T. N. Jackson et al. Vol. II M. 1995.

20. V. L. Yanin, A. G. Zaliznyak. Novgorod texts written on birch bark (from the excavations 1977-1983). M. 1986.

See also the listings noted by asterisk, in the Historiography section.

HISTORIOGRAPHY

1. Beliaev S. A. "Basilica on the hill" in Kherson and "church on the mountain" in Korsun', built by prince Vladimir // Byzantinorussica. M. 1994. № 1.

2. Beliaev S. A. The march of Prince Vladimir on Korsun' (its consequences for Kherson) // Byzantine Vremennik. T. 51. M., 1990.

3. A. Z. Berthier-Delagard. As Vladimir laid siege to Korsun' // News from the Department of Russian Language and Literature, Academies of Sciences Press. Vol. XIV, book 1. St. Petersburg 1909.

4. Danilevskiy I. N. Ancient Russia in the eyes of contemporaries and descendants (IX-XIII centuries). Lectures. M. 1998.

5. *Veselovskiy A. N. Vil'tins and Russians in the saga about Tidrek Bernsk (Veronese) // Dept.of Russian Language and Literature, Academies of Sciences Press. Vol. XIII. Book 1. St. Petersburg 1906.

6. *Veselovskiy A. N. Southern Russian bylinas. Vol. I -III. St. Petersburg 1881-1884.

7. *Glazyrina G. V. Ilya Muromets in the Russian bylinas, German poetry and the Scandinavian saga // The study of the earliest sources for the history of the peoples of the USSR. M. 1978.

8. Gorbovskiy A., Semenov Ju. Without a single shot. From the history of Russian military intelligence. M. 1984.

9. Gumilev L. N. Ancient Russia and the great steppe. M. 1989.

10. Gumilev L. N. The Black Legend: Friends and Foes of the great steppe. M. 1994.

11. Golovko A. B. Ancient Russia and Poland: political interrelations in the X-first third of the XIII centuries. Kiev. 1988.

12. Golovko A. Who killed Boris and Gleb?/ /Science and Religion. 1988. № 2.

13. *Golubinskiy Ye. Ye. The history of the Russian church. Vol. I., books 1-2. M. 1996.

14. Grekov B. D. The "Povest' vremennykh let" about Vladimir's march on Korsun' / / Grekov B. D., Selected works. Vol. II, M. 1959.

15. Grimberg F. L. On Riurik's descendants; or the half-century of "eternal" questions. M. 1997.

16. *Jackson T. N. Iceland's royal sagas about Eastern Europe (from the earliest times up to 1000). M. 1992.

17. Zhirmunskiy V. M. Popular heroic epos, Moscow-Leningrad, 1962.

18. Ilovayskiy D. I. Hero-cossack Ilya Muromets as a historical figure. A proposal of a study of Vsevolod Miller's "Excursus into the region of Russian people epos". M. 1892 / / Russian archive. 1893.

19. *Il'in N. N. Annals article of the year 6523 and its source (an attempted analysis). M. 1957.

20. Kardini F. Sources on medieval knighthood. M. 1987.

21. *Karpov A. Yu. St. Vladimir. (From the series, "Lives of remarkable people"). M. 1997.

22. Kalugin V. I. Heroes of Russian epos. Descriptions on Russian folklore. M. 1983.

23. *Karamzin N. M. History of the Russian state. Vol. I. M., 1988.

24. Kvashnin-Samarin P. I. Russian bylinas in historico-geographical relations / / Beseda. 1871. № IV, V.

25. Kvashnin-Samarin P. I. New sources for the study of Russian epos / / Russian vestnik. 1874. № 9,10.

26. Kirpichnikov A. I. A Comparative Study of Western and Russian Epos: Poems from the Lombardian cycle. M. 1873.

27. Kuchma V. V. The Padabromi Method: the phenomenon of military theory and combat practices of the Xth c. / /Byzantine descriptions. Russian scholars' participation in the XIX international congress of Byzantine Studies. M. 1996.

28. Korolyuk V. D. Western Slavs and Kievan Russia in the X-XI centuries. M. 1964.

29. Kotlyar N. F. Old-Russian statehood. M. 1998.

30. Kotlyar N. F. Did Svyatopolk kill Boris and Gleb?/ / Ukrainian historic journal. 1989, №. 12.

31. Likhachev D. S. Aleksandr Popovich, in the Chronicles / / Works by the division of Old-Russian Literature, at the Institute of Russian Literature of

the USSR Academy of Sciences. Vol. VII. M.-L., 1949.

32. Likhachev D. S. Russian folk poetic creation. Vol. I. Ocherky on the history of Russian folk poetic creation X - early XVIII centuries. M.-L. 1953.

33. Maksimovich M. A. In what century did Ilya Muromets live?/ / Maksimovich M. A. collected works. Vol. I. Kiev. 1876.

34. Miller V. F. Excursi into the area of Russian popular epos. M. 1892.

35. Miller O. F. Comparative-critical observations of class structure in the Russian epos. Ilya Muromets and the Kiev bogatyr's. St. Petersburg 1869.

36. *Nazarenko A. V. The Events of 1017 in the German chronicles from the early XI c. and in the Russian annals / / The earliest states in the territory of the USSR. 1980. M. 1981.

37. Sketches on the history of Russian international reconnaissance. Directed by Yevgenii M. Primakov. Vol. I. M. 1996.

38. *Ogloblin N. N. Archbishop Brunon's letter to German emperor Heinrich II / / University Proceedings. Kiev. 1873. №8. Sections IV.

39. Ponomarev A. L., Serikov N. I. Year 989 (6496) – The year of the baptism of Rus' (Philological text analysis, astrology and astronomy) / / The Black Sea area in the Middle Ages. Issue 2. M. 1995.

40. Poppe A. V. Genealogical background of Mstisha Svenel'dich / / Annals and chronicles. 1973. M.

41. Poppe A. V. On the reasons for Vladimir Svyatoslavich's March on Korsun' 988-989 yr. / / Moscow University Vestnik. History. 1978. № 2.

42. Propp V. Ya. Russian heroic epos. M. 1958.

43. Putilov B. N. Russian and Southern Slavonic heroic epos. M. 1971.

44. Piatysheva N. V. "The earthen way" in the story about Vladimir's march on Korsun' / / Soviet archaeology. 1964. №3.

45. Rapov O. M. The Russian Church on IX – early XII c.: the Adoption of Christianity. M. 1999.

46. *Rapov O. M., Tkachenko N. G. Russian Proceeding of Tietmar of Merzeburg / / Moscow University Vestnik. History. 1980. №3.

47. Richka V. M. What's behind the chronicles of Kyivs'ki Rus. Kiev. 1991.

48. Rybakov B. A. Old Russia: Legends, Bylinas, Chronicles. M. 1963.

49. Rybakov B. A. Kievan Rus' and the Russian principalities XII-XIII cc. M. 1993.

50. Rybakov B. A. Paganism in ancient Russia. M. 1987.

51. Romanchuk A. I. "The Destruction of the 10th century" in Khersones (a question about the consequences of Vladimir's march on Korsun') / / Byzantine vremennik. Vol. 50. M. 1989.

52. *Rydzevskaya Ye. A. Of Old Rus' and Scandinavia in IX-XIV centuries M. 1978.

53. *Sakharov A. N. Svyatoslav's Diplomacy. M. 1991.

54. *Serebryanskiy N. I. Old-Russian princely lives. Survey of manuscripts and

texts. M. 1915.

55. *Sverdlov M. B. Writings about Rus' by Tietmar of Merzeburg/ / The earliest states in the territory of the USSR. 1975. M. 1976.

56. Sverdlov M. B. Political relations of Rus' and Germany X – XI cc. / / The history of international relations. L. 1972.

57. Solovyev S. M. History of Russia from the earliest times. Book I, Vol. 1-2. M. 1993.

58. Tatishchev V. N. History of Russia. Volume I. M.

59. Tolochko P. P. Old Rus'. Sketches of the Sociopolitical history. Kiev. 1987.

60. Toporov V. N. Sainthood and the saints in Russian Spiritual Culture. Vol. I. First century of Christianity in Rus'. Moscow - St. Petersburg 1995.

61. *Philist G. M. History of the "Crimes" of Svyatopolk the Damned. Minsk. 1990.

62. Froyanov I. Ya. Ancient Russia. A study of the history of social and political struggles. St. Petersburg 1996.

63. Khalanskiy M. G. The Great Russian Bylinas of Kiev cycle. Warsaw 1885.

64. Charopka V. Innocent or Guilty. Svyatopolk "the Accursed" / / Rodnik. Minsk. 1991.

65. Cherniak Ye. P. Five centuries of secret wars. M. 1991.

66. *Shakhmatov A. A. The Korsun' legend of the baptism of Vladimir. St. Petersburg 1906.

67. *Shakhmatov A. A. Research on the earliest Russian annalistic archives. St. Petersburg 1908.

68. Jacobson A. L. Early Medieval Khersones. M. 1957.

69. Yanin V. L. "I sent you a birch bark." M. 1998.

70. Yarkho B. I. Ilya, Ilias. Khiltebrant // Izvestia of IInd Department of the Academy of Sciences. Petrograd 1917. Vol. XXII, book 2.

ИСТОЧНИКИ

1. Былины. Сост. Ф.М.Селиванов // Библиотека русского фольклора. М. 1988.
2. Добрыня Никитич и Алеша Попович // Литературные памятники. М. 1974.
3. Илья Муромец. Сост. А.М.Астахова // Литературные памятники. М. 1958.
4. Полное собрание русских летописей. Т.Т. I (Лаврентьевская), М., 1997; II (Ипатьевская), М., 1998; III (Новгородская первая старшего и младшего извода), М., 2000; IX-X (Никоновская), М., 1885; XV (Рогожский летописец; Тверской сборник), М., 2000; XXXVIII (Радзивилловская), Л., 1989; XII (Летописец Переяславля Суздальского (летописец русских царей)). М., 1995.
5. Татищев В.Н. История Российская. Т. I. // Татищев В.Н. Собрание сочинений. Т.I, М. 1995).
6. Радзивилловская летопись. Т. I. Факсимильное воспроизведение рукописи. Т. III. Кукушкина М.В. Исследование. Описание миниатюр. СПб-М. 1994.
7. Сказание о Борисе и Глебе (Сильвестровский сборник) Факсимильное воспроизведение рукописи. . М. 1985.
8. Библиотека литературы Древней Руси. Т.I. XI-XVII века. СПб. 1997.
9. Жития святых мучеников Бориса и Глеба. Подг. Д.И.Абрамович. Пгр. 1916.
10. Украіно-руські пам'ятки XI-XVIII вв.про князів Бориса та Гліба. Состав. А.Бугославський. Київ. 1928.
11. Афанасий Кальнофойский. Teratourgema. Киев. 1638 (на польс. языке).
12. "Великая хроника" о Польше, Руси и их соседях XI-XII вв. М., 1987.
13. Галл Аноним. Хроника и деяния князей или правителей Польши. М. 1961.
14. Древнейшие иностранные источники по истории Древней Руси. Сост. Е.А.Мельникова и др. М., 1999.
15. Немецкие латиноязычные источники IX-XI вв. Сост. А.В.Назаренко. М., 1993.
16. Латиноязычные источники по истории Древней Руси. Германия. IX - первая половина XII в. Перевод и сост. Б.Свердлова. М.-Л. 1989.
17. Лев Диакон. История. (Прилож.: Иоанн Скилица. Отрывок из хроники). Перевод М.М.Копыленко. М., 1988.
18. Скорри Стурлусон. Круг земной. М., 1980.
19. Исландские королевские саги об истории Древней Руси. Т.Т. I-III. Сост. Т.Н.Джаксон и др. Т. II. М. 1995.
20. В.Л.Янин, А.Г. Зализняк. Новгородские грамоты на бересте (из раскопок 1977-1983 гг.). М. 1986.

См. Также сочинения, отмеченные звездочкой в разделе Историография.

ИСТОРИОГРАФИЯ

1. Беляев С.А. "Базилика на холме" в Херсонесе и "церковь на горе" в Корсуни, построенная князем Владимиром // Byzantinorussica. М. 1994. № 1.
2. Беляев С.А. Поход князя Владимира на Корсунь (Его последствия для Херсонеса) // Византийский Временник. Т.51. М., 1990.
3. Бертье-Делагард. Как Владимир осаждал Корсунь // Известия отделения русского языка и словесности имп. Академии Наук. Т. XIV. Кн. 1. СПб. 1909.
4. *Веселовский А.Н. Вильтины и русские в саге о Полдреке Бернском (Веронском) // Извести отделения русского языка и словесности имп. Академии Наук. Т. XIII. Кн. 1. СПб. 1906.
5. *Веселовский А.Н. Южнорусские былины. Т.Т. I-III. СПб. 1881-1884.
6. *Глазырина Г.В. Илья Муромец в русских былинах, немецкой поэме и скандинавской саге // Методика изучения древнейших источников по истории народов СССР. М. 1978.
7. Горбовский А., Семенов Н. Без единого выстрела. Из истории российской военной разведки. М. 1984.
8. Гумилев Л.Н. Древняя Русь и Великая степь. М. 1989.
9. Гумилев Л.Н. Черная легенда: Друзья и недруги Великой степи. М. 1994.
10. Головко А.Б. Древняя Русь и Польша в политических взаимоотношениях X - первой трети XIII в. Киев. 1988.
11. Головко А. Кто убил Бориса и Глеба? // Наука и религия. 1988. № 2.
12. *Голубинский Е.Е. История русской церкви. Т.I. кн. 1-2. М. 1996.
13. Греков Б.Д. "Повесть временных лет" о походе Владимира на Корсунь // Греков Б.Д. Избранные труды. Т. II, М. 1959.
14. Гримберг Ф.Л. Рюриковичи или семисотлетие "вечных" вопросов. М. 1997
15. *Джаксон Т.Н. Исландские королевские саги о Восточной Европе (с древнейших времен до 1000 г.). М. 1992.
16. Данилевский И.Н. Древняя Русь глазами современников и потомков. (IX-XIII вв). Курс лекций. М. 1998.
17. Жирмунский В. Народный героический эпос. М-Л. 1962.
18. Иловайский Д.И. Богатырь-казак Илья Муромец как историческое лицо. По поводу исследования Всеволода Миллера "Экскурс в область русского народного эпоса". М. 1892 // Русский архив. 1893.
19. *Ильин Н.Н. Летописная статья 6523 года и ее источник (Опыт анализа). М. 1957.
20. Кардина Ф. Истоки средневекового рыцарства. М. 1987.
21. *Карпов А.Ю. Владимир Святой. (серия "Жизнь замечательных людей"). Т. 1997.
22. Калугин В.Н. Герои русского эпоса. Очерки и русском фольклоре. М. 1983.
23. *Карамзин Н.И. История государства российского. Т. I. М., 1988.
24. Квашнин-Самарин П.И. Русские былины в историко-географическом отношении // Беседа. 1871. №№ IV, V.

25. Квашнин-Самарин П.И. Новые источники для учения русского эпоса // Русский вестник. 1874. №№ 9,10.

26. Кирпичников А.И. Опыт сравнительного изучения западного и русского эпоса: Поэмы ломбаруского цикла. М. 1873.

27. Кучма В.В. Метод Падабромы: феномен военной теории и боевой практики X в. // Византийские очерки. Труды российских ученых к XIX международному конгрессу византинистов. М. 1996.

28. Королюк В.Д. Западные славяне и Киевская Русь в X-XI вв. М. 1964.

29. Котляр М.Ф. Древнерусская государственность. М. 1998.

30. Котляр М.Ф. Ин Святополе убив Бориси и Глеба? // Украиньский iсторичный журнал. 1989, № 12.

31. Лихачев Д.С. Летописные известия об Александре Поповиче // Труды отдела древнерусской литературы Института русской литературы АН СССР. Т. VII. М-Л. 1949.

32. Лихачев Д.С. Русское народное поэтическое творчество. Т. I. Очерки по истории русского народного поэтического творчества X - начала XVIII веков. М-Л. 1953.

33. Максимович М.А. В каком веке жил Илья Муромец // Максимович М. А. Собрание сочинений. Т. I. Киев. 1876.

34. Миллер В.Ф. Экскурсы в область русского народного эпоса. М. 1892.

35. Миллер О.Ф. Сравнительно-критические наблюдения над слоевым составом народного русского эпоса. Илья Муромец и богатырьство Киевское. СПб. 1869.

36. *Назаренко А.В. События 1017 г. в немецкой хронике начала XI в. и в русской летописи // Древнейшие государства на территории СССР. 1980. М. 1981.

37. Очерки по истории российской внешней разведки. Под ред. Е.М. Примакова. Т. I. М. 1996.

38. *Оглобин Н.Н. Письмо архиепископа Брунона германскому императору Генриху II. // Университетские известия. Киев. 1873. № 8. Отд. IV.

39. Пономарев А.Л., Сериков Н.И. 989 (6496) год - Год крещения Руси (Филологический анализ текстов, астрология и астрономия) // Причерноморье в средние века. Вып. 2. М. 1995.

40. Поппэ А.В. Родословная Мстиши Свенельдича // Летописи и хроники. 1973. М.

41. Поппэ А.В. О причинах похода Владимира Святославича на Корсунь 988-989 гг. // Вестник Московского Университета. История. 1978. № 2.

42. Прони В.Я. Русский героический эпос. М. 1958.

43. Путилов Б.Н. Русский и южнославянский героический эпос. М. 1971.

44. Пятышева Н.В. "Земляной путь" рассказа о походе Владимира на Корсунь – Советская археология. 1964. № 3.

45. Рапов О.М. Русская церковь в IX - первой трети XII в. Принятие христианства. М. 1999.

46. *Рапов О.М., Ткаченко Н.Г. Русские известия Титмара Мерзебургского // Вестник Московского Университета. История. 1980. № 3.

47. Ричка В.М. За летописным рядком. Усторичнi оповiдi про Кыiвську Русь. Киiв. 1991.

48. Рыбаков Б.А. Древняя Русь: Сказания. Былины. Летописи. М. 1963.

49. Рыбаков Б.А. Киевская Русь и русские княжества XII-XIII вв. М. 1993.
50. Романчук А.И. "Слои разрушений X в." в Херсонесе (К вопросу о последствиях корсунского похода Владимира) // Византийский временник. Т. 50. М. 1989.
51. Рыбаков Б.А. Язычество Древней Руси. М. 1987.
52. *Рыдзевская Е.А. Древняя Русь и Скандинавия в IX-XIV вв. М. 1978.
53. *Сахаров А.Н. Дипломатия Святослава. М. 1991.
54. *Серебрянский Н.И. Древнерусские княжеские жития. Обзор редакций и тексты. М. 1915.
55. *Свердлов М.Б. Известия о Руси Титмара Мерзебургского // Древнейшие государства на территории СССР. 1975. М. 1976.
56. Свердлов М.Б. Политические отношения Руси и Германии X - первой половины XI в. // Проблемы истории международных отношений. Л. 1972.
57. Соловьев С.М. История России с древнейших времен. Кн. I. Т.Т. 1-2. М. 1993.
58. Татищев В.Н. История Российская. Т. I. М.
59. Толочко П.П. Древняя Русь. Очерки социально-политической истории. Киев. 1987.
60. Топоров В.Н. Святость и святые в русской духовной культуре. Т. I. Первый век христианства на Руси. М.-СПб. 1995.
61. *Филист Г.М. История "преступлений" Святополка Окаянного. Минск. 1990.
62. Фроянов И.Я. Древняя Русь. Опыт исследования истории социальной и политической борьбы. СПб. 1996.
63. Халанский М.Г. Великорусские былины Киевского цикла. Варшава. 1885.
64. Чаропка В. Без вины виноватый Святополк "Окаянный" // Родник. Минск. 1991.
65. Черняк Е.П. Пять веков тайной войны.
66. *Шахматов А.А. Корсунская легенда о крещении Владимира. СПб. 1906.
67. *Шахматов А.А. Разыскания о древнейших русских летописных сводах. СПб. 1908.
68. Якобсон А.Л. Раннесредневековый Херсонес. М. 1957.
69. Янин В.Л. Послал тебе бересту. М. 1998.
70. Ярхо Б.И. Илья, Илиав. Хилтебрант // Известия II Отделения Академии Наук. ПГ, 1917. т. XXII, кн. 2.

Also from Algora Publishing:

HENRI TROYAT
TERRIBLE TZARINAS

Who should succeed Peter the Great? Upon the death of this visionary and despotic reformer, the great families plotted to come up with a successor who would surpass everyone else — or at least, offend none. But there were only women — Catherine I, Anna Ivanovna, Anna Leopoldovna, Elizabeth I. These autocrats imposed their violent and dissolute natures upon the empire, along with their loves, their feuds, their cruelties. Born in 1911 in Moscow, Troyat is a member of the Académie française, recipient of Prix Goncourt.

RICHARD LABÉVIÈRE
DOLLARS FOR TERROR — The U.S. and Islam

"A riveting, often shocking analysis. Labévière shows how radical Islamic fundamentalism spreads its influence on two levels, above board, through investment firms, banks and shell companies, and clandestinely, though a network of drug dealing, weapons smuggling and money laundering. This important book sounds a wake-up call to U.S. policy-makers."
— *Publishers Weekly*

CLAUDIU A. SECARA
THE NEW COMMONWEALTH
From Bureaucratic Corporatism to Socialist Capitalism

The notion of an elite-driven worldwide perestroika has gained some credibility lately. The book examines in a historical perspective the most intriguing dialectic in the Soviet Union's "collapse" — from socialism to capitalism and back to socialist capitalism — and speculates on the global implications.

IGNACIO RAMONET
THE GEOPOLITICS OF CHAOS

The author, Director of *Le Monde Diplomatique,* presents an original, discriminating and lucid political matrix for understanding what he calls the "current disorder of the world" in terms of Internationalization, Cyberculture and Political Chaos.

TZVETAN TODOROV
A PASSION FOR DEMOCRACY –
Benjamin Constant

The French Revolution rang the death knell not only for a form of society, but also for a way of feeling and of living; and it is still not clear as yet what we gained from the changes.

DOMINIQUE FERNANDEZ
PHOTOGRAPHER: FERRANTE FERRANTI
ROMANIAN RHAPSODY — An Overlooked Corner of Europe

"Romania doesn't get very good press." And so, renowned French travel writer Dominique Fernandez and top photographer Ferrante Ferranti head out to form their own images. In four long journeys over a 6-year span, they uncover a tantalizing blend of German efficiency and Latin nonchalance, French literature and Gypsy music, Western rationalism and Oriental mysteries. Fernandez reveals the rich Romanian essence. Attentive and precise, he digs beneath the somber heritage of communism to reach the deep roots of a European country that is so little-known.

JEAN-MARIE ABGRALL
SOUL SNATCHERS: THE MECHANICS OF CULTS

Jean-Marie Abgrall, psychiatrist, criminologist, expert witness to the French Court of Appeals, and member of the Inter-Ministry Committee on Cults, is one of the experts most frequently consulted by the European judicial and legislative processes. The fruit of fifteen years of research, his book delivers the first methodical analysis of the sectarian phenomenon, decoding the mental manipulation on behalf of mystified observers as well as victims.

CLAUDIU A. SECARA
TIME & EGO –
Judeo-Christian Egotheism and the Anglo-Saxon Industrial Revolution

The first question of abstract reflection that arouses controversy is the problem of Becoming. Being persists, beings constantly change; they are born and they pass away. How can Being change and yet be eternal? The quest for the logical and experimental answer has just taken off.

JEAN-CLAUDE GUILLEBAUD
THE TYRANNY OF PLEASURE

Guillebaud, a Sixties' radical, re-thinks liberation, taking a hard look at the question of sexual morals -- that is, the place of the forbidden -- in a modern society. For almost a whole generation, we have lived in the illusion that this question had ceased to exist. Today the illusion is faded, but a strange and tumultuous distress replaces it. No longer knowing very clearly where we stand, our societies painfully seek answers between unacceptable alternatives: bold-faced permissiveness or nostalgic moralism.

SOPHIE COIGNARD AND MARIE-THÉRÈSE GUICHARD
FRENCH CONNECTIONS –
The Secret History of Networks of Influence

They were born in the same region, went to the same schools, fought the same fights and made the same mistakes in youth. They share the same morals, the same fantasies of success and the same taste for money. They act behind the scenes to help each other, boosting careers, monopolizing business and information, making money, conspiring and, why not, becoming Presidents!

JEAN-JACQUES ROSA
EURO ERROR

The European Superstate makes Jean-Jacques Rosa mad, for two reasons. First, actions taken to relieve unemployment have created inflation, but have not reduced unemployment. His second argument is even more intriguing: the 21st century will see the fragmentation of the U. S., not the unification of Europe.

ANDRÉ GAURON
EUROPEAN MISUNDERSTANDING

Few of the books decrying the European Monetary Union raise the level of the discussion to a higher plane. *European Misunderstanding* is one of these. Gauron gets it right, observing that the real problem facing Europe is its political future, not its economic future.

PHILIPPE TRÉTIACK
ARE YOU AGITÉ? Treatise on Everyday Agitation

"The 'Agité,' that human species that lives in international airports, jumps into taxis while dialing the cell phone, eats while clearing the table, reads the paper while watching TV and works during vacation – has just been given a new title." — *Le Monde des Livres*
"A book filled with the exuberance of a new millennium, full of humor and relevance." — *Le Parisien*

PAUL LOMBARD
VICE & VIRTUE — Men of History, Great Crooks for the Greater Good

Personal passion has often guided powerful people more than the public interest. With what result? From the courtiers of Versailles to the back halls of Mitterand's government, from Danton — revealed to have been a paid agent for England — to the shady bankers of Mitterand's era, from the buddies of Mazarin to the builders of the Panama Canal, Paul Lombard unearths the secrets of the corridors of power. He reveals the vanity and the corruption, but also the grandeur and panache that characterize the great. This cavalcade over many centuries can be read as a subversive tract on how to lead.

JEANNINE VERDÈS-LEROUX
DECONSTRUCTING PIERRE BOURDIEU
Against Sociological Terrorism From the Left

Sociologist Pierre Bourdieu went from widely-criticized to widely-acclaimed, without adjusting his hastily constructed theories. Verdès-Leroux has spent 20 years researching the policy impact of intellectuals who play at the fringes of politics. She suggests that Bourdieu arrogated for himself the role of "total intellectual" and proved that a good offense is the best defense.

JEAN-MARIE ABGRALL
HEALING OR STEALING — Medical Charlatans in the New Age

Jean-Marie Abgrall is Europe's foremost expert on cults and forensic medicine. He asks, are fear of illness and death the only reasons why people trust their fates to the wizards of the pseudo-revolutionary and the practitioners of pseudo-magic? We live in a bazaar of the bizarre, where everyday denial of rationality has turned many patients into ecstatic fools. While not all systems of nontraditional medicine are linked to cults, this is one of the surest avenues of recruitment, and the crisis of the modern world may be leading to a new mystique of medicine where patients check their powers of judgment at the door.

DR. DEBORAH SCHURMAN-KAUFLIN
THE NEW PREDATOR: WOMEN WHO KILL — Profiles of Female Serial Killers
This is the *first book ever* based on face-to-face interviews with women serial killers.

MICHEL PINÇON & MONIQUE PINÇON-CHARLOT
GRAND FORTUNES –
Dynasties of Wealth in France

Going back for generations, the fortunes of great families consist of far more than money—they are also symbols of culture and social interaction. In a nation known for democracy and meritocracy, piercing the secrets of the grand fortunes verges on a crime of lèse-majesté . . . *Grand Fortunes* succeeds at that.